In Face of Reality

In Face of Reality

The Constructive Theology of Gordon D. Kaufman

Thomas A. James

PICKWICK *Publications* · Eugene, Oregon

Pickwick Publications
An Imprint of Wipf and Stock Publishers
199 W. 8th Ave., Suite 3
Eugene, OR 97401

www.wipfandstock.com

ISBN 13: 978-1-60899-401-4

Cataloging-in-Publication data:

James, Thomas A.

    In face of reality : the constructive theology of Gordon D. Kaufman / Thomas A. James.

    xii + 138 p. ; 23 cm. Including bibliographical references.

    ISBN 13: 978-1-60899-401-4

    1. Kaufman, Gordon D. 2. Theology—History—Methodology—20th Century. I. Title.

BR118 J10 2011

Manufactured in the U.S.A.

Contents

Acknowledgments

THIS SHORT BOOK HAS a long history, beginning as a doctoral dissertation under the wise direction of Douglas F. Ottati, now Craig Family Distinguished Professor of Religion and Ethics at Davidson College. As with many of his students, Professor Ottati's mentorship of me was not limited to advising a dissertation and passing on the canons of theological scholarship. He welcomed me into his home on many occasions, introduced me to the delights of single malt scotch, and through his humor, hospitality, and relentlessly constructive habits of mind, demonstrated what sort of person a theologian can be. I am also deeply grateful for the mentorship of Charles M. Swezey, Distinguished Service Professor of Christian Ethics at Union Seminary, who piqued my interest in the relationship between modern knowledge about the world and theology, and, more importantly, refused to countenance easy answers; and to Dawn DeVries, John Newton Thomas Professor of Systematic Theology at Union and now my colleague, who provided the needed encouragement to me to pursue publishing this book and provided advice along the way. I am grateful also to Paul Capetz of United Theological Seminary in the Twin Cities, whose urged me to limit my obsession with Reinhold Niebuhr at least long enough to pursue this topic; and to Gordon Kaufman, whose appreciative and critical reading of the original version of this book did a lot both to affirm my work and to press me toward greater clarity. I am also grateful to my friend David True, and to other members of the Theology and Ethics writer's group, including Elizabeth Hinson-Hasty, James Calvin Davis, and Hal Breitenberg, all of whom read and commented on drafts of part of this book.

Many thanks, with admiration, to students at Union Presbyterian Seminary with whom I have continued to read and ponder Kaufman's work, and who have often surprised me with their interest and openness to such challenging ideas. I have learned a great deal from them, and this work is better for having participated in their struggles with the idea of God.

As with many authors, I could not have seen this project through without the support and encouragement of my family. First, thanks to my wife, the Rev. Michelle James, who has lived with this project almost as closely as I have, and whose love, support, and friendship have made the years spent working on it inconceivably richer than they would have otherwise been. Thanks also to my mother and father, Sue and Don James, for their support, patience, and months of meticulous proofreading!

Finally, this book is dedicated to the memory of my late grandmother, another Sue James, who supported my education from college through graduate school, and whose generosity called for more gratitude than I managed to express during her lifetime.

Introduction

L UDWIG FEUERBACH FAMOUSLY ATTEMPTED to reduce theology to anthropology by reinterpreting classical theistic language as the embodiment of a deep commitment of its users to human flourishing and to humane values. His efforts may well have succeeded in describing a piety that is influential if not dominant in the modern world. Nevertheless, it is a hardly disputable fact that claims about a *real* God who really acts in the world (and, hence, who really places claims on us) have been a touchstone of Christian theology throughout its history, and continue to be. Shaped by a broader Western religious tradition which has emphasized the world's temporality and contingency as well as the personal nature of it creator, Christian theology has consistently placed a series of objective claims about God's activity at the center of its interpretation of human life in the world, and those claims are precisely what make its interpretation distinctive. If projection theories like Feuerbach's are true, or at least if they succeed in demonstrating that there is no objective reality behind invocations of divine activity, then certainly theology as an intellectual discipline is a hopelessly confused and pointless enterprise.

One may be consoled by the thought that the practical orientation afforded by the Western religious tradition is far more important than the viability of theology as an academic field. Theistic faith has its social usefulness, with or without solid theoretical foundations. But where does the practicability of Western religion come from, if not its capacity to construe the enormously complicated welter of events in both nature and history as governed by God's gracious will—in other words, by claims that fall within the provenance of *theology*? Over the centuries, faith in an objective divine governance of events has supported a high degree of confidence that the world is a meaningful whole in the context of which it makes sense for human beings to act with purpose and resolve.

Since the rise of modern historical study and of the intellectual dominance of the natural sciences, however, these kinds of convictions have seemed increasingly problematic to the majority of persons in the West. While projection theories remain influential in some quarters, a more pervasive and troublesome difficulty has to do with the almost universally shared way of seeing the world that has emerged in our era. According to the modern picture, the world is governed by efficient rather than final causality, scientific law rather than divine purpose. The thought of a personal agent who intends and then executes a series of benevolent purposes does not seem to square with experiences of ambiguity and evil, and the explanations it suggests seem to be fated to a losing competition with those based on natural causes.

In response, modern theology has often significantly qualified claims which were made unapologetically by theologians in the past. Adjustments have been either piecemeal or more drastic. Sometimes, claims about decisive and unilateral divine action have yielded to theories of divine suffering: it is *humans* who act, and it is God whose task it is patiently to bear it. Or, in some less drastic versions, God truly does act, but never unilaterally. In some proposals, claims about divine action are sectioned off from the wider world as we know it, relegated to a series of social movements in which certain benevolent purposes may be apparent to the interpreter. In others, God is a purposive but not intentional power whose purposes are buried within the fine-grained details of cosmic and human events, resistant in their particularity to an overarching theory of divine providence.

In terms of the problem of relating the modern world picture to distinctively theistic claims, modern efforts have generally fallen somewhere between two extreme positions. Taken together, these extremes may be understood as the embodiments of a deeper polarity within the subject matter which may not, in the end, be susceptible of being overcome. The first of these embodiments secures the integrity of traditional claims about divine activity by strategically curtailing interaction with contemporary knowledge about the world. This strategy finds expression in efforts to interpret God's action solely from the point of view of one or more privileged sources of religious insight. While promising in its ability both to protect to integrity of theistic traditions and to confront the often unexamined assumptions of modern thought, this approach yields a twofold difficulty. First of all, it undermines the intelligibility of traditional claims by severing them from the world of everyday experience. Secondly, and perhaps more importantly, it tends to leave the world itself insufficiently interpreted by claims about divine activity.

The embodiment of the second polar option, on the other hand, collapses talk about God's activity into a preferred version of modern cosmological theory. While promising in its ability to reestablish the intelligibility of theistic claims, it also yields significant problems. The most important one is that the distinctiveness of theistic interpretations of the world tends to be lost, rendering the strategy's very success in harmonizing modern knowledge and historic religious language a measure of religion's intellectual dispensability.

As I will argue less telescopically in the first chapter of this book, each of these types of positions, in one way or the other, faces serious difficulties in the very fundamental task of bringing distinctively theological insights about divine action to bear upon our contemporary experience of the world. As strategies, they may very well succeed in what they intend (faithfulness in the one case, intelligibility in the other), but the cost is great. The very success of theological programs that move toward either of these poles, in truth, displays the fact that the modern world picture has wreaked havoc upon theology.

This book is written in the hope that this polarity, though it is likely a permanent feature of theological discourse, does not constitute a complete dead end. There are no Pollyanna expectations defended here. Nevertheless, it is hoped that creativity, openness to ancient wisdom, and a persistent willingness to face the facts of human experience are the sort of intellectual skills that may enable theology to avoid the more disastrous temptations of religious thought in the modern and postmodern age, and also to mitigate difficulties which surface within any proposal. It is possible, I will argue, to offer a genuinely modern interpretation of God's activity in the world which, if not steering a middle course between the polar extremes I have outlined, at least avoids some of the worst pitfalls associated with either one or the other.

The case-in-point for our purposes will be the work of Gordon D. Kaufman, but I believe that other programs could be enumerated and analyzed. What is especially felicitous about Kaufman's work is that, particularly in his 1993 magnum opus *In Face of Mystery: A Constructive Theology* and other more recent writings, he has put forward an account of divine activity which draws heavily upon a broad range of modern intellectual resources, while at the same time bringing them into a disciplined relation to a set of normative criteria derived from the classical monotheistic strand of Western religious tradition. His theology represents a monumental effort to interpret the world we actually know, experience, and explain it in terms of the practical wisdom of theistic faith. This is not to say that he finds a way to neutralize or to avoid the polarity described above, but it is to say that the normative criteria with which he begins and finally ends do not function in abstraction, but in real relation to the breadth of human experience and knowledge.

Kaufman's allegiance both to modern knowledge and to religious tradition yields a proposal which is, as we will see, highly revisionary. In the course of making use of the resources of modern knowledge and experience, Kaufman's interpretation of divine activity departs from classical interpretations at significant points. As a result, and predictably, Kaufman's theology has been widely criticized for jettisoning important features of classical Christian theology in the service of modern intellectual and moral commitments.[1]

The central thesis of this book, however, is that the revisionary features of Kaufman's program are the outworking of deep theological commitments that he actually shares with the classical theistic tradition. More specifically, the rather sweeping revisions of classical theism in Kaufman's account of God's activity result from a theological method which embodies a concern, shared with several theologians who have been universally regarded as classical exponents of Christian faith, to establish what we may call a broad "reflective equilibrium"[2] between theological insight and contemporary knowledge about the world. Like these earlier theologians, I will argue, Kaufman seeks to establish this coherence or "equilibrium" in order to render interpretations of God's power and faithfulness that refer realistically to tangible events and processes which are the warp and woof of human experience.

It is important to delimit the import of this claim. Kaufman is not trying to do science, nor is he resuscitating the grand metaphysical ambition of Hegel. The integration of knowledge about empirical realities

---

1. Examples could be multiplied. Criticisms on this point have come from philosophers and theologians, confessional and liberal thinkers, those friendly to his program as well as antagonists. Some representative examples are McClendon, "Four New Theologies," 183–91; Alston, "Realism and the Christian Faith," 37–60; Cobb, "Human Historicity, Cosmic Creativity and the Theological Imagination," 174–77; and Brown, "Mystery and History in Kaufman's Theology," 1209–18. One critic goes so far as to characterize Kaufman's theology as a "monument to modernity": Stoesz, "Gordon Kaufman's Thought: A Monument to Modernity," 37–50.

2. The phrase is borrowed from John Rawls. See Rawls, *A Theory of Justice*, rev. ed.

is important for Kaufman, as it was for many classical theologians, not in order to underwrite the speculative value of Christian belief, but in order that a well-articulated faith may function in religiously appropriate ways. "Saving knowledge" of God, to recall John Calvin's language, provides comfort, motivation and guidance for living because it teaches us to construe the world we know and experience as the arena of God's faithful activity. But this means that a theology which seeks to foster "saving faith" must not refer only to "strange new worlds"[3] borne in sacred texts, but preeminently to this one, which we handle, and observe, and measure, and where both the creative and the destructive realities of life which impinge upon us need to be interpreted.

This thesis is bound to be controversial among readers of Kaufman, in part because it emphasizes a measure of continuity between Kaufman and several prominent classical theologians. Any reader of Kaufman will be aware that he is not a kind of reincarnation of Augustine or Calvin. His theology is profoundly modern—perhaps even a "monument to modernity."[4] Some effort will therefore need to be expended near the outset to establish my admittedly counterintuitive claim that Kaufman's work stands in significant continuity with the classical tradition.

Let me make it clear at once, however, that I do not wish to minimize the radically innovative character of Kaufman's theology. I will not try to argue that it is continuous with classical theologies in all respects. Karl Barth and his followers are ordinarily seen as the defenders of classical Christian orthodoxy against the acids of modernity, and I will not challenge this viewpoint in its broad outline. I regard Barth as among the greatest of modern theologians, in respect both to his faithfulness to tradition and to his systematic rigor. Regarding the insistence of classical theologians that divine activity refer to tangible, empirically describable realities in this world, however, I will argue that Kaufman, even in his unabashed modernism, is distinctively representative of classical Christian theology; and further, that this central feature of the classical tradition has been abandoned by most modern theologians, even by those whose work has earned the label, "neo-orthodox."

My thesis may be controversial for another reason, particularly among more philosophically-minded critics of Kaufman. A persistent

3 See Karl Barth's famous address, "The Strange New World within the Bible," printed in *The Word of God and the Word of Man*, 28–50.

4. See note 2.

question about Kaufman's theology has been whether his concept of God refers to an objective reality, or whether it is merely the projection of human aspirations.[5] A seemingly obvious reading of Kaufman, given his insistence that theology is not a straightforward description of an object, but, as he puts it, an "imaginative construction" of symbols which serve practically to orient human life toward humane ends, has him embracing a Feuerbachian interpretation of theistic language, which I have already denounced as an end-game for theology.

A large part of the argumentative burden of this book, accordingly, will be that a careful examination of his account of God's activity demonstrates that there are indeed objective components to the task of orienting persons and communities in the world which resist easy assimilation to human aspirations, however important, noble, or pressing. As we will see, there are ambiguities that persist throughout much of Kaufman's writings which seem to leave the question unresolved. I will argue, however, that the direction of his recent thought demonstrates with particular clarity that the task of constructing a practically orienting vision of God and the world in fact requires grappling with the constraints imposed by the realities of nature and history as they are experienced in all their firmness and implacability, and that it is this "trajectory" (to borrow from Kaufman's own vocabulary) that embodies the creativity required for responsible theological work today.

The opening chapters of this book will be something of a propaedeutic to the overall argument. In the first chapter, I will examine in more detail the challenges and difficulties faced by interpreters of divine activity today, calling upon the work of Karl Barth and Ralph Wendell Burhoe as witnesses. In chapter 2, I will consider Kaufman's theological method in some detail, clearing away the objection that his constructivism automatically commits him to an unrealistic account of God and the world.

The remainder of the book will be devoted to a detailed analysis of Kaufman's account of God's relation to the world, especially his reinterpretation of divine activity. Since our central concern is that of relating the modern world picture to theological claims and arguments,

---

5. Kaufman's doctrine of God has changed over the years, but this question has consistently worried critics. An early expression of this concern is McLean, "On Theological Models," 155–87. Later expressions include Harvey, "Feuerbach on Religion as Construction," 249–68; and Alston, "Realism and the Christian Faith," 37–60.

my analysis of Kaufman's theology will pay particular attention to his use of modern scientific knowledge in relation to his leading religious convictions. In order to make this rather large problem somewhat more manageable, I will specify it in terms of three smaller, related problems: (1) construing the world as the arena of divine action, (2) assessing and reconstructing the concept of God as agent, and (3) relating human aspirations to what can be credibly affirmed of God's purposes. Important and quite particular conceptual issues lurk beneath each problem. After examining Kaufman's theological method in the second chapter, therefore, the argument of the book will unfold in three major steps, each of which tracking the commerce between traditional religious insight and contemporary knowledge about the world in relation to one of these three somewhat more fine-grained theological problems.

Interpretations of the world as the arena of divine action, first of all, require consideration of the appropriate weight to be given to various descriptive accounts of natural and historical processes. What warrants, the theologian needs to ask, are there for construing the physical universe as in some sense governed, and how do the particular features of our knowledge of the world qualify and shape what is appropriately meant by "governance?" Should theological concerns compel us to look for perforations or gaps in the ordering of nature as understood by modern science? How, further, might any qualifications of traditional affirmations of divine governance made on the basis of empirical knowledge affect heavily emphasized insights about God, such as God's goodness or faithfulness toward the created order? Chapters 3 and 4 will be preoccupied with these questions.

Secondly, assessing and reconstructing the traditional theistic concept of God as agent is closely related to interpreting the world as acted upon, but it involves slightly different conceptual problems. At issue here is the coherence and appropriateness of models of agency drawn from human life to portray God. The analogy is affected not only by modern knowledge about the world as the context of divine action but also by recent scientific and philosophical analyses of agency. What modifications of the concept of agency, if any, are required in order to relate divine activity to the sort of governance that can be credibly discerned amidst events and processes in the known world? Chapters 5 and 6 will consider these issues.

Finally, the task of discerning the place of human beings amid the aims, trajectories, or purposes associated with divine activity raises further difficulties. Granted that we can construct some intelligible account of divine governance, what can we appropriately say about its implications for human life? If considerable weight is given to modern cosmological and evolutionary theories about the world, so that they constrain and positively shape our account of divine activity, we may need to adjust traditional claims about God's faithfulness toward human beings. What price are we willing to pay, in the end, for a theology that moves in this direction? These questions, I will argue in the final chapter, are the ones that lurk throughout Kaufman's recent work. They give voice to the promptings within Kaufman's program that lead him to continue thinking and writing.

The task of constructing an interpretation of the world-before-God which does justice to the wisdom of theological tradition, the compelling insights of modern knowledge, and the demands of the day, as we shall see in the course of dealing with these issues, is a highly complicated one. For the theologian, it is not enough to be well-informed. Alongside a great deal of knowledge about modern science as well as theology, a theologian needs the gift of judgment. An intuitive sense of balance is called for, and Kaufman's effort ought probably to be appreciated as an artistic or even poetic accomplishment at least as much as it is applauded for its conceptual rigor.

That is not to say, however, that attempting to uncover the conceptual moves in the details of his theology will not illumine his overall artistry. Indeed, as I will attempt to show, doing so will demonstrate not only the profundity of Kaufman's interpretation of God's activity, but it will also bring to light the various stresses and strains which drives his theology further toward clarity and completeness, and which may lead beyond his own insights—as the interminable conversation of theology continues.

1

God the (Methodological) Problem

GORDON KAUFMAN'S THEOLOGY HAS been animated from the start by a traditional preoccupation: the problem of God. Indeed, some of the essays which most clearly indicate the line of inquiry which has come to dominate his writing appear in a collection titled *God the Problem*. The "problem" is that of joining a recognizable concept of God to a whole range of shared assumptions about how to describe the world, what it means to act, and what is to be valued. In simplest terms, it is the vexing difficulty of simultaneously securing integrity and intelligibility within a coherent theological program.[1]

The problem is handled in Kaufman's writing by positively relating theistic language to concepts and insights which frame our thinking more generally. In many cases, these insights come from the natural and social sciences. Often they are the result of philosophical reflection upon concepts and their import. Sometimes their origin is, broadly speaking, political. In all cases, however, the insights Kaufman deals with are regarded as compelling to the modern mind, placing claims upon theology that cannot easily be avoided. Kaufman's project has been to receive these claims as a basis for reconstructing theology from the ground up, so that it may once again claim both to do justice to the wisdom of religious tradition and to maintain an intelligible relationship to contemporary knowledge and experience. Only then can the problem of God's reality be resolved in the affirmative.

The aim of this book is to monitor and evaluate his attempts to carry this ambitious program through on a range of topics related to the problem of God, with particular attention to the decisive issue of divine activity. These topics include: theological method, problems involved in interpreting the world as an arena of divine activity, the question of what

1. Ottati, *Meaning and Method*, 171–83.

9

it means for God to act, and the role of human action in relation to
God's activity. My central argument is that Kaufman's attempt to resolve
the problem of God, even though it is quite innovative, is driven by a
quest for coherence with human experience that is not only shared with
a number of important classical Christian theologians, but that is fundamental to any adequate response to theological problems.

Before we begin examining Kaufman's theological program, however, much of this first chapter will be devoted to an analysis of different
ways of attempting to secure both the integrity and the intelligibility of
language about divine activity. As we will see, classical theologians, such
as St. Augustine and John Calvin, were able to move back and forth between empirical knowledge and religious insight with relative comfort,
resulting in a picture of God's governance of the world which connected
with and distinctively interpreted or framed the knowledge and experience available to them. Modern efforts, on the other hand, have tended
toward one or the other of two extreme positions. They have in many
cases curtailed consideration of knowledge and human experience in
order to preserve the integrity of theology. Or, in the opposite extreme,
some of them have simply collapsed theology or religious insight into
scientific theories.

Of course, few of those occupying either extreme or any of the possible positions in the middle have wanted to abandon the reality status
or referentiality of the idea of God. While there have been attempts to
reinterpret God-language nontheistically or even to theorize about a
"Christianity Without God,"[2] these efforts will not be our concern here.
All of the positions to be treated in this chapter may be understood
as attempts to underwrite the claim that a real God, who bears some
recognizable relation to some strand of Western religious symbolism,
genuinely interacts with the real world. However, it will be pointed out
that, for a variety of important reasons, modern efforts have had a more
difficult time holding on to both the distinctiveness of religious insight
and the interaction with contemporary knowledge which characterized
the theological work of earlier ages.

2. Geering, *Christianity without God*.

THE COHERENCE OF CLASSICAL THEOLOGY

As I have suggested, it was not only thought possible but in fact expected by many important classical theologians that theological reflection relate talk about God to what is known about the world. That is not to say that this task was easy. Cherished theological insights regarding God's governance of all things and God's faithful benevolence toward the created order had to be related to a world characterized by a broad range of conflicts, diseases, and injustices. This dissonance between deeply held religious beliefs and contemporary experience made the relation of traditional religious and experiential sources of knowledge and insight difficult, even in a prescientific era.

Several of the staunchest defenders of divine providence, however, were quite confident in asserting coherence between talk about God and knowledge of the world. St. Augustine did not hesitate to ascribe to such diverse empirical realities as "the bird's feather," the internal organs of animals, and the "life of the intellect" a basic and beneficial harmony or order. God's faithful governance of the world provides all creatures with the appropriate means for flourishing in their assigned contexts: for even the simplest living creatures, the powers of reproduction; for most animals, the powers of perception; for human beings, the powers of intellect; and for all creatures living and nonliving, the power to continue in existence.[3]

The benevolent ordering of the world was evident to Augustine in the harmonies of nature and human life, and the observation of these lent credibility to his interpretation of divine providence. The particularities of this perceived order, moreover, actually shaped his account of what God is doing in the world. Indeed, one might say that Augustine's convictions about divine benevolence were given definite form by his identification of a number of empirical examples, and that this procedure enabled him to render an interpretation of the world as governed by divine goodness.

This procedure of giving shape to theological convictions by means of interpreting experience, however, requires the theologian to struggle with the evident ambiguities of history. Augustine's theology does not shrink from this requirement. In *The City of God*, he maintained that "earthly kingdoms" owe their sovereignty to the divine pleasure, which

---

3. Augustine, *City of God*, 196.

can never, he argued, be out of accord with divine justice. He also noted, however, that the world is "liable to be tempest-tossed" with such destructive and costly realities as protracted warfare. God is not to be blamed for the disordered, misdirected nature of human governments (the "city of man") which gives rise to war. But the duration as well as the outcome of wars reflects the workings of the divine will, which supervenes upon the evident disorder of human life in order to absorb it into a wider, benevolent ordering of history. God's "permissive" will allows free creatures to direct themselves wrongly and thereby to distort themselves and the broader social fabric, but the elective will of God mysteriously directs even the events resulting from this distortion toward the fulfillment of God's benevolent purposes. These purposes may well not be apparent, however, and may not be in accord with our own desires.[4]

The point I wish to stress is that Augustine's theology did not simply assert some preferred account of God's providential goodness in the face of all evidence to the contrary, demanding a sacrifice of observational powers if not intellect in general. Rather, his distinction between God's elective and permissive wills embodied an effort to adjust claims about the ultimate harmony of the world's ordering to the experience of historical events. This procedure, therefore, allowed what we normally think of as negative features of human experience also both to qualify and to shape his account of God's activity.

Confidence in the coherence of talk about God and knowledge about the world came to especially vivid expression in John Calvin's doctrine of providence. For Calvin, all events and processes in both nature and history were purposefully determined by God's will. His adoption of a rigorously personalistic conception of divine activity, in preference to talk of "orders" and "natures" that mediate God's purposes in a partially autonomous world, tended to undercut any concessions to the natural freedom of human beings to determine the course of history, concessions that enabled Augustine to attribute the ultimate cause of wars to human perversion rather than to God's elective will.[5] More so than Augustine, Calvin was willing to risk implicating God in the evident disorder of human life by identifying actual events as expressions of God's will. Like Augustine, however, Calvin also saw in the continual ordering of the

4. Ibid., *City of God*, 215–18.

5. Calvin, in fact, repudiated Augustine's distinction between God's elective and permissive wills (Calvin, *Institutes* 1:228–31).

universe testimony to (even a "mirror of") God's benevolent purposes, directed especially toward the well-being of human beings.[6] In nature, creatures were fed, the young were cared for, and procreation sustained the various biological species.[7] In history, moreover, the requisite governance of human society was provided not simply by the creation of a governable human nature but by the "ceaseless activity" of God's all-determining will.[8]

It is important to point out that, far from inculcating dread before an impersonal and ineluctable fate, Calvin's doctrine of providence was designed to direct attention to God's paternal faithfulness in providing for creatures and watching over the details of their lives. Providence is provision and care, and knowledge of it was regarded as beneficial to persons and communities, evoking a corresponding trust and confidence in the midst of the precarious business of life in the world.

Appeals to nature and history as mirrors of divine faithfulness are not without a shadow side, however, particularly when they are made with the rigor of Calvin's. The easily discernible inequalities, and apparent inequities, sustained and supported by events and processes in nature and history are held, in Calvin's theology, to reflect God's purposes just as clearly as do evidences of support and care. If inanimate objects, for example, are "nothing but the instruments of God,"[9] then the falling branch which kills a hapless passer-by is an intentional divine act.[10] If, as Calvin reads Psalm 8, infants receive providentially arranged nourishment from their mothers almost immediately after birth,[11] the inequalities in the amount of milk available to them reflects God's intentions to feed them unequally.[12] If the wicked are in authority and oppress the righteous in a particular place, then the unjust suffering of people there is part of God's inscrutable plan. The threats, ambiguities, and even disharmonies

---

6. Ibid., 52, 179–80.

7. Ibid., 198, 205–6.

8. Ibid., 60.

9. Ibid., 199.

10. Ibid., 205.

11. Calvin, *Commentary on the Book of the Psalms*, 95–96, where in commenting upon this psalm, Calvin asserts that God "wonderfully changes blood into milk" immediately upon the birth of an infant, whose tongue God fits, "by a mysterious instinct," for nursing.

12. Calvin, *Institutes* 1:200–201.

in nature and history play, in other words, a considerable role in Calvin's interpretation of what God is doing in the world.

To be sure, one may want to raise serious questions about the normative adequacy of Calvin's account. What is important for our purposes, however, is that there is a strong and even courageous affirmation of coherence between knowledge of the world and theological insight in Calvin which enables him to identify tangible referents of his claims about divine providence. Faith in providence is not a vague sentiment which fails to join issue with particular human experiences, but rather it is a way to construe actual, empirical events and processes in the world as expressions of God's benevolent will. And so, although the import of Calvin's affirmations of God's faithfulness is not exhausted by observable events, it is of necessity qualified and shaped in important ways by, as he phrased it, "what experience plainly demonstrates."[13]

Before we launch into a somewhat mournful account of modern theology's seemingly inevitable failings in this regard, a quick and merely suggestive comparison of this classical strategy and Kaufman's program can be offered. Though it is not motivated by the need to underwrite strong claims for divine sovereignty to the degree that Augustine's and Calvin's are, Kaufman's theology is characterized by a similar insistence that language about divine activity be related and applied to ordinary empirical realities. For Kaufman as well as for these earlier theologians, affirming the reality of God means relating theological claims to the breadth of human experience. It also means that a portion of the benefits of thinking along these lines will be practical: it provides a coherent context to orient human action and a basic trust or confidence to motivate it.

This fairly obvious way of thinking about the theological task is, as we will now see, not universally shared in the present era. Indeed, attempts to make it work face severe stresses and strains. That is perhaps why the simpler and cleaner, though to my mind less promising, strategies we will examine next have been so influential.

MODERN THEOLOGY AND ITS DISCONTENTS

A major obstacle to extending the classical trajectory in theology is that intellectual commerce between theology and knowledge about the

13. Ibid., 200–201.

world is no longer as easily managed as it was in the fifth and sixteenth centuries. For one thing, the success of science in describing the world apart from appeal to divine activity has tended to make claims about divine intervention in causal processes look rather quaint. Moreover, this rise of scientific thinking has colluded with our growing awareness of enormous evils in history and of disturbing cruelties and deprivations in nature to render traditional claims about divine power and benevolence severely problematic. Calvin, for his part, bravely interpreted tragedies, inequities, and deprivations as expressions of God's faithfulness, but this interpretive task has become vastly more difficult in the face of knowledge of mass extinctions, genocide, and the much longer time frames which now condition our reflection upon the world.[14] Modern theology has faced unprecedented challenges, therefore, in coming to terms with empirical realities.

Many theologians have attempted elaborate theologies of history and of nature in response.[15] However, a prominent strategy in modern theology has been to sever claims about divine activity from empirical descriptions of events and processes in the world. This strategy tends toward the first of the two polar extremes indicated at the outset. Karl Barth's theology exemplifies this strategy, and we will therefore examine his thought in order to bring its features to light.

Rejecting Experience: Karl Barth

Barth's early theology is dominated by a concern for the objective over against the wiles of human subjectivity. It was forged in the context of his Church's participation in the ambiguities of German national politics, in which the subjective emphasis of liberal theology seemed to Barth to be guilty of causing the church to lose critical leverage against the demands of the state. The witness of the church fails, he believed, when it trades its allegiance to the Word of God for the vagaries of human religious sensibilities. The Word of God is objective, and stands over against religion and all human aspirations as their judge. Only faithful adherence to the Word can prevent the church from lapsing into idolatry and cooptation by the secular state.

14. Regarding the effect of the "colossal expansion of our picture of the world" upon theology see Troeltsch, *The Christian Faith*, 34–35.

15. Langdon Gilkey, for example, produced both. See *Reaping the Whirlwind*; and *Nature, Reality, and the Sacred*, 79–204.

This new (or renewed) insistence upon the independence of theology from cultural assumptions and expectations cleared the way for a radically new interpretation of the world. According to Barth, history could no longer be seen as an inevitable march upward toward greater humaneness and civility. The collapse of liberal optimism occasioned by historical events in Europe corroborated Barth's growing conviction that history is actually quite meaningless. Meaning can be found only in a God who must be conceived as radically independent of history, he argued.[16] Based on a reading of the Pauline dialectic of law and gospel, his *Epistle to the Romans* portrays temporal human existence as futile, but also, in and through its very futility, as a signpost to the meaning which can only be granted by God's free grace. Characteristically human attempts to realize meaning in and for our own various and conflicting temporal projects inevitably fail.[17] But this perpetual failure of historical meaning opens us to the possibility of being grasped by a meaning which is beyond history, as we are struck "vertically from above" by divine revelation. God's self-disclosure brings salvation by enabling us to see our temporal lives with the eyes of faith, whose object is not the inherent meaningfulness of history or of some particular feature of history, but the eternal God who utterly transcends it.[18]

Barth's later theology, systematized in his *Church Dogmatics*, is in many respects less austere than his commentary on Romans, but the independence of God from the ambiguities of human experience remains a central feature. In the *Dogmatics*, God's independence is supported by a full-orbed doctrine of revelation, as readers of *Romans* might have expected. It is now supported, however, by an explicitly existentialist account of divine agency. In his classic interpretation of Barth's theology, Hans Urs von Balthasar describes Barth's overall conceptual framework as "actualist." By this he means that, for Barth, agency is not merely the outward expression of a independently subsisting substance, as it was understood by medieval scholastics. On the contrary, the nature of an

16. Barth, *Romans*.

17. The dialectic of judgment upon human pretension, on the hand, and God's bestowal of unmerited grace, on the other, runs throughout Barth's commentary but is especially vivid in two chapters near the beginning, titled "The Righteousness of Men" (55–76) and "The Righteousness of God" (77–114).

18. Resurrection points to the emergence of a "New Man" and a "New Day," the possibilities of which, however, are completely absent from the world as we experience it under divine "Judgment" (Barth, *Romans*, 149–86).

agent is grounded in the particular actions that the agent undertakes.[19] This is true of human beings and true of God. Divine agency, therefore, is not to be understood as the expression of God's nature, which is otherwise kept secret within God's inner life. Rather, God's action is what actually constitutes the divine nature. God's being is not only fully disclosed in God's act—it is definitively realized by it.[20]

The importance of Barth's existentialist account of divine agency to his overall program is generally epistemological: to appeal to the divine nature apart from God's action, according to Barth, would invite confusion about the content of the God's will.[21] This assertion may seem paradoxical, since talk about God's nature has traditionally served to fend off nominalist interpretations of divine agency which have tended to reduce God's freedom to pure arbitrariness. Barth's existentialist account of agency does not commit him to theological nominalism, however. On the contrary, he agrees with the scholastic tradition that God's will is always directed toward ends consistent with the divine nature. The important point for Barth, however, is that this nature is not something reserved behind a series of actions which only indirectly and imperfectly reveal it. Were this the case, human reason would be left free to make inferences and to invent analogies based on human experience of the world in its thinking about divine activity. Human experiences of power, for example, might be (and have been) projected upon a conception of God. Barth warns that thinking of God in this way, according to the analogies of being allegedly characteristic of liberal Protestantism as well as scholastic theology, inevitably leads to the idolatrous reversal of the preferred analogy—particular forms of human or cosmic power will be deified, and persons will become uncritically attached to idealized projections of their own, finite experiences. For Barth's actualism, as we have emphasized, God's nature is fully and uniquely disclosed in what God does, as this is attested in Scripture. No analogies from human experience are therefore needed to discern God's purposes, and none are to be trusted.[22]

19. Balthasar, *The Theology of Karl Barth*, 165.

20. Barth, *Church Dogmatics*, II.2, 27–30.

21. Barth contends that God's power is always a "definite power," defined exclusively by God's particular act of love toward the creature in Jesus Christ (ibid., 50).

22. Barth, *Church Dogmatics*, I.1, 23–27.

Balthasar also characterizes Barth's theology as motivated by a "passion for the concrete."[23] We can certainly see why. Actions are not formed by the confluence of general laws, but by particular decisions which respond to particular temporal conditions. According to Barth, the divine nature is exhaustively defined by a concrete event. He therefore insists relentlessly, even in the face of the classical tradition, that abstract talk about God as the "supreme being" is dangerous and unscriptural.[24] God must rather only and always be spoken of as "this God," the God whose being is neither an object of philosophical speculation nor an utterly unknowable "X," but fully disclosed in a single, concrete choice.

This decision which defines God's being is the eternal election of Jesus Christ to which Scripture bears witness.[25] Though eternal, this decision determines the meaning and purpose of both nature and history. It does so because the election of Jesus Christ is also the election of humanity in and through him, and it is thereby also the election of the whole creation as the context of God's history with humanity in covenantal relationship.[26] Moreover, as an eternal decision, it is firmly established and irrevocable, and not therefore in any respect contingent upon events in the temporal sphere. From eternity, it is determined that the contours of the world ruled by this God will take on *this* character and will serve *this* purpose.

Barth's doctrine of providence is elaborated subsequently to his doctrine of election. This order is significant because, for Barth, the doctrine of election is not merely a specification of a more general doctrine of providence which can be understood on independent grounds. Rather, providence is God's activity of providing the temporal and spatial conditions necessary to realize his eternal decision to reconcile and redeem lost humanity. It is undertaken by God for the sole purpose of establishing and maintaining the sphere in which God's covenant with

23. Balthasar, *The Theology of Karl Barth*, 164.

24. "[I]t is difficult to imagine of the activity of this [supreme] being can ever become a Gospel. If the distinctive and ultimate feature of God is absolute freedom of choice . . . then it will be hard to distinguish his freedom from caprice" (Barth, *Church Dogmatics*, II.2, 25).

25. Ibid., 53. Barth even goes so far as to say that Christian thought about God is not really "theistic" at all, but peculiarly Trinitarian. God the creator and governor of the world is not to be understood in terms of inferences or causality, but strictly from the standpoint of his eternal election of his Son.

26. Ibid., 94–95.

humanity is realized.[27] This divinely-initiated covenant, therefore, is the inner meaning of all creaturely "world-occurrence," and God preserves, accompanies, and rules events and processes in the world so that they may serves as the "external basis" of this covenant.[28] Providence, therefore, must be understood in terms of election, rather than the other way around.

Barth faults Calvin and the majority of theologians in the Reformed tradition for reversing this order, and thereby portraying divine providence abstractly. An abstract doctrine of providence, he urges, tends toward viewing God's activity brutally, as the exercise of unlimited power in the service of inscrutable ends. This is the error of early Calvinists, who left themselves open, in Barth's judgment, to the charge of resuscitating the ancient Stoic notion of a deterministic fate which overwhelms rather than elicits human freedom.[29] Barth also faults, however, a large number of theologians since Calvin who have retreated from full affirmations of God's sovereignty to the relative safety of various forms of semi-Pelagianism. These theologians misconstrue the real problem with this "hyper-Calvinist" fatalism. He argues that the appropriate response is not to limit the scope of divine providence, securing a space free from God's sovereignty so that human agents may genuinely act, but to define God's providential purposes more adequately in terms of the concrete act which defines God's use of divine freedom: the election of humanity, through Jesus Christ, as God's covenant partner.[30] Creaturely life can thus be understood as determined in all its details by divine decision without destroying human freedom, since the "creaturely mode" of human beings as determined by God is in fact the freedom of partnership with God.[31]

The upshot of Barth's doctrine of providence is not merely that the governance of the world is to be understood in relation to God's revealed intentions regarding God's benevolent purposes for humanity. It is, more

---

27. Barth, *Church Dogmatics*, III.3.

28. Ibid., 6–7, 54.

29. Ibid., 115.

30. Ibid., 116–18.

31. Divine "operation," according to Barth, is "fatherly operation," which moves all things by the "force and wisdom and goodness" of the "spirit of His Word" (ibid., 142). Its mode as fatherly speech requires the allowance of free response on the part of creatures.

radically, that this revelation determines everything that is appropriately said about God's involvement with the world, overriding any supposed evidence which may tempt one to allow human experience to play a constructive role in shaping one's interpretation of divine activity.

Barth allows that "worldviews" which are either cobbled together from experience or rationally derived from metaphysical principles, may be inevitable features of human thinking attempting to situate itself in its surroundings, but he insists that they cannot stand in for God. He takes particular aim at modern theologians who employ such notions as "process," "elan vital," or "mechanism" in order to make sense of divine action. These attempts, he argues, are akin to a sort of paganism which pays minimal allegiance to a high god while assigning all relevant dimensions of world-governance to lesser, more accessible cosmic powers. In each of these efforts at mediation between God and the realities which are directly experienced by human beings, the mediating conceptuality employed is effectively cut loose from the controlling determination of revelation, resulting in a characterization of events and processes in the world which is finally independent of Christian faith. Resisting this "alien" influence, Barth argues, Christian faith must insist upon the irreplaceably of God's revealed purposes in its distinctively christological account of the created order. But this means, correlatively, that it must remain free from final commitment to any particular "view of the world," even if it purports to be Christian.[32]

The real governance of "world-occurrence," then, is for Barth not disclosed directly to observation. Rather, it is profoundly and ineluctably hidden, and therefore never to be equated with human perceptions of order and law. These human perceptions of orderliness, which Barth calls "noetic law," are merely "arrows" which point to the real ordering power of the universe, which is the concealed "ontic law" of faithful divine governance.[33] Knowledge of this "ontic" ordering of the world comes only by the disclosure of divine purpose in Jesus Christ. Barth does not shrink from drawing the most radical consequences from this point. In order properly to construe the divine governance of world-occurrence without falsely equating God's free and gracious ordering activity with some fixed, "general" view of the world, Barth urges, we must "drop the ordinary but harmful conception of cause, operation and effect," which,

32. Ibid., 139–42.
33. Ibid., 126–28.

he suggests, is "godless."[34] Though "ordinary" conceptions of causality may portray the universe as indifferent or hostile and restrictive toward human beings, the real ordering of the universe flows from the will of God to elect humanity as God's covenant partner. The world is neither hostile nor indifferent, therefore, but really a "home" for human beings.[35]

Barth's theology, both early and late, places stringent restraints upon the use of experience to construe God's action in order to preserve what might be called the "humane" dimensions of traditional theology. In so doing it famously succeeds in preserving much of what the classical theistic tradition in the West has intended to say about God. However, I want to underscore the fact that there are a number of ways in which his interpretation of divine activity departs quite radically from the classical tradition. First of all, in spite of his thunderous insistence upon God's objective reality, Barth's claims about benevolent divine action appear to have no tangible referents, and thus they avoid what is perhaps the most pressing question modern persons bring to the discussion about God's activity. To what particular empirical details (or generalities, for that matter) of temporal human life does the providential ordering of events in support of the election of humanity in Jesus Christ refer? What within human experience may count for or against it?

Insofar as answers to these questions are ruled out by Barth's method, the problem is not merely that his theology is too abstract. It is that, ironically enough, it appears in the end to banish divine activity from the world apprehended by human knowledge and experience altogether.

Modern knowledge provides fodder for testing Barth on this question. For example, what is the relation of the vastly longer time frames indicated by modern evolutionary theory to the claim that God administers the world for the benefit of humanity? Or, what is the status of our knowledge of historical evils? Are these natural and historical realities to be dismissed by the theologian as mere "appearance," as opposed to the genuine "reality" of God's covenant with humanity realized in Jesus Christ? While there is no law of logic prohibiting one from speaking blithely about the experienced world as the "external basis" of this covenant, it is hard to see how much of what we actually know and experience can contribute positively to that assertion. In other words, what we know about such matters is prohibited in Barth's theology from

34. Ibid., 118.
35. Ibid., 48.

influencing what we are to believe about the ultimate character of our universe. Under the protection of the Kantian distinction between that which is real and that which is apparent to the observer's eye, Barth's interpretation of the world cuts off all commerce between the two—or rather, it allows it to flow in only one direction.[36]

But what this inability or refusal to appropriate modern knowledge means for Barth is that the tensions and ambiguities involved in the evolutionary process, which must be interpreted in order to lend credibility to the idea of God's presence within the details of nature and history, cannot be incorporated into his account of divine activity. And this in turn means that some important features of classical interpretations of God's activity are lost. Necessarily gone, for example, is the courageous incorporation of the deprivations, limitations, and inequalities characteristic of both nature and history into knowledge of divine purpose by theologians like Calvin. Gone too, therefore, is Calvin's and others' austere realism about the circumscribed role and value of human beings before the power(s) who will(s) deprivations and disharmony. Barth's claims about God's faithfulness toward humanity simply do not join issue with the empirical realities that warranted these sober acknowledgements. The result is that many of the obvious features of the world we know are left uninterpreted by the traditional religious insights which he works so assiduously to protect.

In the end, therefore, modern knowledge of deprivations and disharmonies in the world has exacted its price in Barth's theology. In its effort not to contradict modern knowledge and still to preserve what are regarded as central features of the theistic tradition, Barth's standpoint represents a retreat from the experienced world which, from a more classically theistic point of view, might be regarded as a failure of nerve.

---

36. I am here borrowing James M. Gustafson's metaphor of "intersections," formed by the convergence or confrontation of two or more types of account of a single subject matter. "Traffic" at these "intersections" may flow only in one direction, resulting in the dominance of one kind of description over another; it may flow in two directions, resulting in a mutual revision; or it may be "jammed" by ideological differences at the level of method. See Gustafson's *Intersections: Science, Theology, and Ethics*. Although he suggests that human experience and knowledge about the world may be "annexed" to the picture of God and the world given in revelation, we may well wonder how far this "annexation" may extend without seriously disrupting his christocentric account of the world.

The problems here are related to Barth's conception of the theological task. Theology seeks primarily to explicate and unravel the implications of a received theological tradition rather than to interpret the experienced world as the theater of God's activity. Many classical theologians believed that knowledge of God is available by means of numerous sources of insight (reason and experience) which are confirmed, deepened or sometimes transformed by biblical revelation. For Barth, however, revelation is the only reliable source of insight about God, and ultimately about the world under God. Therefore a faithfully Christian theology can only unfold and interpret Christian revelation. Barth does appeal to the classically Reformed notions of the world as "theater" and "mirror" of the divine, but the world is a "theater" only insofar as it serves as the outer context of God's hidden rule, and a "mirror" only as it reflects God's gracious covenant with humanity. It can only be "theater" or "mirror," moreover, in the "moment" in which God freely determines that it will be such.[37] The world as "mirror" has in itself nothing to add to knowledge of the world under God's rule—it merely reflects that which can be truly known only on the basis of revelation. Once again, the traffic in this exchange between revelation and experience goes only one way.

A formal way to characterize the difficulty in Barth's interpretation of divine activity is to say that is discriminate but not interactive. In other words, it employs distinctively religious insights in the formation of an account of divine activity, but these insights are not brought to bear in an interpretation of the empirical world. In order to do this, his theology would have to place these distinctively religious insights into a relationship of interaction with contemporary knowledge and experience. But his overriding concern to protect God's radical independence of the world leads him to employ a method which rules out any such interaction. Barth strategy is to reject human experience as a reliable indicator of divine action. The result, as I have emphasized, is an account of divine activity which keeps faith with the classical Christian tradition's emphasis upon the grace of God only by removing it from the sphere of human experience.

---

37. Barth, *Church Dogmatics*, III.3, 48–52.

Absorbing Theology: Ralph Wendell Burhoe

There have been a number of religious thinkers who, in sharp contrast to theologians like Barth, have sought rigorously to derive claims about divine activity from well-established explanations of causal processes. In the work of these thinkers, the traffic between experience and traditional religious insight is, as it were, reversed. Contemporary experience, often in the form of scientific theory, specifies the allowable meaning of traditional religious affirmations in an exhaustive way. The work of scientist-theologian Ralph Wendell Burhoe is representative of this strategy.[38] Burhoe identifies the cosmic evolutionary process as conceptualized by modern science as the real referent of traditional religious language about God. Modern scientific theory is therefore imported wholesale to replace older conceptualizations of divine agency which were dependent upon a discredited metaphysical dualism.

For Burhoe, God is not, as a more traditional theistic evolutionist might suppose, a personal being who utilizes evolutionary processes as instruments to accomplish consciously determined purposes. Burhoe's theology is naturalistic in a much stronger sense. Not only are particular events in nature and history regarded as inextricably linked with the system of finite natural causes as a whole, but the causal system itself is regarded as closed to external influence. Supernatural agencies have no role to play, and language about a divine reality ontologically distinct from the world can have no literal reference. There is therefore no room in Burhoe's theology for a dualism, or even duality, of God and the world.[39] Empirically describable causal mechanisms are not merely "secondary" causes which point to a higher, all-determining causal power— they themselves *are* the all-determining causal power.

An important implication of Burhoe's naturalism is that there are no cosmic purposes which are in principle hidden and inscrutable. The mysteries of nature and history are the products of our provisional lack of information about their empirical characteristics, not about a supposed teleology which lies behind them, or which supervenes upon them from above. God's purposes for the world, if there are any, are known as any other empirical realities are known—through direct inspection of

---

38. Burhoe, *Toward a Scientific Theology.*

39. Ibid., 74–82.

nature and history in light of the most well-attested cosmological theories available.[40]

Fortunately, according to Burhoe, the widely-shared perception that science excises all purpose from the world is no longer accurate. Though literal reference to a supernatural being is no longer tenable, modern evolutionary science has reintroduced the notion of development in nature and history, a concept which indicates that things in the world are directional. Reality is not "static," he urges, but "progressive." And that means that human purposiveness, as it turns out, is not the free-floating metaphysical surd it has often been portrayed to be by positivists, but an adaptive development of the human organism which enables it to track changes in the natural and historical environment which gave it birth, sustains it, and promises it a future.[41] Science teaches us that there is a larger, dynamic reality (nature) which creates, sustains, and fulfills human life, to which we must align ourselves if we are to survive and flourish. This ultimate reality with which we have to do, according to Burhoe, is precisely what the religious traditions have meant by "God."[42] Science thus enables us to have more precise and credible knowledge of matters symbolized in the religious traditions by claims about divine sovereignty and faithfulness.

It should be noted that Burhoe's theology is just as unabashedly Augustinian as it is naturalistic. Nature's governance over human life is just as omnipresent, all-powerful and unrelenting as any Calvinist's God. Natural selection, a mechanism which for Burhoe operates at all levels of reality (physical/chemical, organic, and even historical), is irresistible and all-determining. It creates by bringing forth new types of ecologically viable complexity.[43] It judges by rejecting "evil" or maladaptive traits and combinations of traits of organisms and social groups. These are simply and ineluctably ruled out of existence by their inability to reproduce themselves in the face of environmental requirements.[44]

40. Burhoe quotes a passage from Charles Darwin's *The Origin of Species* describing the "daily and hourly scrutinizing" of phenotypes by natural selection in order to show how the concept amplifies and clarifies traditional Western intuitions about God exemplified in Psalm 139 (ibid., 109–10).

41. Burhoe, "Prophesying," 23–25.

42. Burhoe scientifically redescribes seven attributes traditionally ascribed to God in *Scientific Theology*, 125–37.

43. Burhoe, *Toward a Scientific Theology*, 78–79.

44. Ibid., 68.

It redeems by selecting the "good," adaptive traits to endure even after individual organisms or social groups which embody them have perished.[45] Though modern human beings have accumulated comparatively vast powers for controlling their destinies, they successfully do so only as their efforts conform to the requirements imposed upon them by the larger, perduring realities of nature. For Burhoe, this fact, recognized by most scientists, points to the viability of the modern concept of natural selection as a confirmation and deepening of traditional religious insights about the sovereign creative and redemptive activity of God.[46]

This confirmation and deepening of traditional religion by modern science is important for human life, according to Burhoe, because for him religion is a sort of "technology" which helps conscious, deliberative human beings successfully to adjust to their surroundings. In less sentient forms of life, the direction and motivation required for the successful navigation of environments are provided by genetic inheritance; but for human beings, genes are insufficient. Greater consciousness, including the acute awareness of death, opens many possibilities for maladaptive behavior which are difficult to manage. Humans depend upon cultural forces, those institutionalized in religions in particular, to provide a sense of meaning which can direct and motivate them in the face of personal loss and anxiety. Religions do this by means of myths and rituals which portray and reenact the meaningful activity of God or gods as the source and fulfillment of human life.

These myths are based in part upon the best knowledge about the available at the time of their formulation, so that the world as experienced is construed as meaningful. The problem for modern men and women, however, is that these necessary functions of the religions have been frustrated by the increasing incredibility of the myths upon which they are based. Knowledge of the closed system of natural causation has rendered supernaturalism unbelievable to educated persons, and theologians and religious leaders have not integrated this pervasive new knowledge with traditional religious insights. The regrettable result in modern Western culture, according to Burhoe, is that alternatively humanistic and nihilistic types of secularism have come to dominate the

---

45. Burhoe, "Prophesying," 18–20.

46. Modern scientific knowledge is therefore for Burhoe a "new gift of revelation about the not-readily-discernible total reality which is our Creator and the Lord of our History" (*Toward a Scientific Theology*, 22).

minds and hearts of persons. Humanists have used the difficulties about credibly conceptualizing the power that creates and judges human life to suggest that we are our own creators and our own judges, finally answerable to no reality outside of our own aspirations. Nihilists, on the other hand, have taken the new scientific accounts of the world as indications of its meaninglessness and even hostility to human life, and therefore have given in to despair of creating and maintaining a viable and humane culture. Both alternatives, according to Burhoe, fail miserably as alternatives to traditional religion, since they lack the power to direct and motivate human beings toward behavior which is adapted to the realities of the natural world.[47]

They are also wrong as descriptions of our actual situation, as, Burhoe suggests, the best of modern science demonstrates. Though nature places limits on the fulfillment of individual aspirations, it is not hostile to enduring features of human life (genotypes and "culturetypes," which collectively make up what Burhoe calls the "soul"), because these in fact have been selected for their conformity to nature's requirements.[48] Human beings, moreover, are not their own creators and redeemers, but indebted and responsible to the natural and historical processes in which they find their life. Science appears therefore to undermine both forms of secularism in a way which more powerfully and effectively echoes the rather feeble protests of historic religions in the face of modernity.

Burhoe argues that a "scientific" theology—one which is based upon established knowledge about the empirical world[49]—can revitalize religion in our time and thereby overcome the alternating moods of arrogance and despair which are maladaptive and which therefore threaten to hasten our demise. Burhoe compares the technological function of religion to that of medicine. Premodern medicine enabled human beings to deal with bodily infirmities because it was based on a great deal of wisdom about the body and its requirements gained through centuries of trial and error. Modern biology, however, has enabled the acquisition of far more precise and reliable information, and the practice of medicine has been thoroughly revolutionized. In the same way, Burhoe

---

47. Burhoe, "Some Prophecies," 50–51.

48. Burhoe, *Toward a Scientific Theology*, 137–44.

49. It is worth noting that Burhoe understands by "scientific theology," not disciplined inquiry into religious communities' speech about God, but religious reflection upon the results of natural scientific research.

suggests, modern knowledge about the world can deepen and revitalize the accumulated wisdom of religious myths and therefore enhance the effectiveness of religious practice in its effort to adapt human conscious-ness to reality. Vital religion, according to Burhoe, is effective because its myths about the divine activity in relation to human begins are coherent with the most reliable current knowledge about the world. A modern integration of science and theology can secure the empirical reference of traditional claims about divine power and goodness which is widely doubted amid caricatures of the universe as indifferent or hostile. In do-ing so it not only renders theology intellectually viable. It also restores it to its rightful place as "queen of the sciences."[50]

Does Burhoe's theology offer a better way of dealing with mod-ern sources of knowledge about the world than Karl Barth's? In sharp contrast to Barth, Burhoe's theology seeks to establish harmony between traditional religious claims about divine activity and modern science. Whether he has finally succeeded in doing so is of course debatable. Perhaps we may grant him that some measure of success is achieved, but any such success here comes at the cost of making historical religious tra-ditions appear, his reverent remarks about the "wisdom" of tradition not-withstanding, normatively superfluous. The strict derivation of theology from science renders such criteria for theological construction as fidelity to Scripture and tradition nothing more than impediments, to be hailed as "wisdom" for a prescientific era but not to be taken as constraining today. By jettisoning these standards on these grounds, Burhoe assumes in effect that historical religious traditions do not convey anything about human life and the world that cannot better be taken into account by the sciences. They illumine, but only after the manner of folk wisdom about the human body before the rise of modern biology. Burhoe's the-ology, therefore, allows the viable meanings of religious ideas simply to be specified by whatever resources the sciences have to offer.

The resulting account of divine activity is little different from sci-entific descriptions of events and processes in the world. It is likely that from Calvin's point of view, Burhoe's affirmation that "nature is God" is made "irreverently."[51] The evolutionary process is affirmed as the real-

---

50. Burhoe, "A Scientific View," 52–59. See also *Toward a Scientific Theology*, 34.

51. Calvin, *Institutes* 1:158. James Gustafson develops an ideal typology for relating theology and scientific theory, which responds to Calvin's enigmatic statement referred to here in Gustafson, *Ethics*, 251–55. In these pages, Gustafson characterizes Burhoe's

ity of God in an unqualified manner—talk about the mystery of God's purposes for the world is retained merely to refer to the ever-shrinking domain of human ignorance about the cosmos. This identification of divine activity and natural and historical processes is able strikingly to portray God's pervasive and relentless power, but the tradition's emphasis upon God's faithfulness is reduced to the regularities of nature and the creation and selection of new forms of existence which can successfully reproduce themselves in a changing environment. Despite Burhoe's approbation of individual sacrifice in the service of greater goods, the "good" toward which God's faithful will is directed is finally reduced to success. This yields a theologically complacent view of the cosmos—one which fails to bring the obvious, most prevalent forms of power and success under scrutiny in light of the specific mode of divine faithfulness attested in the tradition. In Scripture, God's faithfulness is not the faithful guarantee of ultimate success to those who conform to nature's requirements—it is the faithfulness of One who redeems precisely by taking on weakness and failure. The cross is not simply a means to success or power—a symbol of the cost of progress—but the central symbol of a uniquely cruciform conception of power that undermines success as finally normative.[52]

Formally, we may characterize the defect in Burhoe's theology by saying that it is, in radical contrast to Barth's program, indiscriminately interactive. Knowledge about the empirical world is drawn upon to provide tangible reference to such theological concepts as divine faithfulness, but the procedure of deriving the entire meaning of this and other terms from cosmological theory means that they become merely pious metaphors for the character of events and processes in the world as they are understood by the sciences. Ironically, God's faithfulness comes thereby to bear very nearly the opposite meaning of that which has been meant by it in the Christian tradition. The theological value of Burhoe's realistic refusal to turn away from the actualities of nature and history is vitiated, because these realities are not in turn critically interpreted in light of an historic theological frame of reference which orients our attention in

---

work, as I am doing, as attempting to deduce theology from science in a way that finally identifies "God" and "nature."

52. It should be noted, moreover, that from either Calvin's or Barth's perspective, this misunderstanding of divine faithfulness vitiates any potentially helpful understanding of God's power, since the latter is never strictly power in the abstract, but always shaped and constrained by God's paternal faithfulness.

light of the peculiar, counterintuitive notion of divine faithfulness which characterizes the religious vision of the world borne by Scripture and tradition. In this way, Burhoe's theology, like Barth's, forfeits the task of formulating a distinctively religious interpretation of the world.

This brief analysis of the efforts of Barth and Burhoe is intended to indicate that the problem of construing divine activity in relation to modern knowledge and experience involves difficult questions about the relation of theology to other intellectual disciplines. At issue is not only the problem of relating two sorts of inquiry, but also that of conceiving the purpose of theology and of specifying its requirements in the face of modern knowledge. Does theology operate primarily by unraveling the implications of an authoritative and epistemologically privileged tradition? To the extent that it does, accounts of divine activity will not join issue with knowledge about the world, and the actualities of our world will be left uninterpreted. Does it, on the other hand, operate primarily by deriving substantive theological claims from established causal explanations of events and processes in the world? To the extent that it does, divine activity and scientific accounts of world processes are collapsed, the difficulties involved in giving broadly compelling reasons for employing traditional theological language at all are exacerbated, and the genuinely distinctive claims of the tradition are flattened and reduced.

STRIKING OUT ON THE DIFFICULT ROAD OF ACCOMMODATION

The account of divine activity which emerges in the mature work of Gordon Kaufman is governed by a strikingly different methodology than those of either Barth or Burhoe. One way to characterize Kaufman's program in general is to say that it is "constructivist." As we will see in the next chapter, this term represents a methodological stance which embodies a number of controversial epistemological convictions. Epistemology does not govern the program, however. Nor does it short-circuit the hard work of theological thinking. As we shall see in subsequent chapters, one of the most important features of Kaufman's particular constructivist program is the painstaking utilization of contemporary sources of insight about the world in order to formulate an account of divine activity.

Rather than invoking a full-scale epistemology, we may also characterize Kaufman's program by saying that it sets out to "accommodate" contemporary knowledge and experience.[53] The issue is how nontheological sources of insight are used. Rather than rejecting them or using them simply to replace theological frames of reference, Kaufman sets out to incorporate them into an already existing and operative theological framework, making whatever corrections and adjustments that are required.

As his theology unfolds, concepts such as "serendipitous creativity" and "directionality" are proposed not only to characterize certain theologically important features of the world, but to suggest empirical referents for God's activity. This strategy, obviously, marks his program as radically distinct from Barth's, and it is freighted with both promise and peril. But I will argue that the identification of tangible referents for religious language is one component of the important theological task of bringing religious insights to bear upon our experience of the world. It is an important way in which theology may interact with empirical knowledge in order to support the conviction that the world in which we live is in actual fact an arena of grace.

The other component of this theological task is the formulation of some principle of interpretation or some criterion which can bring order to the "blooming, buzzing confusion" of human experience. In a distinctively theological interpretation of the world, this criterion cannot simply be derived from cosmological theory. Kaufman's program, accordingly, stays as far from Burhoe's absorptionist strategy of indiscriminate interaction as it does from Barth's rejectionist strategy of noninteractive discrimination.

As we proceed, we will see that Kaufman's innovative cosmological categories are not derived from modern knowledge per se. Rather, they are the products of a theological imagination which is shaped or formed by distinctively religious convictions characteristic of a particular strand of Western piety, and which makes use of a variety of materials. The language of "shape" or "form" and "matter" can be misleading here, since genuine interaction between theology and empirical knowledge requires that experience also leverage formative influence. But it is important to stress that, in Kaufman's program, modern knowledge about these processes is critically appropriated, shaping, informing, and constraining his interpretation of God's activity, much as (for example) Calvin's ap-

---

53. The term "accommodation" is borrowed from James Gustafson. For other examples of accomodationist theology, see Gustafson, *Intersections*, 100–106.

propriation of that which "experience plainly demonstrates" about the physiological differences in women shaped, informed, and constrained his account of God's providential care of infants. His account of divine governance is therefore not a neutral reflection upon the world, but a critical and constructive interpretation of nature and history which deliberately highlights features of world processes which create, sustain, and redeem human life.

Though the material affirmations of Calvin and Kaufman are radically different, their theologies are characterized by a certain methodological similarity. Neither of them is prone to disinterested speculation, but each is interested in presenting a unified theocentric worldview which accommodates contemporary knowledge and experience without surrendering the momentous claims for divine faithfulness characteristic of their traditions. By means of discriminate interaction with contemporary knowledge about nature and history, they are each able, albeit in very different ways, to formulate an overall vision of human life in the world which retains a tensive balance between realistic appraisal of human possibilities and limitations before the ultimate power(s) with which we have to do and the heartening conviction of God's faithfulness.

As we will also see, however, there are two ways in which Kaufman's theology is quite different from the classical tradition represented by Calvin. First of all, Kaufman accepts the modern naturalistic conception of the world as a unified system of cause and effect. The naturalistic picture of the universe poses major problems for traditional affirmations of divine activity, and it makes the road of accommodation difficult if not hazardous. Kaufman expends a great deal of effort toward a reconstructed account of God's activity that is appropriate to naturalistic assumptions which he believes are shared by most modern persons. This book will be preoccupied throughout with the way in which Kaufman's proposal handles the difficulties which arise in the process.

The following chapter, however, will be preoccupied with a second innovation upon the tradition proposed by Kaufman—an interpretation of the intellectual discipline of theology as one of "imaginative construction." While Calvin's theology was accomodationist in many important respects, it did not venture as far in the direction of innovation and revision. And so, undoubtedly, Kaufman's methodological remarks loosen the theologian's relation to received tradition to a degree that Calvin could not have countenanced. For some, that creates other hazards. However, I will argue that, far from giving him license to depart wholesale from the Western theological tradition, Kaufman's constructive method allows him to reformulate the outlines of the realistic faith in divine activity which has historically characterized that tradition in light of what we now know about the world. It does so, I will argue, because it suggests a way to realize the two-pronged criterion of discriminate interaction which I have identified in the efforts of classical theologians, in contrast to some strands of modern theology.

2

Imagination and Reality

KAUFMAN HAS ACHIEVED FAME and some degree of notoriety as the author of *An Essay on Theological Method*, published in its first edition in 1975. This slim volume features not only an indictment against much of contemporary theology regarding the contemporary chaos of opinion about how to go about thinking theologically—it also includes a radical new proposal for understanding the nature of theological reflection and its proper tasks. Kaufman's proposal is anchored by a claim that, since we have no cognitive access to divine reality, theology is necessarily a matter of the "imaginative construction" of images or concepts of God and of ourselves and the world under God.

As I noted at the outset of this book, his insistence that theological work involves the construction of concepts rather than the description of a unique object raises questions about whether Kaufman views theology as referential. A critic may worry, in fact, whether any or all of the conceptual innovations regarding divine activity that we will analyze in subsequent chapters ought to be understood simply, as he himself puts it in an early work, as "pious noises with no identifiable referent."[1]

In this chapter we will try to understand Kaufman's remarks about proper method in theology both in the context of his epistemological reflections as a whole and in relation to his substantive theological

---

1. Kaufman, *Systematic Theology*, 258. Kaufman uses this phrase here to differentiate his attempt to connect his early reflections about divine purpose to the "actual concrete world round about us" from those approaches (like Karl Barth's, if my analysis in the previous chapter is correct) that relegate divine purpose to a transcendental realm known only through some privileged source of insight. I include this quotation here because I wish to suggest that Kaufman's sustained, polemically-charged rhetoric regarding the role of imagination in theology must be viewed in the context of his equally long-standing interest in securing the referentiality of theological constructions by means of empirical knowledge about the actual world.

concerns. I will demonstrate that "imagination" is an epistemological category that he has consistently employed from the beginning of his publishing career to highlight the constructive character of all knowledge—including knowledge acquired by ordinary sense perception. His use of the concept of "imagination" in the context of theorizing about theological method, therefore, does not by itself preclude the possibility of holding that theology refers.

But epistemological questions are only a part of the story. For Kaufman, the concept of God itself bears on the issue of reference. The possibility of imaginatively constructing conceptualities that make realistic claims about God and the world is turned into a requirement by his assessment of the implicit logic of God-talk. The concept of God, as we shall see, necessarily invokes strong ontological claims about the world. Maintaining these claims, in turn, requires the sort of interaction with and responsibility to empirical inquiry that one might expect from a realistic theology. Theological inquiry, for Kaufman, is a religiously motivated "way of construing the world" (to borrow Julian Hartt's expression), but it is one that requires credible interaction with what we know about it.[2]

THE PRACTICALITY OF KNOWLEDGE

Throughout his career, since long before the controversial claims of *An Essay on Theological Method*, Kaufman has insisted that the knowing process in general is inherently constructive. The most obvious counter example would seem to be perceptions of the external world. Yet Kaufman maintains that even these are not ready-made impressions inscribed upon a *tabula rasa*, but are constituted both by the data of experience and by the powers of the mind to sift and sort them.[3] Even

2. For Hartt, as for Kaufman, theology as world-construal is not merely a "language-game," a way of redescribing the world in biblical or traditional religious categories, thus attempting to shape a community's experience by linguistic training. It is also, "when it is serious," a "reality game," an attempt intelligibly to refer to the world. See Hartt, "Encounter and Inference," 37.

3. In this he clearly follows the tradition of Immanuel Kant. See, for example, Kant's *Critique of Pure Reason*, 98–109. I have no stake in denying Kaufman's Kantianism, or (as will become clear shortly) in downplaying the extent to which this tradition rules out the epistemologically realistic supposition that reality is somehow grasped preconceptually or prelinguistically. I shall only deny that Kaufman's development of this tradition is incompatible with claiming that theology (realistically) *refers*.

sensory knowledge is therefore necessarily the product of a process that involves active construction rather than of one of merely passive reception.

The perduring categories of the mind featured in classical constructivist epistemologies are replaced in Kaufman's account of knowing, however, by historically contingent configurations of language and tradition. His first published book, *Relativism, Knowledge, and Faith*, which grew out of his Yale doctoral dissertation on Paul Tillich, R. G. Collingwood, and Wilhelm Dilthey, was an attempt to deal with the problems raised for metaphysics and theology by historical and cultural relativism.

This aim of this early work reaches beyond establishing the truth or falsity of theories of relativism, toward the formulation of a theory of knowledge that explains both the human experience of epistemic relativity and the responsiveness of our cognitive processes to objective reality. Kaufman argues that the causes of historical and cultural relativity are not themselves by-products of particular historical developments. Rather, he urges, they lie hidden in the complexities of human thought processes themselves.[4]

In a section of the book entitled "The Anthropological Basis of Knowledge," Kaufman argues that the knowing process has to be understood as purposive human activity—a practical process of interpreting the world and ourselves in order to help us make our way amid the particular, changing features of our environments. The fact of diversity among these practical interpretations of the world throughout history and across cultures needs itself to be interpreted. Kaufman concludes that these differences are not, as he puts it, "derived simply from direct contemplation of the Real," but must be influenced in powerful ways by "hidden situational factors."[5]

In order to uncover the ways in which this influence works, Kaufman addresses what he calls the "pre-cognitive bases" of knowledge.[6] Drawing on the work of Wilhelm Dilthey, he suggests that human knowing is rooted in a primitive encounter of organismic drives with the resistance imposed by the external world.[7] The knowing process thus arises out of and remains related to the purposive activity of organisms in which sat-

4. Kaufman, *Relativism*, 17–18.
5. Kaufman, *Relativism*, 27–28.
6. Ibid.
7. Ibid., 30–31.

isfaction of their felt needs is sought in the context of a world that yields to them only reluctantly, imposing various obstacles and restrictions.

Cognition of the external world, therefore, is intertwined from the ground up with feelings and drives characteristic of sentient animal life. Even such basic cognitive distinctions as that between subject and object, for example, are abstractions from the richness of life, derived for the purpose of dealing more effectively with its practical requirements.[8]

On the surface, this account of knowledge may appear broadly realistic. The picture of knowledge arising out of a primitive encounter of organisms with a recalcitrant external world makes it seem as if the world's impingement upon experience provides a basis for knowledge. For Kaufman, however, it is not the world as such that impinges, but rather *life*, the struggle of organisms to survive and flourish in their environments.

To see the difference, it may be helpful to compare Kaufman's analysis with one according to which the world as such imposes itself upon subjective awareness. According to the process philosophy of Alfred North Whitehead, for example, all actualities necessarily affect or alter the experience of other actualities. Knowledge simply, though inadequately, abstracts from the richness of this experience. The limitations of language prevent discursive knowledge from adequately depicting reality, but reality as such is ineluctably present and available to subjective experience.[9] For Kaufman, however, reality is simply not available in this way. What is directly available to the subject is its practical struggle with the external world. The world, in other words, is present to awareness only as a correlate of world-negotiation. It is this complex situation of practical world-negotiation, not the richness of prereflective apprehension of external effects upon the subject, which founds human knowledge. Construing the world, in this account, is less a matter of approximating its givenness to experience than the construction of a kind of map by which to navigate it.

Kaufman's account of the roots of human knowing does suggest constraints upon the constructivity of knowledge, however. If reality is never purely given, it is never purely constructed, either. It is rather the

8. Ibid., 32–35.

9. Whitehead, *Process and Reality*, 256–326. For fuller commentary on Whitehead's epistemology sensitive to its theological implications, see Cobb and Griffin, *Process Theology*, 13–29.

complex product of both the immediate awareness of drives and limitations and the intellectual activity that interprets it. Kaufman develops
this analysis further by tracing the emergence of "higher levels" of consciousness out of the most primitive level (*Erleben*), in which the world
is apprehended as a sort of buzz of undifferentiated sensations.[10] This
"total field" of sensation is first of all narrowed by the selective activity
of attention. Kaufman suggests that attention is a movement of the will,
a deliberate act which selects certain "sensa" out of the total field which
are relevant to the subject's interests.[11] These are then joined with the
memory of other sensa by the constructive power of the imagination.
The sensa are transformed by lifting them from their original experiential context and relating them to the rest of remembered and anticipated
experience. They are thus selectively drawn from immediacy in order to
construct a broader, more inclusive set of cognitive relationships.[12] Since
this cognitive process begins at the very lowest level of consciousness,
human consciousness is constructive down to its roots.

The work of attention and imagination, in Kaufman's analysis,
lifts the raw sensations of *Erleben* to a new level in which they acquire
meaning by being placed in relation to other contents of consciousness.
But this new level is itself a new datum of experience, held together in
memory, inviting new acts of attention and imagination. Memory thus
allows the constructive activities of human consciousness to lift data
of experience to higher and higher levels of consciousness in which an
increasingly broader, more unified set of cognitive relationships gives
meaning to ever wider reaches of experience.[13]

Memory also influences, however, the particular directions this
constructive activity can take. Though selective attention embodies an
emerging freedom of thought with respect to the given, thought is nev-

10. Kaufman, *Relativism*, 39–40. Drawing again upon Dilthey, Kaufman employs
the concept *Erleben* to characterize this most primitive level. Though *Erleben* roughly
translates as "experience" or perhaps "life," Kaufman leaves it untranslated. Our ordinary concepts of "experience" or "life" would be misleading here, since what is denoted
by those terms is already structured by culture and language. The concept of *Erleben*
is intended to denote the very primitive level, not directly accessible to our already-
structured experience and thought, of consciousness, which lies behind and beneath
these more complex forms of experience.

11. Ibid., 39–40.

12. Ibid., 40–42.

13. Ibid., 44–45.

ertheless conditioned by the particular character of the memories with which it joins the data it selects from *Erleben*. The historical character of knowledge is due to this conditioning of thought by memory.[14]

Kaufman suggests that all higher level consciousness is rooted in three sources: the original *Erleben*, the particular memories held in personal history, and the complex of historical and cultural forces which create a collective memory. Through the continual process of transforming the sensa given in *Erleben* by placing them in relation to personal and social memory, and by the corresponding broadening and enriching of memory, a comprehensive conceptual framework for interpreting the self and the world gradually emerges. This framework then serves to orient consciousness and therefore intelligent human action.[15] Kaufman's analysis serves to show, however, that this overall framework does not emerge from direct inspection of experience or logic. It emerges rather as the product of continual constructive activity of human minds in the context of historical and culturally particular memories and meanings.

Of particular importance in this process is the formative power of language. The grammar and syntax of particular languages not only enable the expression of thoughts and feelings—they shape consciousness. Language provides the categories which enable the mind selectively to attend to and lift out a limited range of features of the buzz of *Erleben*.[16] It thus functions much like the *a priori* categories of the mind in Kant's epistemology, conditioning our experience of the world. Again, however, the formalism of strict Kantianism is modified by historicist motifs. The mind's categories are not strictly *a priori*, but are constructed over a long history of experience which is sedimented in language.[17] A particular language is prior to and formative of individuals' experiences, but its categories are themselves formed in cumulative response to historical and cultural contingencies. All human experience and thought therefore transpires within the possibilities and limits imposed by tradition.[18]

14. Ibid., 45–46.

15. Ibid., 47.

16. Ibid., 48.

17. Ibid., 51.

18. Drawing once again upon Dilthey, Kaufman employs the concept of "objective spirit" to describe the epistemologically formative power of historic cultural traditions: "[T]he term aptly refers to the *objectivations* of the human spirit in the manifold kinds of symbolic expressions which somehow seem to 'contain' man's inner spirit within them" (ibid., 61).

One way to characterize Kaufman's early epistemology, therefore, is to say that it is nonfoundationalist. There is no accessible beginning point of thought—thinking is always indebted to prior thought. Though higher level knowledge may be partially justified by demonstrating its adequacy to lower levels, the constructive character of the knowing process makes all such justification only partial.

This ultimate incompleteness of justification, however, does not lead Kaufman toward a postcritical or postliberal posture which characterizes many nonfoundationalists in theology. He does not adopt a complacent relativism which eschews critical appraisal of the language game played by a particular culture. In fact, Kaufman dedicates a chapter to the "marks of knowledge" which give rise to the sense of firm reality, and which therefore serve normatively to distinguish knowledge about the real world from mere fantasy.

Though justification does not appeal to indubitable, foundational experiences, it does require the employment of critical criteria. Two of these are universality and logical connectedness. Thinking is rationally justified if it is communicable, and thus able to relate particular experiences to the wider community of meaning, and if it can relate all elements of experience as parts to some larger, coherent whole.[19] The final standard of thought, according to Kaufman, is the complete unification of all contents of consciousness, including well-established descriptions of the world. This is obviously an unrealizable ideal, but one that creates a normative tension within all thought, preventing an end to the critical process of rational adjudication.[20]

An epistemology oriented by this ideal of knowledge also leads away from the search for secure foundations in the minutiae of experience or *a priori* reason, and ineluctably toward the construction of comprehensive visions of the whole. Kaufman's nonfoundationalist historicism finally leads him, surprisingly to those who associate nonfoundationalism with a refusal to entertain metaphysical proposals, to the sifting of the various comprehensive visions at hand in Western culture.

19. Ibid., 64–80.
20. Ibid., 82–86.

METAPHYSICS, RELIGION, AND THEOLOGY

Historicism in our intellectual climate generally seems to entail a deep suspicion, if not outright rejection, of metaphysics and other "totalizing" forms of discourse. Very often in theology, historicist convictions are invoked in order to back theological programs which simply receive biblical narrative or religious tradition as normative. Rather than being tested against nonbiblical depictions of reality, texts and traditions are construed as whole narrative "worlds" into which believers are absorbed and by which they are trained to experience their own world in particular ways.[21]

A distinctive feature of Kaufman's historicism, however, is that it takes the inevitable entanglements of theological concepts in historically and culturally particular forms of life as warrant for disputing and revising them. If every attempt to depict reality reflects particular cultural and historical conditions, and is therefore not in direct contact with the real, then the even biblical vision of reality also labors under the same difficulties, and is not simply to be received whole.

Kaufman agrees with cultural-linguistic thinkers that the meaning and purpose of religion is not to depict reality in terms of a speculative metaphysic grounded securely in the generalities of human experience, but to shape the consciousness of persons and communities in distinctive ways. Religion orients by enabling us to see our world as governed by a benevolent parental figure (for example), even when such depictions are not obvious from a strictly empirical standpoint.[22]

Where Kaufman differs from cultural-linguists is his insistence upon the decisional character of orienting visions of reality. Since religious beliefs are not derived from some experiential given, Kaufman reasons, an element of choice is involved in their original formulation.

It is possible to claim, of course, that this original formulation ends legitimate choice, but such a claim invokes a normative judgment which

---

21. The classic statement of this position in recent theological literature is Lindbeck, *The Nature of Doctrine*. Lindbeck's "cultural-linguistic" approach, as he calls it, is endorsed most enthusiastically in theological ethics by Stanley Hauerwas (*Against the Nations*, 2–9). Karl Barth's strategy of "annexing" knowledge about the world into a received confessional framework may be seen as a predecessor (Barth, *Church Dogmatics*, II.2, 518).

22. Both are therefore part of large group of theologians who see religion or theology as "seeing-as." See also, for example, Hartt, *Theological Method and the Imagination*; Hick, *An Interpretation of Religion*; and Hardwick, *Events of Grace*.

is not directly warranted by the historicist convictions that he and cultural-linguists share. Kaufman draws the opposite normative conclusion from his historicist convictions: religious concepts and beliefs are, like their nonreligious counterparts, the products of human decisions for which we ought to take responsibility. If it should turn out (as indeed it has, in Kaufman's judgment) that traditional theological notions regarding divine activity in the world no longer make sense in light of modern knowledge, then they are no longer capable of orienting us adequately in the world we experience, and we ought therefore to reconstruct them.[23]

But this imperative pushes theology unavoidably toward the task of constructing new visions of God, humanity, and the world—it requires theology, in other words, to engage self-consciously and deliberately in constructive metaphysical reflection.

Even in his early treatment of relativism, Kaufman links an acknowledgment of historical and cultural relativity to the necessity of metaphysics. The relativity of thought to particular configurations of language and tradition, he argues, demands not a nihilistic disavowal of critical reflection upon reality but a commitment to carry this reflection as far as it will go, assimilating as much of the richness of experience into as comprehensive a framework as humanly possible.[24]

Throughout his corpus, therefore, Kaufman espouses a cosmopolitan as well as practical ideal of knowledge. Genuine knowledge relates parts to larger wholes in order to provide cognitive frameworks necessary for successful human activity. Comprehensive "world-pictures" are the final, though inexorably fallible, expression of this ideal, gathering insights about the whole in which human life transpires from a wide variety of sources. The objectivity proper to such knowledge is attained not through grounding it in some allegedly secure foundation, but through the continual rooting-out of the one-sidedness of perspective into which our inevitably parochial frameworks of interpretation lead

---

23. As we shall see in chapter 4, strict agential models of divine influence provide a pressing example of theological symbols not working properly. Evolutionary thought makes it hard to conceive of agency independent of bodily conditions and of the historical processes that have brought them about. Another pressing example, for Kaufman, is the notion of an all-controlling divine sovereignty in an age in which human beings have the technological capacity to end intelligent life on earth. This idea, Kaufman argues, dangerously abrogates the sense of our responsibility for our own future precisely when it is needed most. See Kaufman, *Theology for a Nuclear Age*, vii–15.

24. Kaufman, *Relativism*, 104.

us.[25] The breadth and the depth of such world-pictures is the measure of their plausibility and, in part, of their viability for orienting human life.

There is a religious or theological dimension of the knowing process as well. In *Relativism, Knowledge, and Faith*, the "anthropological basis" of metaphysics is understood to be the religious, or quasi-religious, quest for meaning. Meaningfulness here is the relation of present experience to the structural system of perceptions and valuations which emerge out of the remembered past of persons and of entire cultures. Meaning is thus a creative, unifying act of human consciousness which draws new experiences into an historic and cultural framework of interpretation which is already operative in construing the world. By means of the ability to construct meaning, persons and communities are enabled to conceive of the context of their lives as in some measure integrated rather than fragmented and chaotic. This creative synthesis of remembered past and novel present underlies every attempt, according to Kaufman, to see life in its totality.[26]

This synthetic function of metaphysical thinking renders some schemes of meaning more serviceable than others. Kaufman argues that the unifying character of this creative act, in fact, makes an irreducibly pluralistic account of meaning impossible, and thus that consciousness is inevitably led toward a final unity of meaning. An adequate metaphysics follows the practical requirements of selves and communities seeking orientation in the world in its effort to make this final unity explicit.[27]

In an essay published nearly twenty years after *Relativism, Knowledge, and Faith*, Kaufman amplifies this line of thought by denying that metaphysics is a speculative enterprise engaged in only for the sake of satisfying curiosity, and affirming instead that it is an attempt to get clear about the "absolute presuppositions"[28] of a culture according to which it understands and orders the world. The metaphysician identifies the particular finite objects or experiences which a culture uses as mod-

---

25. Kaufman, *Essay*, 40.

26. Kaufman, *Relativism*, 96–99.

27. Ibid., 100.

28. Kaufman, *The Theological Imagination*, 245. Kaufman borrows the concept of "absolute presupposition" from R. G. Collingwood. Collingwood attempted to reconceive the nature of metaphysics as an "historical science," uncovering the presuppositions of the characteristic thought patterns of particular historical epochs, rather than a speculative "science of being" objectively describing realities beyond the bounds of empirical verification. See Collingwood, *An Essay on Metaphysics*, 3–77.

els or paradigms for understanding the whole of reality and shapes them into a comprehensive and coherent account of the whole.[29] This effort is indispensable because clarity of thought about received frameworks of interpretation allows the criticism and reconstruction of them for the purpose of navigating the world more adequately and successfully.[30]

This 1978 essay[31] begins with the problem of relating metaphysics and theology. Kaufman argues that theology should not subordinate itself to metaphysics, either by identifying its primary subject matter ("God") with some metaphysical concept (such as "being" or "process"), or by eschewing the metaphysical task all together. The former concedes that metaphysics has a more adequate conceptuality for describing ultimate reality, thus turning to metaphysics for the final legitimation of theological ideas.[32] Like Burhoe's thought, this approach reduces religious language to poetic re-presentation of realities more precisely apprehended by means of other forms of discourse. The latter approach, on the other hand, like that of Barth and cultural-linguistic thinkers, gives up the attempt to relate its many claims to compelling modern depictions of the way things really are. But this strategy thereby abandons the characteristically religious task of construing our ultimate context, leaving it to philosophers and scientists.[33]

Kaufman believes that each of these errors is due to a common confusion about the role and function of metaphysical and theological concepts. Metaphysics, he argues, is often mistakenly assumed to be a "scientific" enterprise: it is understood in terms of a model of intellectual inquiry drawn from the sciences which deal with specific objects or "regions of experience."[34] Since its particular object is the structure of real-

29. Kaufman, *Theological Imagination*, 248.

30. The practical aim of metaphysical reflection, for Kaufman, warrants moving beyond the purely analytical and descriptive conception of metaphysics as a "historical science," championed by Collingwood, toward a normative and constructive conception (ibid., 254–60). This is particularly pressing for Kaufman, as we shall see in the next chapter, in our cultural epoch, in which a number of competing sets of "absolute presuppositions" need to be either adjudicated or somehow synthesized in order to foster coherently oriented human action.

31. Chapter 9 of *The Theological Imagination*, originally published in *Cross Currents* 28 (1978) 325–41.

32. Kaufman, *Theological Imagination*, 238–39.

33. Ibid., 240.

34. Ibid., 241.

ity which is presupposed by all other types of inquiry, it is natural that it should claim to be the final court of appeal for each of them. Theology is seen as requiring adjustment to alleged descriptions of reality, or else it is perforce seen as a non-cognitive or at least non-descriptive enterprise.

But Kaufman urges that this naive realism about metaphysics was decisively undermined by Kant's critique of metaphysics. Kant showed, Kaufman argues, that metaphysical ideas function differently than ideas we have of objects of perception. Conceptions of physical objects, for example, such as "table" or "ball," describe particular features of the experienced world more or less directly. The import of metaphysical concepts such as "causality" and "time," however, does not derive from their relation to particular objects. Their meaning depends instead upon their role in an overall conceptual scheme. They are "regulative ideas" which constructively hold together diverse types of experience in order to give order to a comprehensive picture of the world.[35]

Kaufman cites the idea of "world" as an important example of a metaphysical concept functioning regulatively. We do not, he argues, ever have direct experiences of the world. We experience only some limited segment, portion, or aspect of it. The concept cannot therefore be tested or compared against particular experiences.[36] The concept "world," he suggests, is similar to the concept of "whole," which stands for an overarching unity of numerous parts, but is not in itself an object which can be understood apart from its constituents. Of course many ordinary wholes can be experienced as discrete objects (whole oranges, for example), but these can always be understood as parts of larger wholes (i.e., orange trees, or some class of objects, such as "fruit"). "World," however, is a peculiar kind of whole, since it stands for the whole comprised of all parts and all classes of perceptual objects whatsoever. It cannot logically be made part of some larger whole without trespassing against the meaning of the word in our ordinary usage.[37]

The meaning and import of metaphysical concepts like "world," therefore, is not their reference to any particular objects, but their use in organizing our experience. Characterizing the many diverse objects and experiences which comprise the context of human life as "world" helps

35. Ibid., 242.
36. Kaufman, *An Essay on Theological Method*, 29.
37. Kaufman, *Theological Imagination*, 247–48.

us construe them as in some measure orderly and thus helps us see our context as navigable by purposive human agents.

Moreover, construing "world" in a particular way, using images and models drawn from experienced, tangible realities, helps us construe it as ordered in a particular and in some measure understandable way. The use of mechanistic imagery as paradigmatic of the world, for example, focuses our attention upon law-like regularities in nature and history. Organic imagery, on the other hand, focuses our attention upon growth, spontaneity, and the emergence of novelty. By helping us organize our experiences in particular ways, "root metaphors" such as these do more than provide synoptic pictures of the world appealing to intellectual curiosity. Precisely by providing these pictures, they practically orient our perceptions, affections and actions in the otherwise "blooming, buzzing confusion" of raw sensations, impulses, and possibilities in which we find ourselves.

Since these central orienting metaphors or models are drawn from the accumulated experience of particular cultures, they are shaped in substantial ways by particular histories. They are not, therefore, strictly objective. Metaphysics, then, is not in a fundamentally different epistemological position than theology, which draws explicitly and deliberately upon traditions in order to make claims about ultimate reality. This parity, recognizable once the nonobjectivity of metaphysics is brought into focus, makes the subordination of theology to metaphysics illegitimate.[38]

The major difference between theology and metaphysics, then, is not their respective uses of tradition, but the central concepts which constitute their respective subject matters. For theology, that central concept is "God," and it is not reducible to "being," "process," "evolution," or any other metaphysical or cosmological idea. The latter fail to capture the sense of transcendence and the personalistic connotations of the concept "God" as it functions religiously.[39] For Kaufman, however, the concept of God is like metaphysical concepts insofar as its function is other than that of describing an experienced given in quasi-scientific fashion. Like the concept of "world," the concept of God is not referential

---

38. Ibid., 254.

39. Kaufman suggests that the world seen as "under God" is a "political universe," since it is governed not by impersonal forces, but by a personal (monarchical) agent (ibid., 252).

in a straightforward manner, but "regulative."[40] Its meaning is the role it plays in our conceptual schemes.

On this point, as will become clearer in later sections of this chapter, Kaufman parts company with empirical realists in theology who believe that the word "God" describes a factor in human experience which can be intelligibly discerned. As I will point out, Kaufman picks up a venerable tradition in theology in this wariness about human experience as a basis for theological claims, exemplified in thinkers as widely separated by history and sentiment as medieval negative theology and the radical Barth. To the question of God's reality we now turn.

MYSTERY, REALITY, AND THE LOGIC OF "GOD"

The deepest, most intractable problem for theology, for Kaufman, is also its greatest insight. The concept "God" is a problem for Kaufman not merely because of uniquely modern circumstances. Rather, "God" is a perennially problematic concept because of its unusual logic. Built into it is a strong ontological claim—it purports to represent the most fundamental reality with which we humans have to do. On the other hand, however, the transcendence of its referent implies that any formulation of a concept of "God" will be inadequate, in some respects merely a product of a groping human imagination.[41]

The perplexity arising from this logical peculiarity is complicated by the fact that "God" does not function like the empirical concepts by which we ordinarily signify concrete realities. For one thing, the ordinary relation of subject and predicate in knowledge of perceptual objects is reversed in the formulation of ideas about God. Instead of an immediately perceived object to which descriptive predicates are subsequently applied, "God" is a fully depicted character in a story, which is only subsequently related to realities that we experience in our transactions with the world. The religious and moral predicates which collectively form the central character in the biblical drama are the primary material

---

40. Ibid., 243–44. See also Kaufman, *An Essay on Theological Method*, 25–49.

41. Kaufman, *God the Problem*, 82–100. Here Kaufman distinguishes between the "real" referent of God-talk, forever hidden in mystery, and the "available" referent, the "peculiar imaginative construct" (85) carried in the collective imagination of historical religious communities.

of theological construction, rather than direct perceptions of objective reality.[42]

Once again, however, the irreducibility of narrative (or, more accurately, of "imaginative construction") in theology does not mean that these predicates unilaterally determine appropriate construals of God and world. "God" always functions as part of some conceptual scheme or world-picture which cannot in all its details simply be deduced or otherwise derived from the concept of God itself or from the particular features of religious and moral discourse from which it is constructed.[43] It is, in fact, precisely in relation to some already operating conception of "world" that the concept of God achieves its orienting power. As we shall recall, Kaufman argues that some concept of "world" is required by human beings in order to hold together all of our diverse, seemingly incongruent experiences. The concept of God, on the other hand, is meaningful insofar as it decisively qualifies our conceptions of the world.

It does so in two ways. First of all, "God," as the ultimate reality with which we have to do, *relativizes* "world." This relativizing function of "God" has a formal influence upon the way the world is understood: it now cannot finally be understood in terms of itself, but must be understood in terms of a more fundamental reality which sets its boundaries.[44] The concept of "God" also influences world interpretation materially, however. The personalistic connotations of "God" suggest that the world must be understood in terms of purposes which may not be fully evident in any particular experience of the world. This purposiveness, secondly, *humanizes* the concept of "world."[45] Since the concept of God is derived from predicates or characteristics which describe and embody our (hopefully) most noble human qualities, the claim that this concept refers to the Creator and Ruler of the universe is a claim that a humane moral ordering, or value, is woven into the very fabric of being itself.

---

42. Kaufman, *The Theological Imagination*, 29. The similarity of Kaufman's analysis on this point to that of Feuerbach is of course striking. It should be noted, however, that the subsequent relation of theological constructions to experienced reality provides "quasi-empirical" checks upon the former. Though theological concepts are generated by a "projecting" human imagination, experiences of the recalcitrant realities of the world continually modify them.

43. Kaufman, *An Essay on Theological Method*, 58.

44. Ibid., 61–62.

45. Ibid., 63–65.

Even though the concept of God is constructed out of cultural materials for the purpose of orienting human life, an important logical feature is its tendency to relativize all human thought patterns, and this built-in function keeps it from being easily collapsed into some preferred scheme of value or meaning.[46] In his recent theology, Kaufman employs an epistemologically rigorous concept of mystery in order to protect this relativizing function. Identifying "God" with "mystery" stresses the strict unavailability of God to human experience and knowledge. It therefore functions less as a kind of murky description than as a rule to guide our attitude toward theological inquiry, requiring that we acknowledge the questionableness and the liability to self-deception at every step in the process of theological construction.[47] "Mystery" rules out reification, the confusion of our language about God with the "real God." It identifies God as an ultimately unknown "X," radically unavailable to human language and experience.[48]

Kaufman's austerity on this point is somewhat forbidding, but it sounds a recurrent theme in Christian and Jewish theology. Jewish prophetism, medieval mystics, and the radical Barth also stressed the failure of human language and tradition adequately to represent God.[49] Even Thomas Aquinas' epochal doctrine of analogical reference ends by ac-

46. Kaufman's pairing of relativizing and humanizing functions of the concept of God plays a large role in the initial analyses of both *An Essay on Theological Method* and *In Face of Mystery*. In the present analysis, the former will be considered under the aegis of "mystery" (a predominately formal concept, as we shall see), and the latter will be discussed in the next section as a substantive norm for the theological imagination.

47. Kaufman is careful to distinguish his use of the word from those according to which "mystery" refers to some veiled but in principle revealable object. "Mystery" in these uses is understood on the model of perception. As we have seen, however, Kaufman does not believe that the perceptual model adequately accounts for the conceptual roles that metaphysical and theological ideas play in our thinking (Kaufman, *In Face of Mystery*, 60–61). This "formal" use of "mystery" actually *demystifies* theological claims by pointing to their invincible questionableness, and may be sharply differentiated from the authority-bolstering, substantive use of the word in the thought of theologians like Karl Rahner (*Foundations of the Christian Faith*, 12–13).

48. Kaufman, *In Face of Mystery*, 61, 79.

49. Jewish tradition has protected the objectivity of God vis-à-vis human speech, of course, by prohibiting the pronunciation of the proper name of God in the Old Testament. The classical medieval document invoking the inadequacy of human language for God is Pseudo-Dionysius' *Mystical Theology*, published in *On the Divine Names, and Mystical Theology*. Karl Barth's *The Epistle to the Romans* is not about religious language *per se*, of course, but about the futility of human history in face of a transcendent Other.

knowledging that denials of univocity in theological discourse are more important than affirmations of similarity.[50] This theme in Western religious thought has served to prevent the enclosure of God's being and will in human categories, thus radically qualifying the anthropomorphisms of popular theism and restraining the all-to-human urge to reduce God to a cosmic support of constricted, parochial human interests.

Kaufman adds his own contribution to this legacy by drawing upon modern philosophical analysis. Kaufman agrees with the negative theology tradition that collapsing the mystery of God into finite, human categories is a degradation of divine transcendence. He also argues, however, that it is a "category error."[51] It treats a regulative concept, whose meaning is its function of anchoring a worldview, as descriptive of a concrete object. Kaufman calls this mistake, which arises when we are beguiled by the substantive position held by "God" in the surface grammar of religious speech, "reification."[52]

By placing strictures upon the ordinary, reifying mode of theological reflection, the concept of mystery renders any appeal to a protected sphere of knowledge about theological objects illegitimate. This has several effects in Kaufman's theology. First of all, since theology cannot be privileged knowledge about a special, nonempirical object, the heavy epistemological burden placed upon revelation in traditional Christian theology is removed.[53] Secondly, as we shall see below, a new way of formulating normative criteria in theology is introduced. Reification creates an intractable problem of theological pluralism even within a confessional tradition because conflicting claims about a supposed nonempirical object cannot be adjudicated. The negation of reifying modes of reflection, according to Kaufman, shifts the issue from one of

50. Thomas Aquinas, *Summa Theologiae* I.II, question 13. Anthologized in *Selected Philosophical Writings*, 214–30.

51. Kaufman, *An Essay in Theological Method*, 30.

52. The charge that theology tends to reify is similar to but also stronger than Rudolf Bultmann's critique of mythology. According to Kaufman, Bultmann's charge that myth attempts abortively to describe "the other side" in terms appropriate to "this side" still presumes that it is meaningful to speak of another "side." Kaufman's theology, by contrast, is compatible with strong denials that there is an additional dimension to reality outside of nature and history. Reification is just this attribution of object status to regulative concepts such as "world" and "God."

53. The conspicuous absence of the category of "revelation" in Kaufman's recent theology is, it seems to me, the most obvious way in which Kaufman's later work differs from his earlier efforts.

adequacy of description to one of appropriateness of function.[54] Though it may be difficult to assess the latter, it is at least not in principle impossible. Finally, and most importantly for our purposes here, a widespread tendency in negative theology to appeal to mystery as a shield from criticism is decisively rejected. Kaufman argues, in fact, that the concept of mystery demands a radicalization, rather than diminution, of criticism in theology. We are not able to capture the meaning of "God" in perceptual imagery not because we are need of enlightenment from some unquestionably authoritative source of insight, but because the meaning of "God" is not primarily descriptive. Since the concept of God is regulative within a view of the world which is constructed for broadly pragmatic purposes, Kaufman argues, we must take responsibility for its proper functioning. This rather important task requires unrelenting criticism of reigning theological concepts rather than fideistic acceptance of them.[55]

GOD, INTEGRITY, AND INTELLIGIBILITY

As I noted at the beginning of this chapter, philosophical contentions are not the only ingredients in Kaufman's constructivist theological method. The radical rethinking of theology's purpose and method, for which Kaufman has become both famous and notorious, is partially driven by his understanding of the logical peculiarities of the central substantive theme with which theology has to do.[56] The idea of "God," I will suggest in this section, drives Kaufman to formulate a method that attends to issues of confessional integrity as well as broad intelligibility.

First, since an adequate method for any intellectual discipline is responsible to its subject matter, an adequate theological method is responsible to the idea of "God." For Kaufman, theology must be guided by the requirement that the best insights of Western theism be appro-

---

54. In this way, Kaufman's criticism of reification supports his long-standing emphasis upon the practical nature of theological reflection and the consequent necessity of employing pragmatic criteria in assessing theological proposals. See, for example, his discussions of pragmatic adjudication in *Relativism*, 115–17, and *The Theological Imagination*, 254–62, as well as *In Face of Mystery*, 429–44. In the latter, particularly, the adequacy of a theological program is connected with its "salvific" potential—that is, its ability to orient human beings in such a way that their capacity to exercise responsible agency is maximized.

55. Kaufman, *In Face of Mystery*, 62.

56. This is a central point of Kaufman's prefatory remarks to the second edition of *An Essay on Theological Method* (xvii–xxiii, and also 13–22).

priated. But this is just where, ironically, traditional theology fails. The traditional understanding of theology as a disciplined exposition of received truths, he urges, actually compromises the insights of mono-theism, because it is based upon a serious misappropriation of the idea of "God." In Western religious traditions, "God" is a discriminating and even polemical term, drawing sharp distinctions between that which is ultimate and that which is not (but which may pretend to be). "God" always functions to critique the worship of idols. Built into the concept, therefore, is an acknowledgement that its object is never fully available to experience, but is transcendent and therefore elusive of any attempt to grasp it. This acknowledgement places brackets around the finite models and metaphors by means of which the human mind conceptual-izes God's being or reality. The meaning of the concept of "God" thus includes a relativizing function which persistently invites questions as to the adequacy of any particular account of its referent. The problem with relying solely upon sacred text or authoritative tradition is that it obscures this critical qualification of all finite models and of the sources of insight which supply them, and it thereby co-opts "God" to support an idolatrous attachment to sacred tradition.

The logical peculiarities of "God," in short, both enable and require a resolutely critical posture in theological reflection. Therefore, remaining true to the import of this ancient symbol also requires the formulation of a method which breaks decisively with the way in which the theologi-cal task has been carried out by the majority of theologians in the past.[57]

There is an additional component to maintaining the integrity of Western religious tradition: taking responsibility for its practical and religious function of anchoring an overall interpretation of the world. We have seen earlier in this chapter how Kaufman conceives the task of world-interpretation as both practical and religious. Here it is impor-tant to stress that the engagement of Western religious traditions in this practice leverages normative methodological force in Kaufman's con-structive program. Kaufman insists that theology must adopt a method which is appropriate to the historic "orienting" function of theological

---

57. Most Christian theology throughout the history of the Church, Kaufman sug-gests, has been a rather straightforward, "one-dimensional" hermeneutical enterprise. But this procedure is ruled out, he argues, by the logic of the idea of God. Uncritical appeals to textual authorities, in effect, represent an elevation of these documents that is incompatible with the "jealous" logic of strict monotheism. See Kaufman, *In Face of Mystery*, 7–8, 18–20.

language—i.e., its direction of human attention, affection, and resolve toward some "center of value"[58] or focus for devotion and service.

This religious function, moreover, is always historically situated. Kaufman suggests that theology has never functioned in religious communities simply to expound a faith already present and operative in unproblematic though unarticulated form, but it has always been tasked to reconstruct the content of faith for a particular historical and cultural context.[59] The historical embeddedness as well as the social import of this task of reconstruction requires the forthright assumption of responsibility for its role. Theology may not abdicate its responsibility by appealing to authorities or to past efforts. The historic role of theological inquiry, then, actually qualifies the authority of tradition. Theological work of any age is as subject to criticism, refinement, and reconstruction as any human activity.[60]

There is an interplay of freedom and constraint that follows from this requirement. For Kaufman, responsibility not only places theological inquiry under the constraint of having to receive and respond to criticism—it also frees theology imaginatively to picture the ultimate context of human life in a manner that fits the demands of our own historical and epistemic situation, rather than slavishly following doctrinal formulations fitted for contexts quite different from our own. On the other hand, it is crucial to the understanding of Kaufman's project that we be clear about the fact that the theological imagination is not free from the constraints of embodiment in particular cultural and linguistic patterns of symbolization. Since responsibility is always historically situated, no theological effort can or should evade the influence of culture, and therefore the constraints of particular traditions remain even in a theology which adopts the method of imaginative construction.

Traditions inform theological thinking in two ways. First of all, since no human thinking creates its content *de novo*, broader cultural traditions are indispensable as sources for the theological imagination. The collective memory of a culture, what Kaufman early in his corpus calls "objective spirit," provides the raw material out of which comprehensive and coherent visions of the whole are constructed. Like any hu-

---

58. The terms is H. Richard Niebuhr's. See Niebuhr, *Radical Monotheism*, 100–13.
59. Kaufman, *In Face of Mystery*, 294.
60. Kaufman, *Theology for a Nuclear Age*, 19–22.

man artifact, theological thinking is both animated and limited by the materials available within a particular cultural context.[61]

Second, traditions function normatively, providing criteria for guiding and assessing theological proposals both old and new. Theology is not constrained to reproduce the content of the Western theological traditions that have informed him, perhaps in a new idiom. It is constrained, however, to do justice to the functional genius of the primary symbol carried in Western religious traditions. The dual functions of the Western concept "God," its relativizing and its humanizing of human experience, provide criteria for producing and assessing new theological constructions.[62]

Critics may object that these normative components of Western theism are in some measure abstracted from the tradition, rather than derived from it in a straightforward manner.[63] This process of abstraction, it may be argued, sanitizes traditions, artificially removing particular features that are not consistent with one's preferences at a particular time. It therefore amounts to an evasion of the real normative force of tradition by allowing contemporary beliefs and attitudes to hold sway over its appropriation. Integrity, perhaps, is imperiled.

Kaufman's use of abstraction is consistent, however, with the way in which he understands the general epistemic situation of people who inhabit culture. In his early epistemology, we shall recall, Kaufman argues that tradition is kept alive not through rote repetition of each of its variegated and highly particular details, but rather through a process of continual, deliberate abstraction from the welter of cultural memory. Traditions cannot be appropriated for new historical circumstances without some employing some measure of selective attention.

61. Kaufman, *Theological Imagination*, 30–31.

62. Kaufman, *An Essay on Theological Method*, 59–70.

63. There is, on this point, another obvious similarity to Kant's approach to religion. However, in a book review on an interpretation of Kant's philosophy of religion, Kaufman suggests (with the author of the book under review) that the common interpretation of Kant as a disparager of "ecclesiastical" (historically particular, institutionalized) faith is a caricature. See Kaufman's review of *Kant on History and Religion* by Michel Despland, 400–402. Despland argues, and Kaufman agrees, that Kant's "rational faith" does not simply leave "ecclesiastical faith" behind. The former sifts and reconstructs the latter in a continual "inner mutual relation" in which both are required. Whether or not this interpretation is correct, it at least suggests that Kaufman's devotion to Kant does not, in his own judgment, commit him to an ahistorical, normative interpretation of religious faith.

With respect to Western theological traditions in particular, Kaufman suggests that the functions or logical features of God-talk which are singled out as normative in his theology are central to Western, monotheistic discourse. We have seen how the relativizing function is historically grounded in the struggle of monotheism with the peoples' attachment to idols. In this context, the concept of relativizing is a rather precise translation of the traditional idea of "judgment."[64] Judgment not only smashes various idols on which persons and communities abortively depend—it corrects and transforms the devotees of the defeated idols, opening them to reality in new, previously inconceivable ways.

Another central feature of historical monotheism, paired with judgment, is "salvation." "Salvation" or "humanization" is of particular normative significance for Kaufman. This is largely because this particular functional meaning of the word "God" is taken as a warrant for talking about God in the first place, rather than simply about "world." "God" construes the context of human life in ways which are not empirically obvious, as a world ultimately characterized by a broad creativity which supports humanizing trends toward the development of the most important human capacities. Moreover, since theology is a human creation, undertaken for the purpose of orienting and motivating human life, it may be judged by its effectiveness in doing so. Kaufman's account of what theology is, of what its particular role has been in human life, therefore serves as the central criterion of adequacy for particular theological proposals.

Kaufman believes that this account of theological method has important benefits in the modern/postmodern religious situation. Deriving the central norm for theology from its historical function has the advantage, according to Kaufman, of providing a way to adjudicate the seemingly intractable disagreements in a culture of increasing theological pluralism. As noted above, Kaufman places much of the blame for the chaotic proliferation of theological methods upon the phenomenon of reification. Thinking of theology as a privileged form of quasi-perceptual knowledge about a non-empirical object invites an undis-

---

64. Ordinarily, the "judgment" of God for Kaufman is aligned with the austere "mystery" of the divine, and "redemption" with the "humanizing" features of God-talk. See, for example, *In Face of Mystery*, 405–10. These two concepts, as in many classical treatments, are related, since (for example) the "judgment" of God's impenetrable mystery may break the hold of idolatrous foreclosures upon the human quest for meaning, and thus indirectly foster an enhancement of human well-being.

ciplined mélange of idiosyncratic opinions.[65] Though Kaufman is not
against theological pluralism (the mystery of God and human finitude
collude in his theology, in fact, to make a pluralism of outlooks inescapable[66]), he believes that criteria for adjudicating disputes generated by
this plurality are required in order to maintain the credibility of theology
as an intellectual discipline, and its viability for orienting human life.[67]
Kaufman's theological method is designed to meet this challenge by
(1) undermining certainties based on controversial metaphysical opinions and (2) providing functional criteria that may be widely agreed-
upon yet capable of leveraging critical as well as constructive import.

There is a broader issue at stake whose importance is measurable
outside of narrowly academic debates. In our emerging global context,
Kaufman's strategy also intends to provide a way for dealing constructively with the wider plurality of world religions. The criterion of humanization may appropriately be applied as a norm for all religious
expressions across local cultures. This is because, Kaufman suggests,
not only Western theological language but the spectrum of religious
languages throughout human history have functioned to orient and motivate human life toward the maximal realization of human well-being.[68]

Kaufman believes that the contemporary context of an emerging
globalism, with its attendant threats of nuclear catastrophe, terrorism
and environmental meltdown, renders complacence toward nonwestern
views of reality irrelevant and possibly harmful. The various streams of
culture are flowing together into a single human stream, and the merging currents could either create new opportunities for co-operation and
justice or lead to disastrous new levels of conflict.[69] Religion is a powerful motivating force which may either harm or help. Kaufman therefore recommends moving away from the standard academic practice
of withholding normative judgment upon local religious practices, and
beginning to subject all religious expressions to the critical normative
standard of humanization. This, he believes, would enable interfaith con-

---

65. Kaufman, *An Essay on Theological Method*, xvii–xviii, 1–2.

66. Kaufman, *God, Mystery, Diversity*, 54–67.

67. Kaufman, *An Essay on Theological Method*, 2–22.

68. Kaufman, *God, Mystery, Diversity*, 187–203.

69. Kaufman, *In Face of Mystery*, 131–40.

versations actually to transcend dangerous parochialisms and to make progress toward "a common faith."[70]

Aside from the norms derived from the Western theological traditions, Kaufman's method also places normative constraints upon theological inquiry which are not fully described by the logical features of "God" and the practical requirements of religious tradition. The role that theology has played in interpreting reality in light of religious ideas and sensibilities leverages its own normativity, compelling theology to root out fantastic portrayals of life that fly in the face of what "plain experience teaches us" about the world.[71] Broad human experience and scientific knowledge, therefore, substantially limit what can credibly and appropriately be said about divine activity and other important theological issues. Beside maintaining the integrity of Western religious tradition by appropriating its best insights, Kaufman's method requires establishing a broad intelligibility that necessarily traffics in perceptions, explanations, and interpretations of the empirical world.

The rest of this book will attempt to substantiate this claim, but here it is appropriate to emphasize once again that Kaufman likens the tasks of theology to the construction of "models" or even "maps" of the world. Like maps and models, theological ideas are constructed for the purpose of helping us successfully navigate the terrain of reality. To be sure, theology does not depict reality in an objective, quasi-scientific fashion. But in order to guide us appropriately theological maps must be consistent

70. The phrase is John Dewey's. See Dewey, *A Common Faith*. If the criterion of humanization as Kaufman understands it (with a heavy emphasis upon individual agency freed from traditionalistic constraints) is itself a legacy of monotheism, we may of course raise questions about how seriously Kaufman takes pluralism. From a non-Western perspective, in fact, Kaufman's cosmopolitanism may look rather imperialistic. We may recall that Ernst Troeltsch thought, provisionally, that Christianity was the best religion available, but his historical relativism tended to undercut certainty on this issue (Troeltsch, *The Absoluteness of Christianity*, 85–106). Kaufman's use of an allegedly neutral standard, however, threatens to stack the deck entirely in favor of monotheisms. The abrogation of Troeltschian relativism is warranted, in Kaufman's judgment, by his interpretation of our historical circumstance, according to which the emergence of a global culture makes complacent relativism about religion untenable (Kaufman, *In Face of Mystery*, 24–26). The normative presuppositions of this alleged global culture, clearly, favor interpretations of humanization that stress the freedom of the individual over social belonging.

71. This rooting out of fantasy and narrowly one-sided interpretations of human life, according to Kaufman, embodies the objectivity proper to theological construction. See Kaufman, *An Essay on Theological Method*, 40–41.

with as wide a range of data about the world as possible. A theological interpretation of human disease and healing which fails to take into account undisputed knowledge of the natural causes of diseases, to take an historically poignant example, would risk suggesting that diseases and their cures are matters simply of divine pleasure to reward or punish. Though it is not theology's job to portray the biological processes which lead to disease and health, if it is not informed by knowledge of these it may lead us astray—morally and religiously. Practical orientation therefore requires some interaction with firmly-established explanations and descriptions of empirical events and processes in the world.

A central problem with which modern theology must deal, therefore, is that of provisionally harmonizing the diverging frames of reference according to which we think and in terms of which we therefore carry out the business of living. A viable theology must be "holistic," integrating insights from a broad array of human experiences and knowledge in an effort to portray our ultimate context in terms which are both intelligible and motivating for human life today.[72] Theology must harmonize because its function is to provide a coherent and comprehensive vision of the context of our lives which can orient us consistently and effectively. Such harmonization must be provisional, however, since humans can never achieve certainty about such issues, and since the false assumption of such certainty would constitute an idolatrous foreclosure of the quest for proper human orientation.

As we shall see in more detail in the next chapter, Kaufman believes that modern persons who are religious tend to live by two "faiths" which are in tension with one another. On the one hand, modern theists understand the context of their lives as the expression of a purposive moral will which renders the world a moral universe which is supportive of hu-

---

72. Kaufman, *In Face of Mystery*, 18–31. Here Kaufman contrasts his own "holistic" approach to theology with what he calls "two-dimensional" (or correlational) approaches. These latter theological strategies dominate the liberal theological scene (See, for example, Langdon Gilkey, *Naming the Whirlwind*; and David Tracy, *Blessed Rage for Order*), but Kaufman believes that they wrongly assume that the tradition's resources for speaking intelligibly about the "dimension of ultimacy" in response to cultural perplexities are in good working order. Therefore, he suggests, they leave the Western religious tradition out of which they work more or less intact, when in fact the intelligibility or viability of this tradition is just the thing to be decided. Kaufman believes that his own constructivist or "holist" alternative takes responsibility for every dimension of the theological enterprise to a degree that correlationist approaches cannot, allowing him to reconstruct it more freely in response to the needs of our day.

man values. On the other hand, however, they understand their context as governed by closed causal processes characterized by no recognizable moral order. The reinterpretation of divine activity in this apparently purposeless world, therefore, is an important step toward the (provisional) reconciliation of the faiths competing within the hearts and minds of modern Christians.[73] Once again, the task is not primarily speculative, but practical and religious.

Throughout this book I will argue that this practical task of theology as Kaufman understands it requires a certain kind of relation between the sources of insight available to theology. This relation can be formulated in terms of two formal requirements. These are, briefly, that theology must (1) interact with modern knowledge and experience in such a way as to establish a broad reflective equilibrium between religious insight and human knowledge and experience, and that it must (2) utilize such sources selectively and discriminately in the service of the orienting function of religious ideas which characterizes our Western religious traditions. Our exploration of Kaufman's substantive innovations regarding the problem of conceptualizing divine activity will be guided by these requirements as instruments of analysis and appraisal.

73. Kaufman, *In Face of Mystery*, 434–37.

3

Qualifying Naturalism

THE NATURALISTIC PICTURE OF the world, according to which all events can be explained entirely in terms of the immanent laws of nature, has been all but imposed upon the modern mind by the success of the natural sciences in doing precisely that. This naturalistic picture poses obvious difficulties for theism. Seamlessly deterministic explanations of events and processes in nature allow little or no room for continuous divine action in the world. "Deism," which features a God who sets the initial conditions of the universe and then allows it to develop autonomously, can deal with the modern picture with relative ease; but the intelligibility of theistic faith in a God who continues to act is not as easily maintained.

In a classic article, Langdon Gilkey notes the difficulties involved in speaking of God's "mighty acts" in an age in which modern cosmological assumptions furnish the conceptual resources for reflection upon the world. These difficulties revolve around the collapse of the implicit ontology of the Bible, which accommodated intrusions into the natural order and thereby supplied talk about divine activity objective content.[1] Current attempts by theologians to revive biblical language falter on their

---

1. Gilkey, "Cosmology," 194–95. The object of Gilkey's criticism here is the "biblical theology" movement, which sought to abandon modern, liberal categories and return to a biblical emphasis upon the "mighty acts" of God. The trouble with this strategy, Gilkey points out, is that modern assumptions about the way the world works inevitably impinge upon the interpretation of these "acts." Biblical ontology construed the world as open to intrusion by special acts of God, and talk about God's "acts" therefore has an identifiable, objective content in the Bible. But the modern, scientifically-informed ontology assumed by the biblical theologians is closed to supernatural intrusions, and God's "mighty acts" have therefore to be interpreted *subjectively*, as *interpretations* of events that are, objectively speaking, no different from other events. This procedure removes the objective content to biblical talk about divine activity, which was supplied by the Bible's implicit ontology.

inability to specify its objective reference in the absence of a supernaturalist ontology. In order to solve this problem, he argues, an "ontology of events" which can press modern knowledge into a specification of God's relation to ordinary events in the world is required. The development of such an ontology, Gilkey admits, is a tall order.[2] Presumably, any such effort would have to (1) incorporate, or at least avoid inconsistency with, modern scientific knowledge about the ordering of the world by inviolable natural laws, while (2) specifying a "causal joint"[3] or nexus in the natural ordering where divine causal efficacy can occur.

THE SEARCH FOR "CAUSAL JOINTS"
IN A WORLD GOVERNED BY LAW

As I see it, two sophisticated, overlapping discussions in modern theology have taken the lead in recent years in the development of an "ontology of events" which at least leaves openings for the sorts of claims about divine activity which are demanded by Gilkey's analysis. The burgeoning science and theology discussion, having gained momentum with the writings of thinkers like Ralph Wendell Burhoe, has generated numerous more sophisticated proposals regarding God's activity in the world, including a five-volume set of papers detailing various "Scientific Perspectives on Divine Action."[4] In addition, process theology continues to develop the metaphysical program of Alfred North Whitehead, including scientific insights regarding quantum mechanics, complexity, and biological evolution within its recent formulations. Before turning to Kaufman's proposal, this chapter will briefly review a sampling of these perspectives in order later to highlight the distinctiveness of Kaufman's view. To anticipate, all of the proposals to be reviewed may be seen as attempts to underwrite the objectivity of claims about divine governance by specifying "causal joints" in the natural ordering by in one way or another calling into question the completeness of naturalistic accounts of the world. Some of these, in fact, may be said to mine the alleged openings or gaps in naturalistic explanations of various kinds of

2. Gilkey, "Cosmology," 42–43.

3. The phrase is Austin Farrer's (*Faith and Speculation*, 142–55).

4. Two of these, which contain essays commented upon in this chapter, are *Chaos and Complexity: Scientific Perspectives on Divine Action*, and *Evolutionary and Molecular Biology: Scientific Perspectives on Divine Action*.

cosmic events—though, as we shall see, they generally avoid the pitfalls of crude "God-of-the-gaps" strategies.

Kaufman's theology, however, does not secure objectivity by locating a causal nexus between the God and the world, but instead constructs a model of divine activity upon the assumption that naturalistic accounts of the reign of natural laws in the world are complete. The metaphysical steps in his theological construction do not, however, flow uncontroversially from modern science. The central thesis of the next chapter will be that the key to Kaufman's theistic interpretation of the world is his metaphysical decision to take the present state of our local environment as a clue to the fundamental character of the universe. This allows him, I shall argue, to construe the world as the arena of objectively real divine activity without having to specify an "ontology of events" in the objectivist sense demanded by Gilkey. I shall also note, however, that there are costs to be paid for employing this strategy, particularly with reference to the strongly apologetic ambitions cherished by many to assign divine activity an irreplaceable explanatory content.

The Science and Theology Discussion

Mining the Gaps in Naturalistic Explanations

In the course of briefly examining a few attempts to mine the gaps in naturalistic explanations of events and processes in the world, it is important to be clear about what sort of "gaps" we are talking about. It will be helpful to distinguish three different categories of gaps.[5] First of all, there are "explanatory gaps." These may be divided into two groups: (1) temporary gaps in scientific knowledge, and (2) permanent or invincible explanatory gaps. Appeal to the former as the locus of divine activity yields the familiar, ill-reputed "god-of-the-gaps" strategy, vitiated when the gaps in question are closed by further research and theorizing. Appeals to the latter, however, are at least secure from this embarrassment, since the gaps in question cannot in principle be closed by further scientific progress. Famous examples of this type are connected with quantum uncertainties and the unpredictability of chaotic systems. Invincible explanatory gaps may or may not be taken to indicate (3) "causal gaps," or breaks in chains or webs of causality. These are dis-

5. Tracy, "Particular Providence," 290–92, provides a fuller account of these types. The following is an adaptation of his discussion.

puted, but the "indeterminacy" interpretation of quantum mechanics entails that there are elements of real chance in the universe, at least at the quantum level. In each of the science-and-theology and process perspectives on divine activity in the world discussed below, some type of causal gap in natural processes is identified and mined. In each case, as we shall see, some invincible explanatory gap which surfaces in scientific research is seized upon in order to locate a "causal joint" at which God can influence events and processes in the world without breaking known scientific laws. This will eventuate, in each case, in a large-scale construal of the world as fundamentally indeterminate or open.

The Flexibility of Dynamic Systems: John Polkinghorne—One possible "causal joint" at which divine activity might be claimed to influence natural processes without violating the laws of nature is indicated by recent developments in the physics of dynamic systems. John Polkinghorne has championed this approach. The basic idea is that even relatively simple dynamic systems (for example, the mutually interacting motions of a number of billiard balls on a pool table) involve "infinitesimally balanced sensitivity to circumstance" which makes prediction of subsequent states of the system after even relatively small time intervals impossible.[6] The slightest imprecision in the calculation of initial conditions or of subsequent environmental influences are quickly amplified rather than averaged out by correcting mechanisms. Since infinite precision of measurement and calculation is impossible in principle for finite minds, Polkinghorne points out that we are "necessarily ignorant about how such systems will behave."[7] The epistemic gap here is invincible— no amount of observation or rigor of calculation, and no advance in scientific theorizing, can conceivably close it.

Polkinghorne relies on a "critical realist" commitment, which he believes to be widely shared among scientists, to advance an ontological interpretation of chaotic unpredictability. Since, he suggests, "epistemology models ontology," a permanent gap in our knowledge must point to a hidden openness in the causal mechanisms described by science.[8] The permanent unpredictability of dynamic systems is thus taken to have momentous metaphysical consequences. The world, a critical realist is

6. Polkinghorne, *Science and Providence*, 28.

7. Ibid., 29.

8. Ibid.

allegedly compelled to admit, is stranger even at the "classical" (macroscopic) level than understood by Newton. The causal mechanisms described by Newtonian science are really special cases of a more subtle, flexible ordering. The "unrelenting grip of mechanical determinism" is relaxed, and, in the face of the recognition that the future is not fully implied in the present, room is made for genuine becoming.[9] Most importantly for our purposes here, a "causal joint" where God can influence the world described by science is identified, hidden within the permanent unpredictabilities of nature. God, according to Polkinghorne, can influence the world without disrupting its demonstrable conservation of energy by supplying information in order to determine the future course of world processes left undetermined by the relevant causal mechanisms. Of a number of possible futures of a dynamic system, in other words, one is chosen by God in such a way that no energy is expended.[10] God's purposes are thus secured in a world left thermodynamically intact.

The latter point will inevitably be controversial.[11] Here, however, I want to focus on Polkinghorne's move from invincible explanatory gaps associated with chaos theory to his suppositions about causal gaps or openings in the fabric of nature. It is noteworthy that the move depends upon a somewhat unusual use of critical realism. We are accustomed to imagining that scientific descriptions of discrete objects or events refer to corresponding realities, however imperfectly, but it seems unusual to suppose that what we might call the "gappiness" of scientific explanations of particular events must refer to a corresponding "gappiness" in nature. Is not the former simply ignorance, made invincible by the infinitude of relevant causal factors? The most widely accepted interpretation of chaos theory, in fact, is that unpredictable dynamic systems are

9. Ibid., 30.

10. Ibid., 32–35. See also *Belief in God in an Age of Science*, 62–63. Polkinghorne believes that this picture of divine activity, crudely represented here, has distinct theological advantages. Causal influence by information-input only (with no exertion of energy) is said to highlight rather well the theological tradition's insistence upon God's unique mode of action as disembodied "spirit." It should be noted in this connection, however, that Polkinghorne has recently modified this account upon reflection of "kenotic" themes in Christian theology. He is now led by the Incarnation to affirm that God enters nature and history as one (partially defeated) causal efficacy among others ("Kenotic Creation and Divine Action,"104–6).

11. See, for example, Willem B. Drees' complaints, to the effect that information inputs without expenditures of energy are inconceivable in naturalistic viewpoints (Drees, *Religion, Science, and Naturalism*, 97).

instances of a "deterministic chaos" in which the unfolding states of the system are fully determined by antecedent causal influences which are, however, too numerous and too subtle to allow prediction.[12] The move from unpredictability to indeterminacy, in other words, may not only be insufficiently warranted by appeals to "critical realism," but actually ruled out by predominant interpretations of current scientific theory. The point I wish to make here is that Polkinghorne's attempt to locate a causal joint for divine activity in the unpredictabilities of dynamic systems requires defending a highly controversial ontological reading of them. Even without considering specifically theological problems that arise in this view, any putative theological gains here will be made at the cost of a measure of credibility.

Quantum Indeterminacy: Thomas Tracy—The classical-level unpredictabilities associated with chaos theory, as I noted above, are not the only possible openings for divine causal influence in nature allegedly heralded by current scientific theory. If Polkinghorne's move from unpredictability to indeterminacy in the theory of dynamic systems is controversial, the indeterministic interpretation of quantum mechanics is, if not undisputed, at least far more widely accredited. Theologian Thomas Tracy, in a contribution to the volume of papers on "Scientific Perspectives on Divine Action" entitled Chaos and Complexity, seizes upon the indeterminacies of the quantum world as the "good luck" of theology.[13] Current theories on quantum mechanics are fortunate for theists, Tracy argues, because the ontological openness of nature appears to be a conceptual requirement for the claim that God acts in the world.

Tracy notes, as I have in chapter 1, that claims about divine action within the tangible world of human experience are central to the theistic religious traditions, and furthermore that modern science's success in constructing complete naturalistic explanations of world processes has therefore seriously challenged the very heart of theistic belief.[14] The

---

12. As Drees points out, it is probably in fact inaccurate to say that these processes are left unexplained by science, since mathematical equations have been invented that describe the behavior of chaotic systems. Far from diminishing the scope of naturalistic explanatory accounts of nature, therefore, chaos theory has increased it, since a broader range of phenomena can now be explained in terms of mathematical equations (ibid., 99).

13. Tracy, "Particular Providence," 315.

14. Ibid., 292–94.

dominant response among "liberal" theologians, he suggests, has been "uniformitarianism," the construal of the unfolding universe as a single great act of God.[15] Uniformitarianism deals with the difficulties involved with particular actions of God within the naturalistically-described world by dispensing with the notion of particular divine actions altogether. All activities within the cosmos are divine actions indirectly insofar as they are "subacts" of God's one overarching act, but none is directly, in its particularity, an act of God.[16] Tracy points out that, apart from being perhaps religiously unsatisfying, this viewpoint threatens to undermine the integrity of secondary causes in its very zeal to uphold them. This is because two sufficient explanations of an event or process inevitably seem redundant—the secondary, instrumental causes tend to wane in significance, and it becomes difficult to give reasons why all events and processes should not be seen forthrightly as acts of God. Uniformitarianism therefore tends, in Tracy's judgment, toward "occasionalism," the view that God is the only effective agent within world-processes, secondary causes being merely a shadow of the divine will. In this way, God's purposes and the whole range of natural and historical events are rather closely aligned, and the problem of evil, already troublesome for theistic belief, is exacerbated.[17] The argument here, Tracy himself points out, has nothing to do with knowledge about the world. The theist is compelled to hope for gaps in nature on the basis of a distinctly theological concern to uphold the integrity of talk about divine activity in a world to which some degree of autonomy is ascribed.[18]

A degree of indeterminacy, however, is not enough to support theism. Tracy briefly notes further cosmological requirements for a coherent account of divine activity in the world. Included among these are: (1) the embeddedness of indeterministic processes in a broader ordering, and (2) the amplification of microscopic indeterminacies so that they make differences in the macroscopic world. Without the former, the potential

15. Ibid., 295–97. Tracy identifies this type of proposal as a shift in emphasis from providence to creation. The concept of creation is enlarged so that it may perform the work traditionally left to the idea of providence. God is said to "enact history" in a single creative effort. Tracy highlights the accounts of Friedrich Schleiermacher and, interestingly, Gordon Kaufman, as examples.

16. The language of "acts" and "subacts" is Kaufman's (see the essay titled, "On the Meaning of 'Act of God,'" in Kaufman, *God the Problem*, 119–47).

17. Tracy, "Particular Providence," 300–301.

18. Ibid., 292–93, 324.

gains of novel events cannot be sifted and preserved. Indeterminacy becomes mere randomness, strictly incompatible with the realization of divine (or any other) purpose.[19] Without the latter, novelty at the quantum level is statistically averaged out. The determinism of classical Newtonian mechanics is therefore not broken, and divine influence is muted.[20] Fortunately, Tracy suggests, quantum theory provides a possible conceptuality for conceiving of nature in a way which fulfills these more specific requirements. Tracy believes that the embeddedness of chance in a lawful order is indicated by quantum mechanics by the probabilistic distribution of causally underdetermined events. Tracy urges that, though quantum events are "not uniquely specified by antecedent conditions," their probabilities are predictable.[21] He also believes that chaos theory offers reasons to believe that microscopic indeterminacy can be amplified, so that chance at the quantum level is translated into causal gaps at the classical level.[22]

Tracy admits, however, that "it remains to be seen whether a single account can be given of quantum physics and chaos that would allow for a chaotic amplification of quantum events."[23] The account suggested here, therefore, seems to be a speculative extension of current scientific theory in the service of a theologically-preferred cosmology, rather than a reflection upon the picture of the world currently warranted by science. As Tracy himself admits, this strategy ties his theology in a very fundamental way to scientific discoveries that are yet to be made.[24] Moreover, requirements (1) and (2) in Tracy's account appear to be in an uneasy relation to one another. To the extent that the statistical regularity/predictability of quantum events is confirmed, the possibility of the requisite amplification of indeterminacy would appear to be diminished.[25]

19. Ibid., 316.

20. Ibid., 317–18.

21. Ibid., 316–17.

22. As an example of how this might work in biological evolution, Tracy points to the work of Robert John Russell, who argues that quantum events may trigger mutations, which may in turn play an important role in providing for novelty in nature. See Russell, "Special Providence," 191–224.

23. Tracy, "Particular Providence," 318.

24. Ibid., 324.

25. Widespread doubts about the amplification of quantum indeterminacy, in fact, make quantum theory a generally unpopular choice in the search for a causal nexus between God and the world. Generally, macro-level predictability is taken to indicate that

It is a genuine question, therefore, whether Tracy's speculative extension of scientific theory can coherently do the work he believes to be required for the defense of theism.

Whole-Part Constraint: Arthur Peacocke

Another perspective from the science and theology discussion acknowledges the discoveries of the openness or flexibility of world processes associated with both chaos theory and quantum mechanics, but does not take these as illuminating for the "causal joint" problem. Like Polkinghorne, Arthur Peacocke takes a strongly ontological reading of chaotic and quantum unpredictabilities—these are thought to indicate genuine randomness or chance in the universe. In contrast to Polkinghorne and Tracy, however, he finds in the indeterminacies of nature inexorable limits to God's providential activity, rather than opportunities to exercise it.[26] This is not to say that chance is simply a kind of second god operating (as it were) unrelentingly to foil God's purposes. For Peacocke, chance is a feature of the universe, created by God along with the ordering of nature, which can search out the God-given potential of the fundamental constituents of the universe. Chance continually "experiments" with natural materials, eventually producing more and more complex, emergent realities such as life, consciousness, and, finally, humanity. The ongoing experiment of creation is not therefore the pandeterministic unfolding of divine purpose through micro-managed secondary causes, but a risky venture which produces richness and complexity at the cost of extensive failure and suffering.[27] Peacocke argues, however, that chance is just the sort of creative mechanism one

quantum indeterminacy is averaged out. See, for example, the cautionary comments by Polkinghorne in *Belief in God in an Age of Science*, 59–60.

26. Interestingly, Peacocke argues that Polkinghorne's exploitation of gaps created by the unpredictabilities of chaos theory renders his account of divine providence quite as interventionist as the scientifically unsophisticated views of divine providence deplored by most participants in the science and theology discussion. Polkinghorne's more subtle ordering pointed to but not grasped by modern science, Peacocke argues, is presumably known by God, and the exercise of particular influences over this ordering is just another (necessarily hidden, in this case) intervention into world processes that normally unfold of their own accord, albeit mysteriously (Peacocke, *Theology for a Scientific Age*, 154–55).

27. Peacocke, "The Cost of New Life," 21–42.

might expect in order to produce greater complexity in a law-governed environment.[28] It is the "search radar" of God.[29]

The causal nexus between God and the world, therefore, cannot be located among the set of pervasive indeterminacies in nature. Chance is a chosen means of God to explore the world's potential, but it is not the locus of specific divine influences upon world processes. Peacocke attempts to resolve the problem of how God exercises causal influence by appealing to the notion of "whole-part constraint," or "top-down causation." The idea here is that in at least some natural systems, features of the system as a whole exercise constraints upon its constituents. Causation need not flow only from "bottom up," the motions of particles of matter influencing the state of large-scales systems, but may also flow "downward."[30] The most controversial, and most germane, example Peacocke provides is the causal efficacy of selves upon the component parts of human bodies. God's interaction with the world is likened to the causal power of a self with respect to its own body.[31] The causal joint or nexus is not within the world governed by natural laws, but between the world and God-as-agent. The problem of the "causal joint" is not thereby resolved, but it is located in what Peacocke takes to be its proper place.[32] God exercises causal influence upon the world-as-a-whole, creating and sustaining its regularities, ordaining chance as the divine "search radar," and continually tweaking the system "from above" in response to the indeterminacies in nature amplified and gone awry.[33]

This approach may have an advantage over those which attempt to mine the gaps in naturalistic explanations of particular types of events and processes in nature, insofar as it leaves the widely-assumed completeness of these accounts more or less intact, and exploits known effects in

---

28. Peacocke, *Intimations of Reality*, 70–71. See also *Theology for a Scientific Age*, 115–121.

29. Peacocke, *Theology for a Scientific Age*, 120.

30. Ibid., 45–54.

31 Ibid., 160–164.

32. Ibid., 164.

33. An interesting feature of this scheme, pointed out by Peacocke himself, is that there is no need for the controversial category of particular providence over against general world-governance. God may act here in a general manner, on the world-as-a-whole, in order to accomplish specific objectives, since alterations in the character of the whole seep down to the level of particular parts. Thus, although the model may initially look uniformitarian, it is not (ibid., 157–59, 162).

nature, rather than invincible explanatory gaps, in the construction of a model for divine activity. Peacocke's attempt to assign an explanatory role to the notion of divine activity by ascribing to it a unique causal function runs into difficulties, however. As Willem Drees points out, it is debatable whether "downward causation" ought to be considered causation at all. It is true that some type of top-down analysis of a particular physical system illumines its pertinent features more fully than a bottom-up analysis. For example, to understand the motion of a barrel rolling down a hill, it would be more fruitful to try to understand the motion of the barrel in terms of its environment than in terms of the molecules that make it up. Still, Drees urges, this epistemological point should not necessarily be raised to the level of ontology. From a naturalistic perspective, all causal influences are local, and "can be traced locally as physical influences within the system (the rolling barrel, for example) or between the system and its immediate environment" (the slope of the hill, the weather, etc.).[34] Such a perspective in no way impedes a top-down analysis, when it is called for.

Moreover, Drees suggests that when Peacocke moves from the relation between particular systems and their local environments to God's action upon the world-as-a-whole, a significant degree of extrapolation is required. Drees points out that in the examples Peacocke and other proponents of top-down causation supply there is always an important role for the physical environment. When the world-as-a-whole is taken as a particular system within a larger environment, however, the notion of environment changes. It is no longer physical, and therefore subject to physical laws described by science.[35] It becomes unclear, then, just how the analogy is supposed to illumine divine causal influence when its terms shift so drastically. To the extent that the idea of divine activity is made to do explanatory work, therefore, controversial, and perhaps unclear, claims are made—even in a view, like Peacocke's, which does not require gaps.

Process Theology

Indeterministic chance is not the only sort of openness or flexibility capable of being ascribed to world-processes in order to render them

---

34. Drees, *Religion, Science, and Naturalism,* 102–3.
35. Ibid., 104.

malleable to divine influence. Thomas Tracy mentions an alternative approach to the problem of divine causality which takes *freedom* as a fundamental feature of reality, appealing to process theology as the most visible example of this strategy.[36] Like Tracy's own approach, process thought attempts to locate the flexibility of nature in its minute details. Whitehead's cosmology is, as he puts it, "atomistic," since he derives the large-scale features of the world from an array of discrete entities he calls "actual entities" or "actual occasions."[37] Unlike materialistic forms of atomism, however, Whitehead's "organismic" cosmology construes these ultimate constituents of the world as in varying degrees both bearers of experience and purposive agents. Each actual occasion is comprised by a "physical" pole which "prehends" or receives the causal influence of other actualities, and a "mental" or "conceptual" pole which formulates a response to these influences, called a "subjective aim." It is the latter which finally constitutes the unique character of the individual occasion.[38] Each occasion is thus in principle underdetermined by efficient causal influences from the past. From the welter of influences, it must select one course or another. The world's influences may be relatively constricting, and the "mental" response correspondingly small (as in the life of a boulder, for example), or they may present a wide array of options which require a relatively high-grade consciousness to adjudicate them (as in more complex animals). But in any case, the fundamental constituents of the world are characterized by some degree of freedom. There are problems, however, involved in actualizing one possibility under the influence of a nearly infinite number of efficient causes. How is the relevance of each influence to the well-being of particular occasions to be determined? Moreover, how are the novel possibilities, sometimes actualized by particular occasions of experience, themselves brought into being? These are metaphysical questions left over by Whitehead's construal of the world as a congeries of "dipolar" occasions of experience, and his concept of God provides the answer to both of them. As Whitehead puts it, "In the place of Aristotle's God as Prime Mover, we require God as the Principle of Concretion." In other words, Whitehead's cosmology does not require (as Aristotle's did) a divine being to supply a special, external cause to "sustain the motions of material things," but

---

36. Tracy, "Particular Providence," 311.
37. Whitehead, *Process and Reality*, 22ff.
38. Ibid., 38.

it does require the concept of a God who "grades" the relevance of the welter of causal influences impinging upon any particular occasion, and, in presenting them to in ordered form to each occasion, allows for its "concrescence" out of a myriad of abstract possibilities. John Cobb and David Griffin emphasize that in this scheme God also provides, out of the infinite wealth of the divine vision, novel possibilities for the enrichment of each occasion which are not anticipated by the finite causal influences impinging upon it.[39] The continuing activity of God is thus the source of both the order and the openness which are required to keep the world process moving forward in a creative advance.

Process thought thus ascribes to God an unrelenting, particular providential activity, ordering the world and "luring" it forward toward richer, more intense forms of experience. This activity consists primarily in providing "initial aims" to each unfolding occasion of experience which both grades or orders finite causal influences and suggests novel possibilities which may be actualized. The self-constituting "subjective aim" of each actual occasion is thus aided and initiated by God, though it may choose to ignore or contravene God's purposes by actualizing possibilities not favored by the divine will.[40] John Cobb and Schubert Ogden each press the Whiteheadian scheme into an account of divine activity which portrays the latter as a type of "self-constitution," rather rigorously analogous to the self-constitution which lies at the heart, according to process thought, of finite agencies.[41] God acts in the world by constituting God's self in a particular way in response to finite realities. As the supreme reality among others that impinge upon the actual occasions that make up the world, God must, above all other influences, have an effect upon unfolding mundane events and processes, which nevertheless remain relatively autonomous insofar as their own responses are not coerced. This account, according to its advocates, has the advantage of explaining how divine activity may influence the world without in-

---

39. Cobb and Griffin, *Process Theology*, 57–61.

40. The exercise of God's power is seen, therefore, as strictly analogous to the efforts of noncoercive human love on the behalf of the beloved object. Cobb and Griffin contrast process theology's construal of divine power as "persuasive love" to those which they regard as privileging raw coercive power (ibid., 52–54). For Kaufman, as we shall see below, the strict application of any analogy, including even that of persuasive love, is theologically problematic.

41. Cobb, "Natural Causality and Divine Action," 207–22; and Ogden, *The Reality of God*, 164–87.

tervening disruptively in its causal ordering and without absorbing its autonomy into a uniformitarian pan-determinism. It provides an objective ontology of events which leaves the world's autonomy intact.

The persuasiveness of this picture of the world is allegedly secured by its consonance with modern knowledge and its ability to explain features of world which are inexplicable to materialistic interpretations of it. One of these apparent inexplicables, pointed out by Langdon Gilkey, is the causal influence of the past.[42] How is the causal legacy of the past preserved, and how is its complexity ordered, so as to influence the present? In Whiteheadian schemes, "God" functions in part to explain this pervasive, though perplexing, feature of the experienced world. Process theology does not, therefore, merely locate "causal joints" in the empirically-described world at which divine activity may occur, but it locates features of any event whatsoever in which divine ordering activity is metaphysically required. God (the provider of ordered possibility in the form of "initial aims") and world (the free actualizer of possibility) are both necessary ingredients in the world process, utilized by the divine "creative advance" to promote greater complexity, richness, and intensity.[43] It has been frequently noted that there are theological costs associated with this view which are not happily paid by many theists.[44] Here, however, in keeping with our particular concern with the issue of credibility in this section, I want to underscore some difficulties which a naturalistic view of the world poses for the panpsychist character of process thought. As Willem Drees points out, process thought tends to upend the customary order of scientific disciplines, since it explains the ordering of nature in psychological categories, alleged counterintuitively to be more fundamental than the categories of physics.[45] To press the point further, we might add that the picture of large-scale physical phe-

42. Gilkey, *Reaping the Whirlwind*, 303. Particularly problematic in this regard is the causal efficacy of the past in history, given its constitution by the interplay of free agents.

43. Whitehead, *Process and Reality*, 410–11.

44. Chief among these, undoubtedly, is the metaphysical demotion of God implied in the previous sentence. See, for example, the caveats of such an enthusiastic proponent of Whiteheadian categories as Langdon Gilkey, in *Reaping the Whirlwind*, 311–12. Gilkey argues that the divine necessity can "only be understood ontologically if God also be the source of all ontological factors and so *ultimately conditioned by none of them*" (italics added).

45. Drees, *Religion, Science, and Naturalism*, 257–58.

nomena emerging from the processes of (low-grade) mind appears to be not so much an enrichment or elaboration upon scientific explanations of cosmic and biological evolution as a competing explanatory account of it. The evolutionary account of mind sees mentality as the result of a fortuitous arrangement of matter, brought about by natural selection[46] in a world governed fundamentally by the laws of physics. To the extent that this account succeeds, it would seem that the explanatory role of panpsychism is diminished. Though the emergence of mind may well illumine the propensities of matter, or of the world as a whole,[47] the equiprimordiality of mind with matter is undermined by evolutionary theory as it is almost universally understood. This is quite serious for attempts to use process thought to illumine the causal nexus between God and the world, because the fate of appeals to the latter's freedom would appear to be tied up with the fate of panpsychism. As in other strategies briefly examined here, the benefits achieved by using process categories in order to qualify the naturalistic account of the world are paid for by a some strains in terms of credibility in the face of current science.

Conclusion

The purpose of this section has not been to discount each of the perspectives discussed, whether on scientific, philosophical, or theological grounds, but to suggest that each of them is obliged to defend quite controversial interpretations of scientific theory in order to support claims that a credible "causal joint" in the natural ordering of the world has been found which can help make sense of divine activity. All of them may be seen as attempts to use modern knowledge to achieve distance from the allegedly bland, religiously unsatisfying uniformitarianism of liberal theology. Each does so by substantially qualifying naturalistic explanatory accounts of world. Room is made for explicitly theistic explanations of mundane events and processes, and these in turn give intelligible content to traditional claims about particular divine actions in the world. As I have attempted briefly to show, however, in each case there are problems attending attempts to locate causal joints for particular divine activity. Though the strategies described here seek intelligibility, their various attempts to salvage the tradition's picture of God's ceaseless, particular and

46. And, according to a controversial thesis, by dimly-understood tendencies toward self-organization latent within matter. See Kauffman, *At Home in the Universe*.

47. This, as we shall see, is Gordon Kaufman's suggestion.

local activity in the ordinary world of cause and effect as described by modern science seem inevitably to pay a price in the very commodity which they are trying to save—broad intelligibility.

In the opening chapters of *In Face of Mystery*, commenting upon the current popularity of Whiteheadian thought among theologians seeking to understand the relation between God and the world, Kaufman notes that he will "not move in that direction with the theological construction in this book." He goes on to write, "Doubtless there is much to be learned from Whitehead about contemporary conceptualizations of the world, but in my opinion *we theologians must do our own work* with respect to the question of God, not simply take over someone else's. We must explore carefully the basic conceptual scheme within which the inherited notion of God had its place and meaning, and then see whether it is possible to reconstruct that scheme in such a way as to take account of contemporary experience and knowledge."[48]

The latter part of this quote indicates the shape of Kaufman's alternative strategy to process thought for dealing with problem of relating God and the world, but does not really provide reasons why Whiteheadian categories are to be left aside. The italicized clause seems to offer a reason, but an apparently weak one. Building both upon our earlier discussion of Kaufman's method and upon our analyses of attempts to locate causal links between God and the world, however, we may now specify in more detail the reasons why Whitehead's conceptual scheme is of only limited usefulness to Kaufman. In doing so, moreover, we shall uncover his reasons for eschewing any strategy of attempting to qualify naturalistic interpretations of the world.

The primary reason theologians must "do their own work," for Kaufman, is related to his understanding of proper constructive method in theology. As we have seen, Kaufman's theology proceeds by analyzing the functional logic of "God" in historical religious traditions and then connecting it to current understandings of ourselves and the world. Whitehead, by contrast, understands God in terms of a needed role in a metaphysic constructed without reference to religious tradition. Methodologically, therefore, Whitehead's theological ruminations reverse the proper order of constructive theological thinking. This inevitably means that, substantively, God is understood as an adjunct of the world process. The latter is the real ultimate in Whitehead's system, and

48. Kaufman, *In Face of Mystery*, 46 (italics added).

for Kaufman this entails the unacceptable consequence that the functional meaning of "God" in the tradition (as that ultimacy to which we may give ourselves without reservation) is abrogated. Classical process thought, for Kaufman, is therefore both insufficiently confessional and insufficiently theocentric.

Kaufman's theocentrism and confessionalism support, in addition, skepticism about attempts to specify *how* God impinges upon the empirical world. Beyond the problems of credibility identified here, process thought and other attempts to locate causal joints between God and the world are from Kaufman's point of view inappropriate to the divine mystery.[49] As we saw in chapter 2, part of the meaning of "God," in Kaufman's view, is a prohibition against "reifying" or attributing a kind of scientific objectivity to our depictions of who God is and what God is doing in the world. The referent of "God" is beyond our grasp in principle, not just in fact. Though at least some efforts to locate an objective causal nexus between God and the world (Tracy's and Polkinghorne's, for example) are designed with the intent to conserve allegedly indispensable elements of the theistic tradition (especially particular providence), for Kaufman they in fact run roughshod over a central feature of the logic of "God"—the irreducible mystery and inscrutability of God's ways with the world.

Kaufman's efforts to deal with the problem of divine activity in light of contemporary knowledge about the world, we have suggested, do not eschew metaphysics. Rather, he actively pursues metaphysical reflection as a necessary component of theological reconstruction. In light of what we have said about the various kinds of difficulties associated with locating "causal joints," however, it should be emphasized again that Kaufman's view of metaphysics itself is what we might call "historicist." Following R. G. Collingwood, Kaufman sees metaphysics as less an objectively realistic "science of being" than a critical, historical analysis of the "absolute presuppositions" of a particular culture or cultural trajectory. A realistic "science of being" is simply beyond the grasp of historically and culturally relative human thinking. Kaufman's use of metaphysics, therefore, does not commit him to a task which he finds impossible. Successful negotiation of the problem of divine activity in the empirical world will not involve the construction of an objective view of the world, but the analysis and reconstruction of the overall visions of reality presupposed

49. Kaufman, *God the Problem*, 158–59.

in Western culture. Kaufman's foray into the field of metaphysics is an important component in his overall theological program, but its objective is less an account of a causal nexus between God and the world than the establishment of intelligible connections between what we habitually presuppose about our world today and the logical features of God-talk in Western culture.

NATURALISM AND THEISM: A METAPHYSICAL IMPASSE?

The problem, for Kaufman, is that two grand, inclusive visions of reality predominate in the West. He characterizes the inevitable impasse between them as a religious problem—a conflict of "faiths" which divides and confuses the confidences and the loyalties of a large number of Western persons and communities.[50] In a pivotal article, he argues that the concept of "nature" itself, though now deeply embedded in our working vocabulary, is already metaphysically loaded. The force and meaning of the concept, he suggests, depends upon an ambiguity: "nature" often seems to refer to the world of (nonhuman) animals, plants and ecosystems unspoiled by human interaction, while it is also often used to denote the world as a whole, inclusive of human beings and their artifices. When it is used in the latter sense, however, it has a richer, more concrete connotation than the concept of "world."[51] The concept of "nature," when used inclusively, construes the world, the context of human life, fundamentally as a realm of impersonal, nonmoral, nonpurposive processes. These, rather than human moral agency, become the clue to the character of the world as a whole, and purposive agency must now be understood as their outcome, rather than the other way around.[52]

The implicit, naturalistic metaphysic lurking between our ordinary usage of the word "nature" is troublesome, for Kaufman, because it appears to be incompatible with the inner logic of theism.[53] The worldview

---

50. In *In Face of Mystery*, Kaufman characterizes this problem as a "deep bifurcation" within the "faith that actually orients the lives of many moderns." We are confronted with two conflicting, and equally compelling, configurations of "meanings, values and commitments," and neither can be easily "dropped by the wayside" (*In Face of Mystery*, 434). Kaufman's portrayal of the practical, and problematical, nature of religious faith resembles that of his Yale mentor H. Richard Niebuhr, whose characterization of faith in terms of "confidence" and "loyalty" I am deliberately borrowing here. See H. Richard Niebuhr, *Radical Monotheism and Western Culture*, 11–23.

51. Regarding Kaufman's analysis of the concept of "world," see above, pp. 45–46.

52. Kaufman, "Nature," 213–19.

53. Ibid., 220, 223.

implied in theistic belief is centered around the idea of a God who acts (an "agent-God"[54]) from beyond the world to bring about God's purposes. Ultimate reality is therefore connected with personal moral agency, and a unique rapport with the real is given to our human capacity to act. What we now call "nature" is simply the raw material upon which nonnatural wills (God and our own) impose purpose. Kaufman points out that the theistic world picture inevitably both gives sanction to the "moral side" of human life and denigrates nature, even obscuring our own "embeddedness" in it.[55] But, to whatever degree we may value nature, our embeddedness in it is a compelling feature of our modern view of the world. Kaufman suggests that theologians must come to term with this new view of our close relation to (and dependence upon) the world of impersonal processes, because the modern concept of "nature" and its metaphysical implications now inevitably shape our experience of the world in which theistic belief attempts to orient us, and we cannot in the end help from thinking in terms of them.[56]

Naturalism, however, does not get unqualified endorsement. A construal of the world which privileges mechanistic, impersonal processes has difficulties absorbing the "the subjective viewpoint"[57] of human agency, which is also a real feature of the world. The experience of agency, and the correlated sense of responsibility, is as compelling and ineradicable a component of our mental furnishings as is our connectedness to "nature." When, in fact, we try to think about the world "concretely," Kaufman argues, "the complexities of the self simply cannot be subsumed under 'nature' without giving nature at least as much (self-reflexive) complexity as a self." For this reason, he suggests, the naturalistic metaphysic implied in the concept of "nature" cannot be fully worked out.[58]

It is just this metaphysically abortive character of an otherwise compelling naturalism that leads to the bifurcated faith characteristic of Western culture. Theism seems implausible as an overall world-picture because it asks us to reverse our ordinary thinking about the relation

54. Kaufman, *In Face of Mystery*, 273.

55. Kaufman, "Nature," 223, 226.

56. Ibid., 226.

57. The phrase is Thomas Nagel's, who makes the same point about objective views of the world in general (Nagel, *The View from Nowhere*, 25–27).

58. Kaufman, "Nature," 233–34.

of agency to impersonal world processes. We now understand personal agency to be the product of a long and convoluted history of interacting natural processes, and it is has consequently become difficult to conceive of a type of personal agency which is not embodied in this history.[59] Naturalistic accounts of the origins of personal agency, on the other hand, are compelling, but naturalism falters as an overall orientation because it cannot make sense of, nor help us develop fruitfully, our subjective sense of responsibility for our actions. The result is an uneasy dualism in orientation among Western persons and a consequent frustration of our capacity to engage in fruitful courses of action.

At the end of "Theology and the Concept of Nature," Kaufman suggests that new categories are needed to account for the conceptual complexity of our current understanding of the world. The physical universe is evidently a congeries of nonpurposive, impersonal entities and processes, but one which has given rise to purposive, perspective-holding beings. Since theism highlights the centrality of agency, it continues to offer the promise of successful orientation in the world for human agents.[60] But in order to come to terms with the reality of "nature," he argues, it will not suffice for theists simply to tweak their religious traditions by adding this or that bridge concept. Rather, theism must be reexamined down to its roots,[61] and a concept of God which does not ask us implausibly to believe in a disembodied agent who directs the course of the world from without will have to be constructed. In short, a new sort of (non-agential) theism will have to be invented, one which coheres with the (for us) incorrigible reality of a self-directing, natural law-governed universe. The substantive result, as we shall see, will be a "transformation" of theistic faith itself.[62]

Kaufman also believes, however, that in the course of doing so a new, richer conception of "nature" will also have to be invented, one which does justice to the anthropic character of our knowledge, inevita-

---

59. Kaufman, "On Thinking of God," 410.

60. Kaufman often associates the continuing promise of theism with the *orienting function* performed by the word "God" throughout Western religious history. Though the "form" of theistic belief may need drastic revision, its functional components remain promising, and for Kaufman they are in fact normative for the reconstruction of its form. See, for example, the constructive role played by a functional analysis of the word "God" in *In Face of Mystery*, 301–21.

61. Kaufman, "Nature," 230.

62. Ibid., 226.

bly highlighting the emergence of self-conscious agents as an important
feature of the physical world. For this, a new "history-nature" concept will
be required. This requirement for a two-fold innovation, of course, lays
a heavy conceptual burden upon theology, but Kaufman suggests that a
conceptual developments may already be underway which will enable a
"more unified view."[63] The fulfillment of this requirement would amount
to no less than a rapprochement between Western theism and naturalism. This, it seems to me, is the central desideratum of Kaufman's work
since the initial publication of his essay on the problem of "nature."

An important methodological implication of this diagnosis and
proposed cure of Western religion, to be tracked as we examine his
constructive proposal, should be perhaps be mentioned at this point by
way of anticipation. Kaufman himself mentions it at the end of the essay
under discussion: a theology which ventures upon a reconstruction of
theism in light of modern ideas about nature will not be able to do so
"intramurally."[64] A "unified view," required for successful orientation in
the world, cannot be achieved simply by expanding upon some theme
within the traditional theistic cosmology (such as "creation") in order to
absorb the insights of the modern knowledge. Rather, if theism is to be
reconciled with naturalism, nontheological sources of insight will need
to play a substantial constructive role. Claims about divine governance,
for example, will have to be reconstructed from the ground floor, with
the aid of generalizations from well-established scientific theories such
as biological evolution and "big bang" cosmology. This, we shall recall, is
for Kaufman precisely what is implied in the notion of a "constructive"
theology—its task is to sift modern knowledge and experience in order
to see whether a viable concept of God, and an intelligible account of the
world as governed, may be constructed for today. Though Kaufman, as
we have noted, eschews any appeal to particular "causal joints" in nature
in order to render traditional language about divine activity intelligible,
his recent efforts to account for divine activity do involve the difficult
and controversial task of establishing positive connections between
modern cosmology and religious faith.

63. Ibid., 236–37. These include, according to Kaufman, (1) the characterization of
nature as in some sense "historical," and (2) the growing recognition that history is
rooted in nature.

64. Ibid., 230.

4

Radicalizing Naturalism

RADICAL NATURALISM AND THE SIGNIFICANCE OF TIME

IN AN ARTICLE PUBLISHED in *Zygon* slightly before the release of *In Face of Mystery*, Kaufman announced that he had now found a way "through or around" the impasse between naturalism and theism.[1] This breakthrough involved the construction of a "history-nature" concept (a "biohistorical" interpretation of human beings)[2] and the outlines of a new metaphysical interpretation of the world as the context of the unfolding of "nature-history." This perspective is eventually called by Kaufman "radical naturalism"—"naturalism" because it accepts the presupposition of modern science that complete causal explanations of events and processes in the world are possible (and therefore supernatural and teleological explanations are ruled out); "radical" because it allegedly resists the reductive implications often derived from this claim, refusing to eclipse the experience of historicity as a distinct, emergent order of reality.[3] For Kaufman, as we have noted, reductive or mechanis-

1. Kaufman, "Nature, History, and God," 380.

2. Kaufman's anthropological reflections are worked out in some detail in a lengthy section of *In Face of Mystery* titled "Constructing a Concept of the Human" (pp. 97–234). These reflections play an important role in his theology, since they provide content to his normative criterion of humanization to which any theological effort is subject. I will not discuss Kaufman's anthropology in detail in this book (though I will return, in the final chapter, to the question of how the formal criterion of humanization might be filled out substantively). Its central features, however, may be summarized briefly: human beings are (1) inseparably connected to and dependent upon their physical environment, and (2) characterized by the capacity to make deliberate, considered choices, and consequently to set the course, to some extent, of their own destiny, and even the destiny of the planet. These features together, for Kaufman, yield both an adequate *description* of human experience and the outlines of an appropriate *ethic* for human beings today.

3. Kaufman, *In Face of Mystery*, 458. Actually, Kaufman employs the phrase to

tic forms of ontological naturalism do just this, and a viable naturalism will therefore need to construe ostensibly mechanistic processes in the world in terms of a broader framework which does not. Kaufman's effort turns upon a decision to take the present, locally observable outcome of natural and historical processes, rather than their origins, as the clue to the fundamental character of the universe which environs them. This decision, as we shall see in this section, involves disputed questions about the metaphysical significance of time.

Metaphysics and Faith

The ultimate context of human life is, for Kaufman, a matter which is intrinsically mysterious. Like talk about "God," talk about the fundamental character of the universe extends human thinking beyond its proper competence. Kaufman's appeal to the concept of mystery at the beginning of part 3 of *In Face of Mystery*, titled "Constructing a Concept of the Context of Human Existence: The World," functions, therefore, to place cautionary brackets around the whole of his metaphysical discussion.[4] "Mystery" does not, however, function positively to protect the integrity of traditional claims about either God or the world from scrutiny. It is significant that the very next point Kaufman makes in part 3, after his cautionary remarks about the "mystery" of the world, is that through common sense as well as modern knowledge and experience we do in fact know some things about it. We know, he suggests, that the world is not a given structure that is impervious to change. It develops, and to some extent it is even plastic to human interests and purposes.[5] This knowledge, rather than some perceived causal gap or some limit question, is the starting point for Kaufman's effort to construct a viable account of divine governance.

The metaphysical interpretation of widely accredited factual knowledge, of course, is perennially disputed. Kaufman suggests, in fact, that

characterize the naturalistic, though non-reductive, understanding of the relation of empirical fact and value or meaning that flows from his theology. Human values and meanings are not extraneous to natural ordering, he suggests, but belong to it intrinsically. Being and value are therefore inseparable. We will have more to say about the valuational dimension of his proposal below (chapter 7). The phrase also belongs here, I suggest, because the being from which value cannot be separated is itself understood naturalistically.

4. Ibid., 238.

5. Ibid.

there is an incorrigible plurality of perspectives, and some basic choices which are not susceptible to proof are therefore inevitably required.[6] He characterizes each of a chain of metaphysical choices as a "small step of faith." Faith in divine governance, therefore, may be seen as built up from a number of somewhat less momentous metaphysical decisions, rather than as a single great leap. In this way, the cognitive details of religious faith can be scrutinized. More importantly, however, faith can also be re-constructed self-consciously and deliberately, so that responsibility may be taken and more adequate orientation may be acquired.[7]

This does not mean that responsible theological reflection upon our world must begin at ground zero with respect to faith. In the first (1975) edition of *An Essay on Theological Method*, Kaufman portrayed theological construction as a series of three "moments," the first being made up of "pure[ly] phenomenological description" of the world.[8] He has since, in the third (1995) edition, pointed out that these moments are more logical than psychological. For an illuminating psychological account of theistic consciousness, he suggests, a "moment zero" must be posited. This initial moment is the concrete faith situation of the puzzling, questioning theologian, already shaped by a religious tradition.[9] The moment of "pure description" is intended by Kaufman to represent the necessary interaction between knowledge and experience of the world with the content of religious traditions in a robust faith in divine activity. That emphasis, as we have already seen, remains in Kaufman's *In Face of Mystery*, but his earlier "moments" are replaced now by "steps of faith." The latter concept is arguably more capable of dealing both with the logical and the psychological features of theological reflection, though, as with the three "moments," one ought not to suppose that each of the steps is clear in the mind of any believer (nor, for that matter, in the mind of any theologian). The point is that the initial steps to be taken

6. This disjunct between established fact and metaphysical interpretation makes Kaufman uneasy about Sallie McFague's claim that modern science has given us a "common creation story." "Creation" is a metaphysical concept, and a number of alternative metaphysical schemes may well cohere with the facts of modern cosmology (ibid., 239).

7. The claim that we must take responsibility for every feature of our theological proposals, rather than simply accepting the authority of tradition, is most forcefully made in Kaufman, *Theology for a Nuclear Age*, 1–15.

8. Kaufman, *An Essay on Theological Method*, 1st ed., 60.

9. Kaufman, *An Essay on Theological Method*, 3rd ed., 92.

in constructing theological accounts of the world are now described as "steps of faith." Even the decision to embark upon metaphysics as a way of clarifying theistic faith, he argues, is a non-coercible response of a historically-shaped religious consciousness to the pressures of modern knowledge.[10]

This procedure, again, may be contrasted to the way in which Whiteheadian categories have been constructed. While process theologians may be similarly motivated by a "faith seeking understanding," the metaphysic they employ is more or less ready-made, not itself a construction guided explicitly by the (functional) norms inherent in the Western religious consciousness. The latter, Kaufman suggests, is rooted historically in the faith tradition of ancient Israel, in which a decision to attribute Israel's liberation from Egypt to an objective, cosmic ground.[11] Both the impetus to embark upon metaphysics as well as the direction to be followed, therefore, come from the logic of the tradition itself (which already makes rather momentous and controversial metaphysical claims), not from any speculative interest or scientific insight. The whole metaphysical apparatus in Kaufman's theology, therefore, may be seen in the broader context of a confession of faith.

Theologians operating out of a theistic historical tradition are not, of course, compelled to engage in metaphysical reflection. In light of the profound difficulties in persuasively supporting any particular metaphysical viewpoint, Kaufman allows, many may reasonably choose to adopt an agnostic attitude toward matters of this highest level of generality. Or, one may take these difficulties as a collective warrant for holding dogmatically to some traditional metaphysical model. Since only loosely pragmatic reasons, rather than rationally constraining ones, can be given for rejecting either of these options, Kaufman points out that his choice to follow an alternative "reflective religious/metaphysical road" is best seen in fact as a first "step of faith."[12] The decision to embark upon such a large-scale construction (which claims to pull together a plethora of factual insights into a coherent pattern) as a theological strategy embodies confidence, historically rooted in Israel's imaginative objectification of its experience of liberation, that talk about divine activity refers to realities in the world also describable in the terms available in nonreligious

10. Kaufman, *In Face of Mystery*, 240.

11. Ibid., 246.

12. Ibid., 240.

vocabularies. Kaufman argues that, by contrast, agnosticism about metaphysical issues entails the rejection of any constructive effort to portray the empirical world as a realm in which God has any significant place.[13] Far from an alien influence, therefore, metaphysical reflection which draws upon and is accountable to modern insights about the world is for Kaufman required in order to sustain the confessional integrity of theistic religious traditions.

The type of theological construction advocated by Kaufman involves more than confidence in the intelligibility and illuminating power of theistic categories, however. It also involves a commitment to take secular portrayals of the world seriously enough not arbitrarily to perforate them when the evidence suggests their completeness. This commitment is also akin to faith, since no coercive reasons can be given for the absolute truth of any framework of interpretation. Kaufman thus suggests that his theological interpretation of the world as governed begins with a two-pronged commitment (a "double act of faith"). It operates from within the sphere of commitment to (1) the modern scientific understanding of the cosmos, and (2) the possibility that theistic categories may be able to orient us successfully in the world so understood.[14] In light of what we have said previously, we may specify (1) by noting that for Kaufman this commitment means accepting the naturalistic metaphysical presuppositions of the contemporary scientific practice. So amplified, it becomes clear that sustaining such a dual commitment throughout the details of a theological program poses challenges. We will need to track Kaufman's use of sources of insight to see whether and how he meets them. I have already proposed that the major point upon which his interpretation of the world turns is a claim about the metaphysical significance of temporality. It is time now to investigate this claim.

---

13. Ibid., 242. We may note that metaphysical agnosticism is widespread among theologians today, and often used to protect language about God's "mighty acts" from rational scrutiny. Barth and cultural-linguists seem to exploit the difficulties involved in metaphysical thinking in this way (For a brief discussion of Kaufman's approach to theology in relation to that of cultural-linguistic thinkers, see above, pp. 40–42). Thus has metaphysical agnosticism become allied, ironically, with dogmatism.

14. Ibid., 243.

Ways of Taking Time

Kaufman's decision to take the reality of human historicity as clue to the real is described as a second step of faith. This second step involves both formal and material considerations. At issue, formally, is the significance of time. Is the experience of time to be taken as merely phenomenal, or as a local variant of an eternal structure? Or does it point to the intrinsically developmental character of the universe? What sorts of knowledge and insight might count for or against either of these alternatives? Materially, Kaufman's decision points toward a construal of the world as a proper home for the human spirit. If the humanly perceivable outcome of cosmic temporal development is seen as the central clue to the meaning of the universe, as we shall see, materialism is reversed, and claims about the meaninglessness and aloneness of human life in the face of "omnipotent matter" are shown to be empirically unnecessary metaphysical elaborations upon the naturalistic picture of the world rendered by modern science.

The Metaphysics of Time

Temporal development is an obvious fact about life on earth. Modern knowledge about geological and meteorological change, biological evolution which tracks it, and the dramas of human history all make static understandings of the world of human experience appear untenable. What is not obvious, however, is the metaphysical significance to be attributed to these facts. It is not impossible, Kaufman allows, that temporal dynamism transpires within an eternal structure. It may be that the developments that have produced human life are actually only local perturbations within a vast, static order. In spite of our own experience in this corner of the universe, in other words, it is possible to take structure as ultimate, rather than process or change.[15] We may note that materialism does something like this. The explicability of natural history in terms of evolutionary laws which are, in turn, reducible to more fundamental principles of chemistry and physics may easily be taken to indicate that reality includes nothing more than physical matter plus the set of unchanging, immutable physical laws, and that evolutionary developments are merely historically contingent, accidental elaborations. This is certainly a possible viewpoint, but for Kaufman it is important to

15. Ibid., 251.

point out that it is a metaphysical choice, not strictly required by science, nor even by the naturalistic view of the world which sees it as explainable solely in terms of matter and physical laws. Neither explanatory nor ontological naturalism[16] entails an atomistic materialism which takes the smallest units of matter as key to the ultimately real.

Because naturalism and materialism are so often identified, it may be necessary to entertain an alternative metaphysical view which remains within the orbit of naturalism to see this. Kaufman's own suggestion, that process rather than structure be taken as ultimate, is such an alternative. Far from being his own, idiosyncratic innovation, however, the choice to take process as ultimate is for Kaufman a central feature of the theistic tradition. In ancient Israel, he suggests, world history was seen not as a series of cycles repeating the cyclical rhythms of the cosmos, but as governed by God's purposive activity and thus characterized by an historical or narrative pattern. Whatever cosmic and institutional structures there are have come into being through divine activity, and thus are not to be understood as permanent and unalterable. Nor are they to be seen as bearers of ultimate meaning. Meaning, rather, is to be understood in terms of God's unfolding purposes in history.[17]

The question about the metaphysical significance of time is finally, according to Kaufman, a religious one. Temporal passage may be understood fundamentally as a threat to human well-being.[18] Knowledge about past events in nature and history, and about prospects for human life continuing in the future, may be drawn upon in support of this way of

---

16. By "explanatory naturalism" I mean the belief that every event in the world can be explained solely in terms of natural causes. By "ontological naturalism" I mean the related but somewhat more ambitious claim that the world of matter and laws is all there is. My point, however, is that even this latter claim does not strictly entail that the world as a whole must be understood primarily in terms of the properties of matter and the physical laws that govern them. As we shall see, the choice to construe the world in terms of origins rather than results remains a non-coercible choice.

17. Kaufman, *In Face of Mystery*, 252. For Kaufman, as we shall see in chapter 6, the important feature about the theistic picture is not its assertion of the existence of some being outside of the world, but the decision to construe the world in terms of developments within it in and through which *extra-human realities* have created and continue to support human life. Therefore theism at its root represents and embodies a decision to take the world we know and experience in a certain way, not a postulation of additional entities that resist being subsumed under the modern idea of an all-encompassing nature.

18. Ibid., 254.

seeing time, but the basic issue is not simply that of describing the world accurately. Rather, taking temporality as a threat is kind of orientation or posture toward the world, a stance of faith or confidence in and loyalty toward that which is enduring and "secure."[19] Practically, this stance may eventuate in fighting social and institutional innovation tooth and nail; or it may lead to a pious regard for the goods of the natural world which we are presently destroying through modern technology and population growth, and perhaps to a critique of the industrial anthropocentrism of Western societies. Either type of response is, in the broad sense, conservative, since it locates value and meaning in natural or social realities now being eroded by the passage of time. More importantly, each is *religious*, a matter of being practically oriented toward some central locus of meaning and value.

Alternatively, temporal passage may be taken as an "instrument of salvation."[20] In ancient Israel, as in much of Western piety which has descended from it, history was seen as meaningful and productive of potentially redemptive new realities. Again, modern knowledge about the past and about future prospects may support this viewpoint, but finally it is not a scientific but a religious stance, a matter of ultimate confidence and loyalty. This history-minded piety, however, is characterized by a high degree of confidence in the historical process.[21] It may, in contrast to the view described above, eventuate in zeal for social and institutional reform, or in taking it as a moral obligation to "improve" the landscape through clearing, building, manufacturing, and otherwise expanding human influence over the world of nature. This is, metaphysically speaking, a progressive faith, since it locates value and meaning not in existing structures of one type or another, but in the prospects for transforming one such structure into something else, in the hope that the future may offer better resources for human fulfillment than the past.

---

19. Ibid., 253.

20. Ibid., 254.

21. It should be noted that confidence in the historical process need not entail the (arguably misguided) trust that history is somehow automatically redemptive. Though belief in the inevitability of progress has at times thrived in the historical aftermath of theistic faith, Kaufman's point about a history-minded faith does not require that history be construed as a continual upward march. It only requires that (nature and) history be viewed as continually productive of new possibilities, some of which may be seized upon for increased human well-being.

As we have said, Kaufman does not believe that one can adjudicate these faith options simply by appealing to the most well-attested knowledge about the world. The adequacy of particular construals of the world as a whole, in fact, is not an empirical matter at all, but a matter of being oriented in such a way that we can go on with life in the face of what we know (as well as what we do not).[22] Nevertheless, at least one empirical matter seems at least to impinge upon the adequacy of world-pictures which view time as central. If temporality is taken to be of ultimate metaphysical significance, we may demand that the universality of time be shown to be at least consistent with modern knowledge about nature. If so, this may constitute a problem. There may be difficulties involved in conceiving of time as unidirectional during the earliest, highly chaotic phases of the universe. In addition, relativity theory appears to require that time be understood locally rather than universally.[23] Construing the ultimate context of our existence in non-temporal terms may deal with these features of modern cosmologically better than a history-minded metaphysic. It should be pointed out, however, that Kaufman's construal of temporality as a fundamental feature of the universe does not require it to be ubiquitous—nor does it require a universal perspective on temporal flow. Rather, it requires only that time be a pervasive feature of the universe as we now experience it. Upon this modest empirical basis, he believes, the decision imaginatively to take temporality as a clue to the meaning of the world is at least not ruled out.

Spirit in the World

The formal issue of time's significance is important, as we have said, because of the opening it creates for talking about the metaphysical significance of realities which have emerged relatively recently, and perhaps only locally. The substantive claim upon which Kaufman's proposal for understanding the world is constructed is the centrality of "spirit," or the "symbolic order of meaning and purpose," in the universe.[24] This claim

22. Kaufman, *In Face of Mystery*, 254–56. Kaufman appeals here to the imaginative character of all cosmological knowledge. Even the idea we have of the sun, he suggests by way of example, is not strictly a product of perception. All knowledge is shaped by imagination, which is in turn formed in part by particular interests.

23. Drees, *Religion, Science, and Naturalism*, 261–66.

24. Kaufman, *In Face of Mystery*, 257. Kaufman's use of "spirit" here is much like his earlier usage, in *Relativism, Knowledge and Faith*, 60–61, 63–72. In neither case does it refer to some Cartesian mental substance but rather to the arena of cultural realities

is a denial of metaphysical materialism, not because the latter denies that spiritual realities are in every case connected to and dependent upon physical processes, but because the concept of spirit intends to refer to features of the "actual context of human life" which cannot be adequately grasped by the concepts of physics and chemistry.[25] Reductive explanations may work, successfully showing that, for example, emotional states are completely explicable in terms of chemical processes within the brain. They cannot, however, grasp the richness of subjective or first-person perspectives of being affected emotionally, nor of rationally devising practical strategies in response. Even more importantly, they cannot account for the centrality of these experiences in any of the inevitably anthropic visions of the world constructed by humans.

A word should be said here about what adequately grasping reality entails for Kaufman. In continuity both with his logical analysis of the concept of "world" as a regulative idea and with his historicist understanding of the knowing process (discussed above, chapter 2), he asserts that we cannot say "what reality is." Reality as a whole is not available to us, and therefore it is inappropriate to ask that a view of the world correspond to it. Rather, we may adjudicate between competing views only by asking which one most adequately interprets the "wideness and richness of human experience."[26] The criteria of adequacy are two-fold: an adequate view must be (1) intelligible in light of modern experience and knowledge, and (2) capable of orienting human agents. In order to fulfill the latter criterion, he suggests, it must construe the world not only as orderly but as meaningful. It must portray human responsibility as one part of a "wider cosmic process" which has been generating increasingly complex, self-directing forms of existence.[27]

Both materialism and Kaufman's historicist metaphysic, he suggests, satisfy the criterion of intelligibility. Either is fully consistent with scientific facts, and with the naturalistic presuppositions of modern science. The metaphors of "matter" and "machine" by themselves, as we have seen, are not in Kaufman's judgment adequate to grasp all of our experience, but they may be augmented by evolutionary/developmental

---

that are borne in traditions and are therefore objective to and, to some degree, formative of human individuals.

25. Kaufman, *In Face of Mystery*, 257–58.

26. Ibid.

27. Ibid., 260–61.

concepts which make room for the emergence of novel properties at higher levels of complexity.[28] The failure of reductive materialism occurs not at the level of intelligibility, but at the level of orienting possibility. Kaufman suggests that the decision to take reductive explanations of spirit as indicative of the ultimacy of impersonal matter and natural laws tends to "dampen our enthusiasm" for the task of taking responsibility for our projects. In effect, it fosters a deterministic attitude which undercuts human responsibility. It thus fails as a normatively orienting vision of the world.[29]

Kaufman further suggests that the deficiencies of materialism as a worldview point to certain correlative advantages of a spiritual view of the world. The former falters as an orienting vision because it attempts to construe the world in terms of its beginnings or foundations. This procedure privileges the simple, primitive, non-sentient features of our universe, and it is should therefore come as no surprise that it fails to highlight the significance of spirit. Purposive human life inevitably appears somehow out of place in such a mechanistic vision of the world. The latter, by contrast, attempts to construe the world in terms of the "point to which it has come."[30] Local, present reality, characterized most obviously by beings who consciously and deliberately carry out purposes, is awarded a higher metaphysical status. Modern biology's successful explanation of human self-sacrificial love in terms of physiological urges driven by the need to reproduce, for example, is taken also to show that these rather amoral urges may be "transmuted" into the sort of humane relations we value.[31] The explanation of complex biological and historical realities in terms of matter and natural laws is taken to show the rich potential of matter, rather than to reduce the significance of human and other animal life. The effectiveness of reductive explanations is not denied, but their significance is reversed. In light of them, the world of matter and laws is taken to be the kind

28. Kaufman suggests, however, that this already comes close to the theological notion of "creativity" he employs in his own metaphysic, and thus invites reflection upon the ultimate significance of process or development (ibid., 258–59).

29. Ibid., 260.

30. Ibid.

31. Ibid., 266. Kaufman acknowledges here the contribution of Paul Ricoeur's work on Freud. The same logic may also be applied, it seems to me, to other, even more ambitious "reductive" accounts of human love, such as those of sociobiology and evolutionary psychology.

of world in which things like human love emerge. This reversal of materialism is important, for Kaufman, because he believes that it allows
him to take what we know about the world and shape it into a vision of
life which can effectively focus our attention upon the humane features
of our world which most directly concern us, while construing them
as supported by the cosmos as a whole rather than as merely unlikely
curiosities in an indifferent world.

The philosophical warrants for attempting to construct this spiritual view, we may note, are coherentist and pragmatic. By invoking the
criterion of intelligibility in support of his view, Kaufman suggests that
it coheres with the most well-established results of empirical inquiry
as well as with commonsense observations about the way the world
works. It need not be held to the stricter standard of correspondence,
since correspondence is not an appropriate desideratum for imaginative accounts of reality as a whole. Kaufman alleges its superiority to
materialist world-pictures, which also cohere with the scientific data, on
a resolutely pragmatic basis. It enables us to see our moral strivings as a
natural and appropriate part of the world as a whole, and thus heartens
us for the struggle that humane existence in the world entails. In addition, it opens the possibility, Kaufman believes, for successful constructive efforts at seeing God as a reality at work in the world we know and
experience. Kaufman suggests that this possibility is all but foreclosed
by the reductively materialist metaphysic often constructed out of modern knowledge. Therefore the decision to take process as metaphysically
significant and "spirit" as an expression of the fundamental character of
our world is both a step toward faith in divine governance, and a move
made already within the circle[32] of faith, justified in part by its promise
of rendering it intelligible.

---

32. I am borrowing here the concept of a "circle" of faith or a "theological circle" from
Paul Tillich. See Tillich, *Systematic Theology*, 8–11. Martin L. Cook (*The Open Circle*)
has also exploited the notion of a theological circle in order to develop a typology of
confessional theologies. Cook distinguishes between "internalist" and "noninternalist"
confessional approaches. The former seek to justify theological proposals on grounds
internal to the theological tradition, and the latter are open to revision or correction
on nontheological grounds. Cook focuses upon H. Richard Niebuhr's theology as an
example of "noninternalist" confessionalism, but it seems to me that Kaufman's theology might just as well be cited.

CREATIVITY

Kaufman's second step of faith, as we have seen, involves questions about the metaphysical significance of time and spirit. The third step involves building upon Kaufman's answers to these by asking, in turn, about the particular implications that may be drawn from the fact that non-personal events and processes in the universe have brought forth life and historical existence.[33] As we saw above, the emergence of a new, historical and cultural, level of reality suggests that the impersonal cosmic process is capable of producing realities too complex to be describable fully in natural-scientific terms (though their existence may be so explained). A different set of categories must be invented to deal with the complexities of human history. For a cosmology intent upon construing the world as a whole as fundamentally historical in nature, these historical categories will need to be shown to be relevant to the interpretation of the entire universe, including its "mechanistic" elements. Kaufman's third and fourth steps of faith, therefore, embody an attempt to fashion historical categories of sufficient breadth to illumine all of the world experienced and known by human beings.

Kaufman suggests that, taken together, temporal development throughout the universe and the facticity of "new modes of organization" (complexity) and "new modes of activity" (purposive activity) here on earth warrant a claim that the "irreversible cosmic movement into the future" is no longer "blind" and bereft of purpose, but has in fact become deliberate, intentional, and "permeated with meaning."[34] Kaufman is not arguing here for teleology on a grand scale, attributing a single, coherent set of purposes to the world as a whole. Precisely insofar as human culture, as a realm of intentionality and meaning, is a natural outgrowth of physical processes in a developing world, however, one may intelligibly claim that the world as a whole is characterized by local and quite specific purposes and meanings. This locality of purposiveness does not prohibit one from attributing significance to it. Its emergence amidst the welter of non-purposing events and processes of the world, for Kaufman, warrants making the theologically momentous claim that "creative activity occurs."[35]

33. Kaufman, *In Face of Mystery*, 264–65.
34. Ibid., 266.
35. Ibid., 267 (italics added).

In a recent article, Kaufman argues that the concept of creativity is directly implied in the idea of an evolutionary development from simple combinations of element to complex, sentient life forms, but that it is also a descendent of the biblical concept of creation.[36] In a unique way, "creativity" thus appears to bridge biblical and modern cosmologies. Indeed, Kaufman suggests elsewhere that the Hebraic cosmological vision and what he calls the "evolutionary epic" are quite similar in form, despite radical differences with respect to details. Both of them, he argues, portray the world fundamentally as a "temporal historical process of development." The basic substantive difference between the two is that biblical cosmology alleges an intimate connection between "how things are" (being) and "which things matter" (value), secured through the continued activity and presence of God in the world.[37] The source of the unfolding order of the cosmos is also the source of goodness—the Creator, we might say, is also the Redeemer. This connection of being and value is for Kaufman a central and unique contribution of theistic belief—and though he intends his own project to depart from the reifications that have often accompanied it, his theological program is designed to support this connection rather than undermine it. Kaufman therefore suggests that his usage of the concept of creativity fits modern thinking about the cosmos, while amplifying it in important ways under the influence of traditional theistic belief about the world.[38]

Kaufman's amplification of modern knowledge, we may note, is not a qualification of its naturalistic assumptions, a claim about some extra reality which bears upon human life but which is not perceived by ordinary means. Rather, it is an attribution of moral and religious significance to the modern understanding of cosmic, biological and historical development. Kaufman has made this distinction particularly clear with recent remarks that the idea of creativity ought to be understood in close connection to the concept of mystery. He admits that some of the language about the creativity at work in the cosmos in his previous publications, including *In Face of Mystery*, may be understood to refer to some kind of non-personal, novelty-producing "force" alongside others. Confident talk about this sort of causal agency, however, "presupposes that we know more about the emergence of novelty than we

36. Kaufman, "On Thinking of God," 409.
37. Kaufman, "The Epic of Evolution," 182.
38. Ibid., 183.

actually do." As the traditional doctrine of creation *ex nihilo* affirmed, he suggests, the creation of novelty in the universe is beyond human comprehension. Creativity is mystery, and cannot therefore be reified in terms of either personal agency or impersonal forces.[39] We can affirm that creativity occurs, but the affirmation must remain in the category of an historical judgment rather than a quasi-scientific statement about *causes* of novelty.

Though generalizations about natural history may support the notion of creativity, biological science in fact provides no viable model for understanding it, since it is oriented toward uncovering mechanistic causes. The attempt to locate causal agencies responsible for creativity as such (in contrast to investigations of the specific avenues creativity takes in biological evolution) would be tantamount to vitalism, almost universally acknowledged by biologists to be a misuse of scientific data. Kaufman's remark about thinking we know more than we can possibly know makes the same general point. He proposes, therefore, to look for a model for understanding creativity in the realm of *history*. Historians regularly take pleasure in reporting instances in which particular historical events produce more than what was intended—more even than what could have been foreseen—by the principle historical agents. This feature of history Kaufman proposes to call the "serendipity of history." History can be judged to be serendipitous because retrospective observations reveal that the complex interplay of free decisions of historical agents produces results that often "outrun the expectations" of any or all of them.[40]

Kaufman cites the dynamics of ordinary conversations as a compelling micro-example of serendipity. In conversations, the spontaneous interaction between free participating agents can take on a life of its own, resulting in the participants being led to make responses and ask questions they would not have entertained on their own. In this creative matrix, new thoughts and ideas, not accessible to any of the conversants beforehand, become available. This fruitful "mixture of determinism and indeterminism," Kaufman suggests, does not inherently diminish the agencies of each of the participants by placing them in a sort of zero-sum competition with the others. Rather, the constraints of having to respond to another may spark the imaginative capacities of each, with the result

39. Kaufman, "On Thinking of God," 412.
40. Kaufman, *In Face of Mystery*, 273.

that freedom is enhanced. This does not mean that the outcome will be positive, however—the life of a conversation may just as easily alienate old friends as create new affective bonds. The point is, the unpredictable course of a conversation may produce more momentous results than envisaged, for good or ill.[41]

Along the same lines, it should be emphasized that Kaufman does not think that the attribution of serendipity to the world as an historical judgment commits one to optimism about the course of history. Rational intentions may accumulate and interact to produce profoundly irrational results. The outrunning of expectations by this cunning of history may often amount, therefore, to a perilous diminution of human agency. Kaufman indicates his apprehensions regarding the limits of human control over the creativity at work in human ingenuity by his choice of symbolism for the phenomenon: the "great literary symbol," he writes, is Shelley's Frankenstein, and "the great factual symbol" for our time is the splitting of the atom.[42] Both symbols indicate the tragic possibilities which always attend historical advance. Since history's cunning may also produce more profound sorts of human well-being than could be imagined, extending rather than diminishing human freedom, the concept of serendipity may also serve as a model of divine governance; but it must be emphasized that, for Kaufman, the concept taken alone is inadequate for this purpose. The phenomena it describes are too ambiguous.

Kaufman believes that an advantage of employing the model of historical serendipity to interpret the world as a whole is that it can also throw genuine light on the world of nature described by modern biology, whereas, on the other hand, strictly biological models have little power to illumine the complexities of human history. The serendipitous creation of new ideas in a conversation can serve as a model for understanding the emergence of new species in the evolutionary process. The "mixture of determinism and indeterminism" created by the spontaneous interaction of free agents may be likened to the combination of randomness and the constraints of evolutionary law characteristic of the interaction between mutations and the process of natural selection which sifts them.[43]

41. Ibid., 276–77.
42. Ibid., 275.
43. Ibid., 278.

This applicability of the idea of creativity to biological (and other cosmic) processes, for Kaufman, has important implications for a doctrine of God. First of all, since it indicates that human purposive activity is not the most fundamental type of finite creativity, it suggests that human agency is probably not workable as a model for divine creative activity. Kaufman suggests that Darwinian science, though it does not provide the conceptual resources for understanding creativity as such, has at least demonstrated that the production of novelty can come from impersonal processes.[44] Therefore, as we shall see more fully in the next chapter, Kaufman believes that a kind of personal agency which is not the product of this impersonal, physical processes of nature (and therefore still dependent upon them) has become, since Darwin, inconceivable. This makes straightforward agential models of divine activity conceptually difficult. It is this difficulty which plays a large role, in Kaufman's thinking, in suggesting the promise of pursuing the model of historical serendipity in the first place.[45] Secondly, the applicability of the concept of creativity to cosmic processes supports the decision, made in conjunction with Kaufman's second step of faith, to view the universe as a whole an arena of process or development. Thus, while eroding the intelligibility of one way of taking traditional claims about God's purposes in the world, it supports the development of another.

After drawing upon the serendipity of human history to interpret the processes of nature in the passage from *In Face of Mystery* cited above, Kaufman goes on to reverse the flow of conceptual influence, as it were, by characterizing history in terms of biological categories. In human history also, he suggests, something like a "natural selection" of myriads of idiosyncratic innovations takes place. Many cultural "mutations," brought about by the exuberance of human creativity, turn out to be useless, but some of these prove to be adaptive for new, changing local and global contexts in which they occur. They are then selected by the historical process to shape some aspect of the relevant culture. In addition, like biological phenotypes, some cultural phenomena become obsolete by virtue of changes in their (historical/cultural) environment, and are therefore sifted out.[46] The serendipity of history, therefore, is for Kaufman a model for interpreting nature in light of human history, but

44. Kaufman, "On Thinking of God," 413.

45. Kaufman, *In Face of Mystery*, 273.

46. Ibid., 278.

one which is enriched by the addition of other developmental categories in the process. History is in turn illumined by interpreting it in terms of this biologically enriched historical model. In this back and forth movement between biological and historical categories in Kaufman's thinking, however, history clearly has pride of place. Their mutual interaction seems only to be warranted, in fact, by the supposition that history is a more metaphysically fundamental notion than "evolution." The reach of Kaufman's historical category of creativity is shown its ability to incorporate even the insights regarding mutations provided by molecular biology (among the hardest of biological sciences) into a broadly historical framework.

It should be pointed out how different this interpretation of natural selection is from Ralph Wendell Burhoe's, and how vastly different its theological implications are. Burhoe, we may recall, collapses talk about divine activity into evolutionary categories. One way he does this is to distribute the modes of divine activity over different mechanisms at work in evolutionary processes. Mutation is identified with divine creative activity, for example, and natural selection exercises divine "judgment" as well as "redemption." For Kaufman, however, this straightforward identification of the mystery of divine creativity with a quantifiable, tangible feature of the natural world would be reifying. Kaufman attempts to qualify the theological relevance of evolutionary categories in two ways. First of all, they are not identified with creativity, but rather they function as tangible models through which the mystery of creativity may be given tentative empirical content. Secondly, and more importantly, in his interpretation of nature, both mechanisms of evolutionary change he discusses are subsumed under the category of creativity.[47] The interactive process of mutation and natural selection is a kind of creative "mixture of determinism and indeterminism" which brings forth and sustains novelty in the world of nature. The creation and sustenance of novelty, however, is not all there is to say about divine activity. As Kaufman points out, the mystery of creativity is known to produce (and sustain) what inevitably look from a human perspective like "horrifying

47. Strangely, however, in the chapter in *In Face of Mystery* presently under discussion, Kaufman suggests a parallel between the relation of genetic novelty or mutation to natural selection and that of serendipity to another concept, "directionality" (293). I will address this ambiguity more fully in the next section.

evils, as well as great goods."[48] Room is therefore left for further specification of divine governance in terms of other, more explicitly historical,
categories.

COSMIC TRAJECTORIES

Obviously, creativity does not simply run amok in the universe, producing and then immediately destroying one curiosity after another. Neither,
however, is it plausibly characterized as immanently teleological, given
the vast numbers of failed species and "jerry-rigged" mechanisms in
the biotic world uncovered by modern biology.[49] Between these two
abortive ways of thinking about the world, some way of accounting for
the existence of perduring realities, particularly complex, self-directing
ones, must be found. For Kaufman, the central development that theology as a search for adequate orientation for human beings in the universe must grapple with is the fact that, through us, "explicit, teleological
activity becomes operational" in the world.[50] Local explanations of this
fact, of course, may or may not be terribly hard to come by—in light
of the difficulties identified earlier in this chapter, in fact, it is hard to
see what explanatory contributions theology or philosophical reflection
could make to the findings of recent science regarding the cosmic and
evolutionary origins of human beings. The question that is pressing for
theology, however, is: what does this fact indicate about the character of
the world in which we live and act? Are there justifiable metaphysical
and/or theological implications to be drawn on its basis which might
enrich and further specify Kaufman's characterization of the world as a
realm of serendipitous creativity?

In order to address this question, Kaufman offers generalizations
about what we know of the evolutionary process that has brought about
human purposive activity. The first of these is that evolution appears to
be irreversible, or even "unidirectional." Though there are many blind
alleys and side-streets, the overall movement appears to be toward

---

48. Kaufman, "On Thinking of God," 416. Kaufman appeals to his "christomorphic"
faith as a warrant for not taking creativity alone, and in the abstract, as a sufficient
account of God's purposes. As I shall argue further in the concluding section of this
chapter, therefore, Kaufman's (particular version of) Trinitarianism provides grounds
for resisting the reductive strategy of Burhoe on this point.

49. Gould, *The Panda's Thumb*, 9–44.

50. Kaufman, *In Face of Mystery*, 281.

organisms and communities of organisms of greater complexity and flexibility. A "certain momentum of development" is set up, though it is only discernible by means of a retrospective judgment. This momentum is embodied, according to Kaufman, in such things as the constraints upon evolutionary possibility represented in the present characteristics of particular genotypes.[51] Specific configurations of genes which make up the genotypes of organisms are compatible with only a limited range of innovations, and thus there is an element of destiny involved in the future evolution of any species.

Kaufman's second generalization is that the evolutionary process "has not stayed on a level plane." Through it a whole new order of reality, history, has emerged.[52] The impersonal causal agencies of the physical universe have brought about an arena of consciously self-directing beings. Kaufman acknowledges that no unambiguous development toward historicity can credibly be affirmed in light our growing knowledge of the halting, circuitous character of natural history, and further that "progress" is a category inappropriate to biological descriptions of this process. From a strictly biological point of view, he allows, human beings may not be the apex of cosmic-historical development to this point because they are not the most obviously viable forms of life on our own planet. Kaufman's theological interpretation of natural history, however, does not take a strictly biological point of view as normative. For Kaufman, theology does not simply describe or explain, as we have noted, but constructs visions of the world which can orient us by highlighting features most pertinent to the responsible exercise of human agency. From this point of view, Kaufman believes, seeing the emergence of historicity as an advance is warranted.[53]

This attribution of creative advance to the cosmos is important, because it allows one to construe time, not as an empty receptacle of events, but as directional. Looking back upon the course of cosmic and biological history from our own (anthropic) point of view, Kaufman urges, we can discern a trajectory toward historicity, a tendency of the serendipitous creativity at work throughout the universe to produce

51. Ibid., 282. Regarding the constraints of genotypes Kaufman appeals to the work of evolutionary biologist Ernst Mayr.

52. Kaufman, "Nature, History, and God, 385. See also Kaufman, *In Face of Mystery*, 282.

53. Kaufman, "Nature, History, and God," 386; Kaufman, *In Face of Mystery*, 383.

self-directing, free and rational creatures. He acknowledges that there is no strictly scientific warrant for this interpretation, but notes also that it is not inconsistent with established scientific facts, either. In fact, he suggests, the quite widespread, though implicit, confidence in the universe's propensity to produce intelligent life among modern scientific cosmologists is indicated by the enthusiasm shared among many of them for the search for extraterrestrial life, even in the face of enormous improbabilities.[54]

Two caveats are in order, however. First of all, Kaufman is careful to differentiate "directionality" from older concepts of "teleology." The latter, as we have noted above, is in his judgment no longer plausible in light of modern knowledge. Understanding the course of the universe in general as directional does not require it. Attributing directionality amounts simply to an historical judgment, not to an attribution of final causality or purposiveness as a causal factor in the world process.[55] It does not, therefore, require that naturalistic accounts of the world be qualified. Kaufman's characterization of the creative advance suggests, in fact, another reason (beyond scientific questionableness) for rejecting strongly teleological claims. Teleology misleadingly translates the mystery of directionality or creative advance into causal language, collapsing causal and metaphysical generalizations about the world, and thus tempting us to believe that we know the ultimate "purpose" of life with a kind of scientific objectivity.

A second caveat has to do with the relation of the humanizing trajectory in the cosmos to other trends. We shall devote the better part of the concluding chapter of this book to this issue, but at this point it should be noted that Kaufman's conceptuality does not require that all of the various trends or trajectories discernible in the universe be in harmony with the one which has produced and continues to sustain human life. Kaufman notes that our human trajectory unfolds in the midst of many others.[56] Nowhere does he suggest that these others somehow serve our own. Indeed, all that is required for Kaufman's purposes is that the humanizing trend in the universe be construed as a "significant expression" of the creativity at work in the whole.[57] To return to traditional

54. Kaufman, *In Face of Mystery*, 283–84.

55. Ibid., 283.

56. Ibid.

57. Ibid., 284.

theological language, the salvific purposes of God must be positively related to God's creative purposes, though the two need not be collapsed. The Creator is also humanity's Redeemer, though more good may be at stake in creation than humanity's own. This theological point is important, because it mitigates the substantial metaphysical strain placed upon the humanizing trajectory in a cosmology which construes it as central to the meaning of life even in the face of a plurality of other (potentially competing) cosmic trends.

The credible attribution of a humanizing trend to the course of the world as a whole is theologically important, in turn, because it allows Kaufman to articulate a decisive fourth step of faith toward a viable conception of divine governance. We have alluded to the content of this fourth step already: it involves construing this humanizing directional trend as a "significant expression" of the creativity at work throughout the cosmos. This way of taking the relation between our own (natural) history and the diversity of trends throughout the universe provides, Kaufman urges, a metaphysical ground for the human spirit. Personal agency need not be construed as a metaphysical surd in an impersonal universe, but may be seen as connected to and even prepared for by the world process as a whole. The world, in other words, may be taken as a genuine and proper home for purposive human agents.[58]

Again, Kaufman acknowledges that there is no strictly scientific warrant for this sort of grand cosmological claim, but he argues that its possibility indicates that humanity's "long, upward march" by means of natural, evolutionary mechanisms need not be understood as due entirely to chance.[59] What he means by this claim is not specified, but it would appear that "chance" for Kaufman means the complete absence of purpose behind and beneath particular cosmic events and processes, rather than a break in the chain of natural causality or a region of indeterminacy somehow exempt from the influence of adjacent causal agents. The existence or nonexistence of the latter is a matter for quan-

---

58. Ibid. The opposite conclusion is of course often drawn by philosophically reflective modern scientists, particularly those with existentialist leanings. See, for example, Jacques Monod's rather famous remark that modern evolutionary science has shattered nature's "covenant" with humanity, in Monod, *Chance and Necessity*, 169ff.; and Steven Weinberg's equally famous remark that increasing comprehension of the universe seems to have the effect of an increasing sense of its meaninglessness, in Weinberg, *The First Three Minutes*, 144.

59. Kaufman, *In Face of Mystery*, 283.

tum and/or chaos theorists to work out. The denial of purpose, however, is a metaphysical judgment which goes beyond the bounds of strict empirical inquiry.[60] Though the success of causal explanations rules out teleology, Kaufman believes that an account of cosmic directionality which does not contradict current empirical knowledge undermines the certainty with which modern cosmologists rule out purpose as a viable cosmological category.

It is noteworthy that Kaufman employs a kind of hermeneutical circle in his cosmological reflections on this point. As I alluded to above, a Trinitarian confidence in the relation-without-collapse between creation, governance and redemption provides a distinctive way of interpreting the relation between the cosmic trend which brings about human good and the creative fecundity of the world as a whole. It provides, to borrow Calvin's language, a "lens" or "spectacle"[61] through which we may understand our experiences of the world, inviting us to regard the powerful creativity at work throughout the universe as positively related to but not collapsed into historical trends toward the realization of humane values. The interpretation it renders, moreover, is both to some degree credible (since it does not overtly contradict or qualify what we know about the natural causalities at work in the world) and capable of orienting and motivating human life (since it provides metaphysical grounding for the responsible exercise of human capacities). The circle moves in the other direction as well, however.[62] The coherence of Kaufman's claim of a relation between creativity and directionality with empirical knowledge warrants the use of theological insights in his cosmology while also constraining and shaping them to a considerable degree. The degree to which modern knowledge shapes Kaufman's understanding God's relation to the world will become clearer in the next chapter, but much of the constraining effect should be clear already. Divine governance cannot mean, in light of the naturalistic perspective of modern science, episodic intrusions into the natural ordering of the world. Nor can it mean, we

60. If this reasoning is correct (and I am extrapolating a good bit here), Monod's and Weinberg's remarks are not strictly warranted by their quite extensive knowledge of the (allegedly) relevant scientific data, and are not therefore to be accorded the authority they seem to presume. Philosopher Mary Midgley has criticized these thinkers, and others, on precisely these grounds in Midgley, *Science as Salvation*.

61. Calvin, *Institutes* 1:69–79.

62. Or, in James Gustafson's language, the "traffic" between scientific and religious perspectives flows "both ways" (Gustafson, *Intersections*, xvi–xvii).

now discover, a natural teleology, a force immanent within the cosmos driving it toward the achievement of prearranged goals.

Kaufman admits that directionality is a formal and rather vague concept. In order to specify it further, he suggests, we need a model. The one which seems immediately to suggest itself is that of biological evolution. Unfortunately, according to Kaufman, the evolutionary model can do very little to illumine experienced historical realities, which are shot through with purpose and intentionality, phenomena for which biological science has no conceptual room. Historical categories, therefore, will be required.[63] Kaufman examines two historical models which have been dominant in the West: (1) the doctrine of historical progress and (2) historical relativism. He argues that the first of these, aside from being ethnocentric in its identification of Western influence with progress, imbibed a teleological metaphysics of history which is no longer plausible.[64] In much the same way as teleological interpretations of nature are undermined by the success of nonteleological causal explanations, progressive interpretations of history are ruled out by the success of modern historical study in explaining historical change in terms of particular causal agents. The metaphysical doctrine of historical progress, in other words, reifies a particular observed historical trajectory into a causal force, and thereby tempts us to believe that we possess quasi-scientific knowledge about an historical process which, in reality, is too mysterious to be so understood.

The second historical model examined by Kaufman is that of historical relativism. This model, he notes, is a clear and self-conscious departure from the imperialism of progressivist theories, and it moreover does not presume to know with quasi-scientific certainty the course of the historical future. Kaufman suggests that historical relativism, however, is actually an attempt to conceive of history on the model of biology. Like modern evolutionary biology's account of speciation, it emphasizes the proliferation of many relatively independent and local "cultural streams." In doing so, again like biology, historical relativism provides an illuminating account of the serendipitous creativity at work in our world, but cannot account for its directionality. But directionality in the historical process, Kaufman argues, is not merely an imaginative interpretation—it is a fact to be reckoned with. Unlike biological spe-

---

63. Kaufman, *In Face of Mystery*, 288.
64. Ibid., 289.

cies, relatively independent cultural streams have the capacity to flow back into one another and therefore synthesize in new and creative ways.[65] While evolution cannot plausibly be thought of as a single interconnected movement, history, Kaufman believes, can. He suggests that from our own historical perspective, shaped by the realities of modern globalization, the history of the world appears to be just that.[66] Not only is our current world a "global village," but world history as a whole can be seen from our perspective as a "single interconnected stream moving forward."[67]

The historical process of globalization in Kaufman's analysis may be likened to his interpretation of the relation between the various physical energies of the human organism and the centeredness of the human spirit. In both cases, the serendipitous creativity which issues in divergent phenomena which are, at best, randomly organized is transmuted into some kind of highly organized pattern. The biological impulses that encourage procreativity, for example, are routed through culturally acceptable means which, *qua* cultural, are the products of rational reflection upon various human needs. Sexual desire is transformed, thereby, into perduring, culturally institutionalized patterns of love. The fact that it is susceptible to this kind of transformation, as we shall recall from our earlier discussion,[68] indicates something about the potentiality of those physical impulses. In the same way, the susceptibility of the various cultural streams to organization in the service of some larger set of (global) purposes indicates something fundamental about them. It means that recent expressions of global consciousness, including the "dream of a new humanity on a new ecologically ordered earth,"[69] are not merely excessively pious aspirations unrelated to the historical realities, but are idealized images of what is in fact going on in the world.

Since, moreover, the cosmic trajectory which has brought about human history has already been admitted to the status of being a significant expression of the creativity at work in the cosmos as a whole, the process of globalization is itself seen as rooted in, and perhaps even supported by, the creativity of the universe. What is important about

65. Ibid., 290, 292.
66. Ibid., 291.
67. Ibid., 292.
68. See pp. 91–92.
69. Kaufman, *In Face of Mystery*, 292.

this (wildly ambitious, it may seem) claim for our purposes is that it suggests the transmutations of both physical impulses and cultural trends into patterns of purposive order as constitutive of a model of the world's ordering in general. To return once again to explicitly theological language , God's ordering activity may be understood as an ongoing transmutation of the richness and diversity of world processes into patterns of order. It should be pointed out, however, that this attribution of ordering to certain trends unfolding in the universe, for Kaufman, is not an explanatory account of either origins or causal mechanisms. Rather, claims about divine ordering indicate a way of attributing metaphysical significance to the emergence of patterns of order which may turn out to be fully causally accounted for by modern science. Indeed, as we have said, the ability of science to connect humanly significant features of the world to physical causes appears to strengthen rather than weaken Kaufman's metaphysical point.

Kaufman believes that, taken together, serendipitous creativity and directionality provide an illuminating and theologically suggestive account of the mixture of creative fecundity and orderliness experienced by human beings in our interactions with the world. Together, they point to a "quasi-teleology" at work in nature and history which is surrounded by mystery.[70] The "quasi-" is important, because it highlights the fundamental openendedness of world processes. The universe does not bring about intelligent, purposive life with the inevitability of a tree arising out of the ontogenetic instructions inscribed in an acorn—or at least Kaufman's conceptuality is not committed to that kind of analogy. There is an aura of uncertainty about the degree of inevitability or of contingency of our present world which is preserved in his view. What it suggests is that the facticity of this trajectory toward the humane be taken seriously as an indicator of what our world is capable of. The "mystery" which surrounds this "quasi-teleology" is equally important, because it highlights the surplus of creativity in the universe, and even in human life, which is constrained by no recognizably purposive pattern. Claims about cosmic purpose" therefore, are limited both by uncertainty and by recognition of realities which burst any organizational pattern we might construct to contain them.[71]

70. Ibid., 293.

71. It is interesting to note that Kaufman's highly cosmological language to describe the relation between mystery and ordering partakes of a logic that can and has been

The conceptual frame which serendipitous creativity and directionality provide, Kaufman suggests, brings together several salutary characteristics not easily combined in coherent cosmological visions. It can (1) portray what has in fact happened in the course of cosmic, biological, and human history, while (2) according a significant, but not dominant place to human life within the world. In so doing, they provide (3) principles of interpretation which can orient our perceptions of and responses to what is going on around us, as well as (4) giving us hope in the meaningfulness of our activity in the grand scheme of things and therefore (5) helping to motivate us to pursue appropriate ends with vigor.[72] It can thus claim to help maintain a broad reflective equilibrium between various kinds of insights about our world, while serving the uniquely religious function of providing an overall orientation in the world for beings, like ourselves, who must actively engage it.

GOD, CAUSALITY, AND EXPLANATION

In concluding this discussion of Kaufman's cosmological innovations, however, we must press once again the issue of "causal joints" between God and the world. We must ask whether a theological cosmology such as Kaufman's entails some specification of God as a causal factor in the events and processes of nature and history. We have stressed Kaufman's refusal to enter God as an explanatory mechanism that competes with or otherwise qualifies the naturalistic picture of the universe with which we have become accustomed. But, we may ask, does not talk about "governance" require some account of God's impingement upon world processes? Moreover, do not Kaufman's cosmological innovations of themselves already indicate one?

It ought to be clear that Kaufman's account of divine governance is motivated more by a concern to address what classical philosophy has called "final causation" than to align theistic belief with any particular account of efficient causes. An account of the purposes behind historical

---

expressed in more overtly theological language. This relation-without-collapse more than faintly resembles, for example, Reinhold Niebuhr's oft-repeated remarks about the meaning of history surrounded by a "penumbra of mystery" as a peculiar logical feature of the biblical view of human life (Niebuhr, *Pious and Secular America*, 123–45). As I have suggested and shall reiterate below, this relation-without-collapse is conducive to, if not directly inspired by, Trinitarian thought.

72. Kaufman, *In Face of Mystery*, 294.

trends in the world, and not an adequate causal explanation of them, is the aim his theological interpretation of the world. Purposes rather than explanations are theologically germane, for Kaufman, because the former indicate the direction or orientation which ought to shape responsible human agency. This is one important reason why no explanatory power is attributed to theological statements in his program, and why it has no stake in questions about particular openings in the fabric of efficient causality which is described by science.

Nevertheless, as we have seen, Kaufman's theology does seek to connect this account of purpose with empirical knowledge. And empirical knowledge, moreover, traffics primarily in matters of efficient causality. Indeed, if the final causality to which Kaufman's theology points were simply bracketed off from efficient causes, we would have a more rigorously Kantian program, which would require no effort spent making the sort of constructive cosmological innovations Kaufman so painstakingly and deliberately makes. We may fairly ask, therefore, about the relation between efficient and final causality in Kaufman's construal of the world. But that is precisely to ask *how*, on Kaufman's account, creative advance occurs.

Kaufman's espousal of agnosticism on this issue should not be taken as an indication that his position is incapable of being characterized. Indeed, his refusal to admit particular causal joints and his agnosticism regarding divine impingement upon the world already suggests a well-tried position on divine causality: that of Friedrich Schleiermacher. As in Schleiermacher, God may be taken in Kaufman's theology as the "whence"[73] to which the finite causalities that operate in our world finally refer. Metaphorically speaking, we may think of divine agency as directed toward the world as a whole, in a manner analogous to Peacocke's "downward causation." The causal nexus between God's and the world processes, if we are pressed to speak of one, may therefore be located in the enactment of the entire cosmic and historical drama, as it is characterized both by serendipitous creativity and by a directional trend toward the humane.

We must remember, however, that theological language in Kaufman's program is not to be taken as descriptive of an object. If we borrow Schleiermacher's "whence," therefore, we must be careful to note that the word may legitimately indicate only an indirect reference. Talk about di-

73. Schleiermacher, *The Christian Faith*, 16.

vine activity is not grounded in any sort of analysis of empirical states of affairs or of human experience. It is, as we have emphasized, constructed in order to provide orientation in the world. There is therefore no basis in Kaufman's theology for a direct, ontological description of God's impingement upon world processes. One may employ causal language to describe Kaufman's position regarding God's impingement upon the world, but such language must, in the end, be understood as metaphor. If one regards the direct, ontological description of this impingement as a requirement for rendering theism intelligible, then Kaufman's theology simply refuses to meet that standard, on the grounds that it would inappropriately reify talk about God. For Kaufman's position, therefore, the conceptual machinations of theologians like Peacocke (close as his position is, in many respects, to Kaufman's) are neither necessary nor desirable.

It is evident that the picture of God's relation to the world which emerges in Kaufman's theological cosmology is quite different from the picture associated with traditional theism. Kaufman is quite forthcoming about the differences. He suggests that his is a "more austere theocentrism" than traditional Western religious faith. This austerity is related to the vastly larger scale ascribed to the universe in modern scientific cosmology as compared to the relative coziness of the biblical world.[74] Our place in the grand scheme of things is much diminished, and proper judgments about good and evil can no longer be made according to straightforwardly anthropocentric criteria. We live in the context of, and are dependent upon, a vast and complicated web of life, and the realization of this fact must shape and qualify our normative judgments about what is good and important, and therefore about what God's purposes are.[75] Within this framework, our relation to God is more remote, less personal; and a childlike trust in God as cosmic guarantor of our interests is no longer available.[76] Our human existence under Go" is no longer immediately dependent upon God, and we are called upon to take a greater responsibility for ourselves.[77]

These relatively drastic revisions of classical theism need to be examined further, and more directly. In particular, we need to ask about

74. Kaufman, "On Thinking of God," 422.

75. Ibid., 421.

76. Ibid., 423.

77. Ibid., 422.

the overriding metaphor or model for God's relation to the world that is suggested by Kaufman's cosmological reflections. The construction of a viable model for understanding God is, after all, the central task of theology for Kaufman. In the last section of this chapter, I shall argue that Kaufman's treatment of this culminating issue is at once most radically revisionary of classical theism and, at the same time, most strikingly reliant upon a peculiar feature of Western religion: the idea of God as Trinity.

GOD AND THE WORLD: A TRINITARIAN COSMOLOGY

Although, as we saw in chapter 2, Kaufman sharply distinguishes his understanding of the purpose of theological reflection from those which see it as a rehearsal or interpretation of religious texts and tradition, the theological cosmology we considered in the previous chapter bears striking resemblances in many respects to traditional Christian reflection upon the world. I indicated how the relation-without-collapse between creativity and directionality or ordering partakes of the same Trinitarian logic which is at work in classical interpretations of the relation between God the Father and the Logos or Son. In classical Trinitarian theology, this relation radically qualifies the monarchical imagery of early Hebrew theology and also of philosophical theism which abstracts from it. God, or the creative power behind the workings of the world, is not to be conceived abstractly as sheer power, nor as sheer creativity. Rather, the power of God is to be seen in relation to the divine goodness demonstrated in God's benevolent ordering and redemptive activity.[78] The Creator must

---

78. See, for example, St. Augustine's account of the relation between God's power and goodness or justice in book 13 of *The Trinity*, 353–58. This is the same theological concern that drives Barth's critique of mere "theism" (see above, p. 20, and H. Richard Niebuhr's critique of a "unitarianism of the Creator" (Niebuhr, *Theology, History and Culture*, 52–53). Kaufman's theology is in some respects radically christomorphic, but he also resists a "unitarianism of the Redeemer." The ultimate mystery of divine creativity resists absorption into God's redemptive purposes. This can be seen in his recent discussion of divine love. "It would be improper," he suggests, "to say simplistically that 'God is love.'" Such an unqualified identification would "project on every feature of the universe what we find significant in our own human sphere." Kaufman goes on to suggest that love may nevertheless remain an important metaphor for God, thought not the most important: that status is reserved for serendipitous creativity (Kaufman, "On Thinking of God," 420). We might also point out, however, that Kaufman's Trinitarian logic also prevents the identification of God with the concept of "serendipitous creativity" from becoming an absolute one.

be seen as the Redeemer, and vice versa. In the same way, the concept of serendipitous creativity in Kaufman's theology is acknowledged to be inadequate as a focus for worship. In order to properly orient human devotion, so that we do not fall into a sort of "pagan" worship of raw creative power, the religious imagination must construe the mystery of creativity as related to and expressed through the benevolent ordering of the world embodied in particular humanizing trajectories.

This Trinitarian logic thus enables Kaufman to engage modern empirical knowledge without collapsing traditional religious insights into it. We shall recall that Ralph Wendell Burhoe identifies the creative activity of God with the emergence of more complex orders of existence, and the judging and redeeming activity of God with the sifting of these emergents through the process of natural selection. In this way, I have argued, Burhoe's proposal for understanding divine action collapses the tradition's claims about God's faithfulness, derived to some degree from christological insights about the redemptive role of suffering and failure, into a kind of oversight over the achievement of evolutionary success.[79] Kaufman, by contrast, by insisting that divine creativity be understood as expressed in the humane, other-regarding, self-sacrificing features of human life, renders a christomorphic account of divine action and purpose which does not identify redemption with evolutionary or any other sort of prudential success." On the other hand, by insisting that divine creativity not be collapsed into the benevolent ordering and redemptive purposes of God embodied in humanizing trajectories, a significant status is granted to empirical knowledge about features of the world which are not capable of being absorbed into a christocentric (or any other sort of broadly humanistic) framework. Kaufman's use of Trinitarian logic, therefore, enables him to bring a confessionally important normative insight to bear upon empirical knowledge, without requiring that the former dominate the latter.

Other modern and contemporary theologians have also, of course, constructed accounts of the world which draw upon Trinitarian logic, but seldom have these efforts attempted to embody this logic within a modern naturalistic view of the universe in the way that Kaufman's does. Jürgen Moltmann, for example, acknowledges that the cosmological reflections contained in his Gifford Lectures do not so much "naturalize

79. See above, p. 29.

human hope" as "eschatologize nature."[80] Kaufman's cosmological proposal may be seen, quite unlike Moltmann's, as an attempt to "naturalize"
the particular sort of "human hope" embedded in the logic of Trinitarian
faith. In this way, the connection between religious insight and the modern view of the world assumed in daily life is assured, and Trinitarian
faith is reclaimed as a genuinely orienting faith.

The attempt to embody the logic of Trinitarian faith in a cosmology, it should be noted, presumes that a significant portion of the import
of Trinitarianism is contained in what it says about the relation between
God and the world (the so-called "economic," as opposed to the "immanent," Trinity). For Kaufman, it may fairly be said that this economic
import exhausts the significance of Trinitarian thought. The immanent
reality of God is a matter too ensconced in mystery for confidence about
the propriety of language about distinct divine "persons."[81] Trinitarian
logic illumines, however, the mixture of novelty and order characteristic of human experience of the world. In the form of the interrelated
concepts of serendipity and directionality, and in conversation with
the aspects of modern human knowledge and experience from which
these concepts are drawn, it allows the intelligible affirmation that the
world is governed. The activity of God the Creator is identified with the
overflowing or "serendipity" of creativity throughout the universe; the
activity of God the Logos with the "very specific modes of order and
meaning" in those cosmic and historical trajectories which support human flourishing; and the activity of God the Spirit with the "immediate
and continuous presence" of creativity in every locality.[82] The idea of the

80. Jürgen Moltmann, *God in Creation*, xi. Moltmann's cosmological reflections,
despite their innovative character, may be seen as an extension of the Barthian tradition insofar as empirical knowledge does not so much restrain and positively shape
theological construction (in a "two-way" fashion) as get absorbed or annexed into a
preferred theological framework. In Moltmann's case, as in Barth's, the radical implications of New Testament Christologies are taken as the point of departure for speaking
about divine governance of the world, and the import of empirical knowledge is kept
to a minimum.

81. Kaufman believes, however, that the distinction between "economic" and "immanent" is based upon a conceptual confusion akin to reification. See Kaufman, *In Face of
Mystery*, 493–94. Nevertheless, Kaufman's reflections upon Trinitarian logic have been
consistently slanted toward an economic interpretation of it throughout his career. For
an early example of this, see Kaufman's *Systematic Theology*, 243–52.

82. Kaufman, *In Face of Mystery*, 296. Interestingly, however, on the previous page
Kaufman aligns serendipity with the traditional idea of grace, and directionality with

Trinity, therefore, is not simply myth, nor a speculative doctrine about God's inner being, but a series of rather momentous metaphysical claims about the character of the actual universe under God.

---

promise. This slightly different way of relating Kaufman's concepts for divine activity to traditional religious functions suggests a flexibility reminiscent of the perichoretic emphasis of classical Trinitarian thought, which protects against rigidly partitioning divine activity and thereby setting some functions in opposition to others.

5

God and Action

T HE VIABILITY OF THE notion of divine agency has been a prime
consideration of Kaufman's theology throughout his career. At the
center of his most recent attempts to reconstruct the idea of God is a rejection of metaphor of agent on the grounds that it is too anthropomorphic. Yet, an analysis of Kaufman's concept of God easily shows that he
picks up on themes drawn deliberately from the classical logic of divine
agency. This becomes especially clear when one compares Kaufman's
relatively early attempts to fashion an account of God's relation to the
world on the basis of a rigorous analysis of the concept of agency with
his later (ostensibly anti-agential) proposal. One would expect that a repudiation of human agency as an appropriate model for God's relation
to the world ought to precipitate a proposal vastly different from one
which relies almost exclusively upon it—but that is not what we find in
Kaufman. Rather, his earlier and later proposals are marked by a surprising degree of continuity.

These reflections, though they remain to be justified, suggest a
method for this chapter and for one that follows. My central claim in
these chapters, bound not to be surprising to the reader who has followed my argument this far, is that Kaufman's revisionary doctrine of
the Trinity, while most certainly not employed to fulfill obligations to
religious tradition, represents the culmination of Kaufman's effort to secure the proper functioning of God-talk by harmonizing it with modern
knowledge and experience. Though by "culminating" I intend a systematic rather than historical point, a substantial portion of my justification
for this claim will be historical. I will (1) analyze Kaufman's earlier proposal, which was forged in order to render traditional, anthropomorphic
claims about God's action intelligible, (2) mine its internal tensions, and
(3) develop an interpretation of his later proposal as an attempt to re-

solve the tensions within his earlier position while preserving its basic logic. The concept of God as intramundane triunity of serendipitous creativity, directional ordering, and pervasive presence, it will be shown, emerges in Kaufman's thinking as a result of the interplay of the forces of the traditional, anthropomorphic piety carried in the Western concept of God, on the one hand, and of modern inclinations to find the sources of intelligibility and meaning within the finite world rather than beyond it, on the other. First, however, we need to examine Kaufman's earlier defense of the concept of God as agent.

DIVINE AGENCY AND ITS APORIAS

Sharp contrasts between the philosophical god of classical theism and the personal God of the Bible have often marked theological literature in the modern period. The former, it is argued, is a static being, and the latter is dynamic, radically temporal, and active. There are, undoubtedly, a variety of motivations for this sea change in theological assessments of temporality: the wish to delegitimate static social structures and to support sweeping reform, new apprehensions of the world itself as dynamic combined with older interpretations of time as linear, and the religious need to see God as intimately involved in the push and pull of history, to name a few. Kaufman's theology is sympathetic to each of these modern concerns. As we have seen, his cosmological reflections embody an emphasis upon dynamism rather than stasis, and his doctrine of God, as we shall see presently, clarifies rather than obscures it.

Though not all twentieth-century advocates of a dynamic God were biblical theologians, the biblical theology movement exerted an enormous impact upon, and provided much fodder for, recent discussions of divine action. Its emphasis upon a "God who acts" successfully connected modern sensibilities to the narrative traditions of the Bible, and thereby provided powerful tools for critiquing the static God of classical theism.[1] As Langdon Gilkey challenged, however, the insistence upon a God who is active in history requires some way of accounting for how God can act in historical processes. Without some ontology of nature and history which allows for divine influence, Gilkey averred, biblically-

---

1. The classic exposition of this point of view is Wright, *God Who Acts*.

minded theologians are liable to fall back upon the "liberal" method of psychologizing talk about divine action.[2]

We have already dealt with some of the alternative conceptualities which have been suggested in order to meet Gilkey's challenge, and especially with Kaufman's historicist or "radical naturalist" alternative. In this chapter, however, we shall be concerned with another way of addressing the question of how God acts lurking beneath biblical theology: the demand to know how an agent can act may invoke not only the problem of the "causal joint" where he or she exerts influence, but also questions about what Thomas Tracy calls the "intentional structure" of action.[3] The latter refers to the discrete, deliberate steps taken in the course of carrying out an action, and to the relations among them. Large questions about determinism and indeterminism aside, we may inquire, for example, about the manner in which Jones realized his dream of becoming a doctor. The sought-after explanation would not involve a complete causal analysis, but a sorting out of the ways in which Jones prosecuted his larger goal by pursuing a series of smaller ones. The act of becoming a doctor, therefore, could be explained as a complex act, having a complex intentional structure. It could be argued, moreover, that we have not fully accounted for the meaning of "becoming a doctor" unless we are able to specify some of the possible intentional structures it would involve. It is perfectly consistent, Tracy argues, to accept a reverentially agnostic response to the question about causal joints while demanding greater clarity regarding the intentional structure of divine action.[4] The causal nexus between God and the world may be in principle beyond human understanding, but this metaphysical mystery does not automatically rid us of the need to account for the possible (surely certainty as to particular instances is impossible here) ways in which God's intentions are structured in order to make sense of talk about divine activity. The problem to be addressed here will be that of deciding how like and unlike human agency God's intentional structures might be, and of making logical sense of whatever model is suggested by this decision.

It is on this front that Kaufman's reflections in God the Problem attempt to address Gilkey's challenge to theologies which stress the notion of a "God who acts." Kaufman sees further reflection upon the concept

2. Gilkey, "Cosmology, Ontology, and the Travail of Biblical Language," 194–205.

3. Tracy, God, Action, and Embodiment, 87.

4. Ibid., 64–65.

of agency as a third alternative between that of (1) abandoning God-talk altogether in the face of modern knowledge about the unbroken web of natural cause and effect and (2) retaining talk about God while jettisoning "act" language in favor of language about "being." If it is possible to retain "act" language, Kaufman suggests, the intelligibility and force of such central theological notions as divine love and mercy are also retained, and the equally crucial notion of divine transcendence is given intelligible content.[5] The principle conceptual move Kaufman makes in his effort to do so involves sharply distinguishing the notion of "action" from that of mere "activity." The latter is said to refer simply to various happenings in the world, to be understood by ordinary causal analysis. "Action," however, refers to activity which is "bound together and given a distinct order and structure by the intention of an agent."[6] Whereas activities are events and processes which are necessarily difficult to isolate, due to their positioning in a seamless web of cause and effect, actions can be understood as both unified and discrete. Though a complete causal analysis of Jones' becoming a doctor, for example, would have to control an unimaginably large jumble of data about upbringing, social circumstances, coincidences, etc., an intentional analysis of the "act" of becoming a doctor would involve demarcating a number of steps which can be coherently ordered according to a single overarching purpose.

Each step identified in such an analysis would therefore need to be understood, *qua* step, primarily in terms of the purpose of the overall act. It should be noted that this places limitations upon what can be known about such purposes by means of ordinary empirical observation. To see this, it is helpful sharply to distinguish, as Kaufman does, a strictly agential account of God's purposes for nature and history from one which stresses an immanent teleology inscribed in the world order itself. The latter, Kaufman notes, identifies divine purpose rather straightforwardly with patterns built into the structure of creatures (especially organisms). Indeed, the "immanent teleology" model privileges the instinctual behavior of lower animal life as most disclosive of God's mode of activity in the world. In such a model, knowledge of the patterns, achievable by disciplined observation, suffices to supply reliable (though perhaps incomplete) knowledge of divine purpose. An agential account, on the other hand, though it does not deny the existence of natural patterns, resists

5. Kaufman, *God the Problem*, 124.
6. Ibid., 126.

identification of these with God's will. According to Kaufman, the ends envisaged by a purposive agent are deliberately imposed upon nature. A "new, historical order" is "superimposed upon life."[7] Understanding divine purpose on this model suggests that an overarching intentional order is deliberately imposed upon the whole world, and that the contours of the divine will for the world (i.e., the intentional structure of divine action) cannot therefore be known by strictly empirical observation. In a (then) characteristically neo-orthodox move, the Kaufman of *God the Problem* suggests that it can only be known by revelation.[8]

These reflections, it may be noted, are reminiscent of the classical Kantian distinction between the world of (causally determined) "phenomena" and the "noumenal" or real world which is not directly accessible to finite perception. It presses this sort of distinction, moreover, in a quite similar manner as Karl Barth's theology does (and, as we shall see, for similar reasons). One crucial difference, however, is that Kaufman's insistence upon strictly pressing the analogy of human agency requires him to make claims about the world as it exists in time. From this point of view, the importance of establishing the outlines of a worldview in *In Face of Mystery* as a preliminary step toward faith in God may be seen as a down payment upon the intelligibility of agential language about God, even though, as we shall see, such language falls out of this later book. My present point is that, for Kaufman, strict adherence to the analogue of human agency requires a positive valuation of temporality. Actions unfold in time. God's action within the world, therefore, must really and not only apparently unfold in the actual push and pull of nature and history. Though the overarching purpose of world processes is necessarily unavailable to empirical observation, the causal mechanisms that drive events and processes in the world must be seen as open to new configurations of reality, rather than eternally returning the world to pre-established harmonies. Empirical knowledge can be drawn upon to confirm this picture, or, alternatively, to refute it.

The inherently temporal character of action also has implications for the notion of divine power. Like many process theologians, Kaufman presses biblical language about divine acts in order to suggest limitations to God's ability to accomplish the divine will. Unlike the former, however, Kaufman does not appeal to an alleged quasi-agential char-

7. Ibid., 126.
8. Ibid.

acter of atomic world processes to support this notion, but to a logical analysis of the concept of action. The idea of God's action in the world entails a lengthy and laborious process, according to Kaufman, because the contrasting idea of "instantaneous action" is incoherent.[9] Action is not only the imposition of purpose, but "bringing order into time," and this process entails "tension" and "struggle."[10] Human experience of the world as incomplete and tensive, therefore, is consistent with a strict interpretation of the notion of God as agent.[11] Kaufman derides strong doctrines of "omnipotence" which "abstract" the idea of God's power from the overarching logic of the concept of action. The idea of a divine "magician" who acts instantaneously and unilaterally, he argues, is the result of focusing attention upon one characteristic of agency and ignoring others.[12] In this way, Kaufman's analysis of the concept of action presses the central affirmation of theism in order to mitigate the force of theism's historically most troubling difficulty.

Kaufman is concerned, however, to retain a significant sense of divine sovereignty. The idea of a God who does not in fact govern nature and history, and direct it reliably toward benevolent ends, cannot orient us in the world in the way Kaufman's theology requires. In order to support such an account of divine activity, Kaufman offers an analysis of the limiting case of action. A series of intentional acts, he suggests, may be bound together in a single, larger action. This larger act is logically more fundamental than any member of the series of smaller acts which comprise it, since they cannot be understood outside of their relations to this larger intention. The act of picking up a pen, for example, cannot be accounted for as an intentional act unless the reasons for picking it up are known. Was it picked up as part of an act of theft? Or perhaps as part of an act of benevolence on behalf of a colleague whose back pain prevents her from comfortably retrieving it herself? Picking up the pen is, in Kaufman's vocabulary, a "subact" of a larger "master act," to be understood in terms of the larger purpose it intends. According to Kaufman, the limiting case of "master acts" would be the enactment of the world as a whole—not as a static structure but as temporal, dynamic reality. This, he suggests, is the most fundamental way of describing divine action,

9. Ibid., 181.
10. Ibid., 183.
11. Ibid., 182.
12. Ibid., 183.

since monotheistic faith presses theological language to construe God first of all as sovereign lord of all the world. The vast series of more limited happenings within the world may not, in fact, be described straightforwardly as divine acts, because in each case their character *as* act can only be understood in relation to God's overall purpose in enacting the world as a whole. Kaufman assigns individual events and processes to the category of "subact," because they indirectly, though genuinely, serve the purpose behind God's "master act" of creative world-enactment. In this way God's sovereignty over the world is strongly affirmed, while distancing God somewhat from an embarrassing variety of worldly happenings.[13]

Kaufman's earlier account of divine activity has been criticized strongly for its alleged "uniformitarianism," or reduction of divine interaction with the world to a single, uniform action. The relevance of this criticism is obvious, and I will address it shortly. Before doing so, however, it should be pointed out that Kaufman's theology risks this criticism in order to develop a broadly intelligible account of divine activity which avoids the perils deism, on the one hand, or of pantheism, on the other. The affirmation of the whole world as God's act may tend to suggest the latter, but Kaufman's distinction between "master act" and "subact" serves to prohibit describing individual events in the world as God's action in any direct, unequivocal sense. He argues, in fact, that any event in the world may be described as God's act only insofar as it enacts divine purposes. The world, however, is given a measure of autonomy, so that non-divine agencies are inevitably involved in shaping (and misshaping) the character of intramundane events. No event, therefore, unambiguously enacts God's purposes for the world, or even for a portion of it. The one exception to this pervasive historical ambiguity, he suggests, is the crucifixion of Jesus. Only this supreme instance of powerlessness directly indicates the workings of divine power in the world. The choice of this particular instance as the only direct manifestation of divine purpose, beside agreeing with the tradition about the uniqueness of the culminating events of Jesus' life, is theologically important in Kaufman's early program because its counterintuitive, perhaps even paradoxical, character as a revelation of divine power constitutes a vivid refusal of

13. Ibid., 140–47.

pantheistic elaborations upon Christian faith in divine sovereignty over the world.[14]

Kaufman's analysis of action likewise enables him to speak intelligibly about divine activity without resorting to deism. Though the divine action upon the world may perhaps be described as "uniform," insofar as it is comprehended in a single "master act," this master act is not temporally positioned outside of the unfolding of events and processes in the world. It is not, as in seventeenth-century deism, a mere act of initiation, allowing the created order to develop with complete autonomy. The autonomy of the world, for Kaufman, is not subsequent to its dependence upon the creator, but contained within it. God allows a measure of autonomy as a necessary feature of the act of creating a responsive world. God's "master act" is still in process of being enacted, and divine sovereignty must therefore be construed as ongoing rather than merely residual.

The charge of "uniformitarianism," as put forward by some of Kaufman's most persuasive critics,[15]does not entail the charge of either pantheism or deism, however. The complaint, rather, is that Kaufman (and other theologians of his ilk) flatten out divine activity in such a way that the God envisioned by the position is remote and unresponsive. God no longer is seen as one who exercises special and specific providential care over such events, for example, as the fall of sparrows. This austere picture, it is sometimes argued, whatever its connection to the supposed logic of agency, does not reflect the personalistic overtones of biblical imagery regarding God. Kaufman is quite frank, however, about the losses to traditional theistic piety incurred in his reconstruction of it.[16] His theological method, moreover, does not commit him to salvag-

14. The contrast with Burhoe could hardly be sharper on this point. For the latter, we may recall, God's governance of the world is describable entirely in the language of natural selection; and, consequently, God's will is identified with that which evolutionary and historical processes crown "successful."

15. See, for example, Tracy, *God, Action, and Embodiment,* xiii–xvi. See also Vernon White's critique of Maurice Wiles' somewhat similar view of divine activity in White, *The Fall of a Sparrow,* 64–70.

16. Kaufman may in fact undersell the capacity of his conceptuality to accommodate much traditional Christian piety. Maurice Wiles'1986 Bampton lectures, published as *God's Action in the World,* are far more articulate about the ways in which a Christian "uniformitarianism" coheres much that is crucial in traditional Christian faith. I shall argue in the final chapter of this volume, moreover, that those who construct theologies from the standpoint of some strands of Christian piety might be inclined to press Kaufman's proposal toward an *even more austere* position than his own.

ing every feature of biblical faith, and to those willing to accept some such loss, this criticism is bound not to be seen as very damaging to his project.

A potentially more serious problem, it seems to me, is what Michael McLean has called the "residual Cartesianism" involved in Kaufman's effort to press human agency as a model of divine transcendence.[17] As we have noted, Kaufman's formal analysis of the Western monotheistic concept of God uncovers a tension between the concepts of God and world. This tension has often been embodied in piety's language about divine transcendence over the world. The trouble, of course, is that such talk has been given content through the ages by a picture of reality which is divided between "nature" and "supernature." In such a context, transcendence is easily specified. Now, however, in an age in which the older cosmological categories no longer prevail, the transcendence of God has become difficult to specify, and the tension between God and world is in danger of being lost in the confusion. One of the functions of the concept of agency in Kaufman's earlier theology, therefore, is to provide intelligible specification of the transcendence of God for an age in which predominant depictions of reality do not divide easily into two distinct realms. The transcendence of God is not understood in terms of the transcendence of one alleged realm over our own, but in terms of the hiddenness of an agent's intentions. God's otherness or being-beyond-reach is analogous to that of purposeful beings we experience. Neither God nor neighbor is fully explicable in terms of observation, however acute. Each may therefore said to "transcend" our own perspectives.

McLean argues, however, that this notion of transcendence replaces cosmological dualism with an even sharper dualism. By likening divine transcendence to the hiddenness of selves in relation to other selves, he suggests, Kaufman invokes a dualism of inner subjectivity and outer bodily states. This "residual Cartesianism" has been widely discredited in light of both philosophical problems about the interaction of mind and body and the development of modern neuroscience, which has suggested a close connection between subjectivity and embodiment.[18]

In the Preface to *God the Problem*, Kaufman responds to McLain's charge of "residual Cartesianism." He agrees that Cartesian dualism is a distorted view of the relation between subjectivity and embodiment,

---

17. McLain, "On Theological Models," 155–87.

18. Ibid., 166–68.

and that in some of his earliest essays he did in fact invoke this imagery. He argues, however, that his use of the concept of agency to describe the transcendence of a self captures what is useful about this dualistic picture without succumbing to its defects. Agency, he suggests, necessarily involves an "inner" perspective: an agent's purposes in carrying out an act or project, though they may be either intentionally or inadvertently revealed through bodily expressions and movements, are not susceptible to direct observation. It is this hiddenness of purpose, Kaufman argues, that explains the ineradicable possibility of deception in human affairs. The hiddenness of purpose characteristic of agents does not require, he argues, dualistic suppositions about the relation between mind and body.[19]

The appeal to the notion of agency, however, raises difficult problems for Kaufman nonetheless. The advantage, purportedly, is that agency does not require discredited dualistic assumptions about the relation between minds and bodies. This dualism, however, does not turn out to be merely an unfortunate accretion to the logically more primitive notion of agency, but a rival account of selfhood. When the notion of agency is pressed, dualism turns out to be unintelligible, since the concept of agent is constructed out of the experience of purposive activity among embodied beings. Embodied agency, Kaufman admits, is the only kind of agency we know, and it is consequently questionable whether the idea of agency without embodiment is even capable of being understood. But if this is so, what sense can be made of the idea of God as disembodied agent?

The trouble here is that Kaufman is claiming two things at once, the compatibility of which may be sharply questioned. On the one hand, he is arguing that the intelligibility of the idea of divine activity can be secured on the basis of an analogy with human agency. God's agency is alleged to be sufficiently like our own experience of action to render claims about the former intelligible. He claims, on the other hand, however, that the transcendence of God can be secured on the basis of the hiddenness of an agent's first-person perspective from empirical observation. The difficulty is that the success of the "intelligibility" argument undermines the "transcendence" argument: the closer the analogy, the more one might expect that empirical observation may mitigate the hiddenness, much like skilled observation of a human agent's bodily states uncovers his or

19. Kaufman, *God the Problem*, xvi–xviii.

her hidden intentionality. Conversely, the success of the "transcendence" argument erodes the analogy on the basis of which the "intelligibility" argument is constructed. The more it is claimed that God's transcendent purposes for the world remain impenetrable by external observers, the more it becomes apparent that the kind of agency we are talking about here is far removed from the human experience of agency from which the analogy draws its force.

Those who wish to press the concept of agency to resolve difficulties about divine transcendence, therefore, face a dilemma: either God must be construed as in some sense embodied, or the agency model must be heavily qualified. The first horn of this dilemma not only threatens claims about divine transcendence, but the way in which it requires the world to be interpreted also creates its own difficulties regarding intelligibility. The second horn, on the other hand, raises serious questions about the adequacy of the model of agency. This difficulty, I want to suggest, is a major problematic for Kaufman, and eventually leads him to abandon the concept of agency as a model for God's relation to the world. Before we turn to Kaufman's revised specification of the God-world relation in the second half of this chapter, however, it will be helpful briefly to examine a couple of contrasting efforts to salvage the model of agency, and to suggest reasons why neither approach succeeds in resolving this problematic in Kaufman's theology.

QUALIFYING AGENCY

The two most obvious strategies for dealing with the dilemma attending attempts to conceive of God as agent which I have identified are resolutely to grasp either of its horns, and to show why the consequences for doing so are acceptable. While the theologies of Grace Janzen and Thomas Tracy are not simply responses to Kaufman's reflections upon the promise and the logical pitfalls of this project, they may be regarded as examples of these strategies. In this section, I shall suggest that Janzen's *God's World, God's Body* embraces the model of embodied agency in order to respond to modern philosophical and scientific insights about the nature of selves, but that her proposal necessarily involves highly ambitious, and in fact quite questionable, claims about the character of the universe. Thomas Tracy's *God, Action, and Embodiment*, on the other hand, attempts to show that a highly qualified model of agency is philosophically and theologically tenable, but I shall argue that his proposal involves a disengagement with ordinary language about agency which is ruled out by Kaufman's theological method. The upshot of this section, therefore, is that the dilemma I have identified constitutes something of a dead end for this phase of Kaufman's work. His abandonment of the model of human agency to construe God's relation to the world, therefore, may be understood as a response to the insoluble character the problems connected with its use in a naturalistic context. As we shall see in subsequent sections, however, his renewed efforts to portray the divine attempt to recapture much of the substance of his earlier affirmations in a new conceptual idiom.

Embodied Agency

In order intelligibly to elucidate the unique character of divine agency, Grace Janzen appeals to a distinction which originates in philosophical reflection upon action. Most human action, she suggests, must take an indirect route: we accomplish a certain goal by performing a series of more "basic" tasks. We cannot catch a ball "immediately," for example, but must operate our limbs (or jaws, if we intend to catch it in our mouths!) in order to do so. The movement of limbs, we might say, is "basic" to the act of catching a ball. Some actions, however, just are the movement of limbs or of some other part of our bodies. These are, properly speaking, basic actions: we execute them "directly" rather than through some mediating act or acts.[20] We may note that, generally, we have a greater degree of control over basic actions, since indirect acts depend not only upon the success of our direct actions but also upon favorable environmental conditions.

Janzen points out that, since all our actions upon our environments require basic actions, it is difficult to imagine how a non-bodily agent could interact with the world at all. Even if this difficulty can be resolved, she suggests that theists would likely want to maintain that none of God's actions in the world are mediated, and thus dependent in some respects upon a favorable environment, but that all are direct and unilaterally sufficient. But this is to say, in Janzen's terminology, that all God's actions are basic. These considerations, she suggests, point toward the conclusion that God must be conceived as embodied.[21]

---

20. Janzen, *God's World*, 85–87.
21. Ibid., 88–93.

Theologians, of course, have generally recoiled from such a conclusion. To portray God as embodied seems to imply a finitization of God: to have a body seems intrinsically to mean having limits. Janzen is aware of the force of this objection, but responds by denying its central underlying premise. Embodiment, she argues, does not entail finitude. In light of the difficulties involved in conceiving how a disembodied agent can act in the world, she suggests that a more plausible alternative to attributing to God a body that must interact with others is to construe the whole world as God's body. The supreme agency of God, in other words, is conceived not by denying embodiment but by affirming it "more completely."[22] Janzen's model suggest that God is more completely embodied than finite agents in two ways: (1) by affirming that the body of God is coextensive with the world, it affirms that no sphere of the world is external to divine embodiment and therefore to be acted upon indirectly (and therefore necessarily fallibly); and (2) by applying a classical theistic logic of analogy, she affirms that the control a finite embodied agent has over bodily moments (direct actions) reflects in only an imperfect manner the supreme and uninterrupted power that God has over the world.[23] God's body, in other words, is never in any sense a recalcitrant given in the way that human bodies sometimes are (and, in the case of certain bodily systems, always are). There are no involuntary bodily reactions, nor any systems within God's body that are not directly willed by God.

Janzen's proposal therefore presses philosophical insights regarding the logic of action toward a picture of God and world which is both responsive to modern knowledge about persons as embodied and surprisingly able to recapture much of the substantive force of classical theism. This accomplishment may appear to represent a promising way for Kaufman to have moved from his reflections in *God the Problem*—but, unfortunately, it is not. The problem with Janzen's proposal, as Austin Farrer pointed out with reference to what he styled "anima mundi" positions in general, is that it presupposes that the world can be objectively described as a coherent whole. According to a more constructivist way of thinking about the world, however,

22. Ibid., 87.
23. Ibid., 108–13.

the diagrammatic unity is in the mind, not in the world...Realities do not coexist by absolute position in a Newtonian continuum; they coexist by constituting a field of conditions for any single piece of organized agency. The universe is indeed organized, or drawn together into unity; but it is so organized or drawn together a million million times over at all the single points where a field of forces finds a focus; and that is wherever any single active existence is present ... (T)o all evidence, there is no world-pattern pulling the universe together; it is pulled together by each of the infinite overlapping multitude of focal patterns, the patterns of actual and active existences.[24]

These words, though couched in a slightly different rhetorical style, convey an account of the status of generalized pictures of the world which is recognizably similar to Kaufman's. For Kaufman, construals of the world as unified are not straightforward, quasi-scientific descriptions, but imaginative constructs which selectively focus the mind in a particular way. Indeed, in Kaufman's theology, "world" is an imaginative construct which is formulated in order to aid the construction of the concept of God. As we saw in the last chapter, Kaufman attempts to piece together a vision of the world for the purpose of portraying it as governed. The unity of Kaufman's "world," therefore, is imposed upon the "blooming, buzzing confusion" of experienced life in order to enable us to see it as subject to God's overarching purposes for it. Janzen's appeal to the world as God's body, by contrast, functions quite differently. The unity of the world is understood not as the subjective unity of God's purposes for it (i.e., its unity is not seen in relation to God), but in terms of the objective unity of the human body. Janzen's argument is based, in other words, upon an analogy which not only operates independently of any theological insight, but which requires an objective, even empirically demonstrable unity amidst the experienced welter of events and processes in the world.[25] It is precisely this assumption, however, which makes her proposal guilty, from Kaufman's point of view, of the philosophical confusion of reifying the metaphysical category, "world." In terms of the argument being developed here, we may say that the attempt to ground the relation between God and the world by means of an analogy with bodily agency requires that excessive claims be made about

24. Farrer, *Faith and Speculation*, 150–51.

25. It is difficult to imagine what sense could be given, for example, to her appeal to the idea of "direct" or "basic" actions without this assumption.

the character of our world. Whether we identify the issue as the logical problem of reification or as simply flying in the face of experience, the general problem is one of intelligibility. Far from resolving Kaufman's dilemma, therefore, Janzen's effort to grasp the horn of intelligibility is impaled upon it.

The Perfection of Agency

The opposite strategy from Janzen's is to recognize the vast difference between the types of agency exercised by embodied beings like ourselves and God, to whom no bodily limitations are ascribed, but to argue for the intelligibility of this heightened conception of agency. Thomas Tracy's proposal in *God, Action, and Embodiment* exemplifies this approach. Tracy's strategy, we may note at the outset, has the advantage of having greater resonance than Janzen's to the classical Western religious traditions. Denying embodiment has a strong standing in theistic traditions, and, like Tracy, the traditions have often done so for the purpose of denying limitation and/or imperfection. Moreover, Tracy's proposal may be said to have even greater resonances with the biblical traditions than do the classical theistic accounts of God, insofar as the latter located the perfection of God in the peculiar mode of God's being, while the biblical traditions and Tracy portray God as the maximal realization, not of being, but of the capacity to act.

Tracy acknowledges that recent philosophy has discredited dualistic accounts of personhood. Talk about "mental substances" existing independently of bodies has been thoroughly undermined, both by empirical knowledge and by philosophical analysis. He believes, however, that the extent of damage this consensus entails for theology is in fact quite limited. There are, he argues, no logically necessary conditions for the attribution of agency. We have no access to other types of agency than our own experience, but there are no *a priori* reasons, he argues, for believing that our experience exhausts all possibilities.[26] Tracy appeals to the widely-accepted formal definition of action as "intentional behavior," and suggests that this definition imposes two formal criteria upon realistic agency-attribution only: (1) the capacity to act intentionally, and (2) identifiability as *this* rather than some other particular agent.[27]

26. Tracy, *God, Action, and Embodiment*, 65, 108.
27. Ibid., 69–70.

But these, he proposes, do not rule out the attribution of a supreme type of agency to God.

In order to defend such an account of divine agency, Tracy's proposal needs obviously to provide a clear concept of non-embodied action that satisfies both of these requirements. He goes about doing this by portraying our human experience of agency as "two-sided," or intentional only in a qualified manner, and then by attempting to show that the notion of agency is still coherent when this "two-sidedness" is removed. Our experience is two-sided, he suggests, precisely because of our embodiment. Our bodies substantially limit the field of possible actions we can undertake. Some activities within ourselves, for example, are carried out by our bodily systems without being detected, much less controlled, by our conscious efforts. Other actions, on the other hand, are impossible for us rather than automatic, and this whether we know about how consciously to perform them or not. Our bodies, moreover, not only enforce limits to our actions, but they "orient" them. Tracy suggests that our capacity to act is itself a function of our biological organisms, and remains substantially tied to the "interests" or "agendas" programmed into us by our "subintentional life patterns." Despite this limitation and orientation of our agency by given factors, Tracy suggests that our action is nevertheless indefinite in scope. Our bodily nature does not prescribe every detail of our behavior, and our capacity to form intentions and to carry them out deliberately expands the possible range of human projects indefinitely. This incongruence in human experience between the power of intentionality and the constraining effect of our embodiment is felt by human agents as a sharp duality within their "natures."[28] For Tracy, this mixed character of the human experience of agency actually provides the fodder for constructing an unambiguous concept of intentional agency as the "enactment of well-formed, carefully articulated projects." Even though the ambiguity of human experience renders the reality of such unencumbered agency the exception rather than the rule in human life, Tracy suggests that human ability to formulate such projects makes the idea of their complete enactment intelligible.[29]

---

28. Ibid., 94. Though couched in a somewhat different philosophical vocabulary, Tracy's account of human agency bears remarkable resemblance to some older accounts. The similarity to Reinhold Niebuhr's interpretation of human agents as ineluctably both "finite" and "free," for example, is obvious.

29. Ibid., 92–102, 125–26.

The concept of intentional action is thus an abstraction from the ambiguities of human experience, but an intelligible one, since its very qualification is felt so intensely precisely as a qualification of our capacities to act. But since Tracy traces the pervasiveness of such qualification to the constraining and orienting character of our embodiment in nature and culture, the concept of a disembodied form of agency is in principle intelligible. The abstraction of a concept of intentional action from our mixed human experience of freedom and limitation, in fact, just *is* an abstraction of intentional agency from embodied life. Embodiment is experienced by human agents acutely as limitation, precisely because it is limitation. This is an important identification, because it allows Tracy to make a very classical move in order to defend the idea of God as agent. According to classical analogical reasoning, God is the most perfect exemplification of the attribute analogically applied to God. Though the content of such notions as "power," for example, is quite obviously derived from human experience, the attribution of power to God requires that God be conceived as possessing it in a more perfect way, not limited or qualified by its opposite. The notion of intentional agency, then, must be attributed to God in such a way that is unmixed with the limits and qualifications experienced in every instance of human action. The supreme instance, or "perfection," of agency, therefore, must be non-embodied.[30] This notion is intelligible, again, because such unencumbered action is experienced indirectly as the never-realized desideratum or ideal of human action.

In order to address the requirement of identifiability, Tracy appeals, not to alleged empirical instances of divine action,[31] but to the plausibility of speaking of a maximal instance at the end of a scale of agency. The maximalization of agency, he argues, would necessarily entail the possession of a number of unique (and therefore identifying) qualities not shared by other agents. These unique characteristics are explicated in terms of three properties which are, according to Tracy, intrinsic to the concept of agency and therefore characteristic of all agents.[32] The first of these is the capacity to regulate one's own activity. In the case of finite,

30. Ibid., 124.

31. As we saw in chapter 3, however, Tracy believes that theism requires that there be openings ("gaps") in the fabric of natural causes, so that the locus of divine activity may in principle be identified (Tracy, "Particular Providence," 289–324).

32. Tracy, *God, Action, and Embodiment*, 125.

embodied agents, this capacity is of course qualified by "subintentional life-patterns." But God, Tracy suggests, as the perfect instance of agency, must be seen as "radically self-creative." The implications of the notion of radically self-creativity, in turn, fill out in some measure what sort of being God must be. In this way, God can be identified from among the various agencies at work in the world. Tracy notes that a number of classical identifiers of divine uniqueness can be derived from the idea of a radically self-creative agent, including lack of temporal beginning, ontological independence or "aseity," pure activity, changelessness, and simplicity.[33] Tracy's second and third characteristics of agency, the attainment of a degree of order in one's sphere of activity and the exertion of influence upon a range of phenomena in the world, are treated similarly, maximizing them for God and thereby deriving unique characteristics of divine agency.[34]

Tracy's argument in *God, Action, and Embodiment* may be judged largely successful on its own terms. He ably and convincingly demonstrates that there are no formal contradictions between modern knowledge (in this instance, of the embodiment of human beings) and biblical portrayals of God as agent. His proposal may therefore appear to be promising extension of Kaufman's early efforts to press the concept of agency into a fresh appraisal of the prospects for an intelligible theism. One might ask, however, just how significant of Tracy's accomplishment is for a program like Kaufman's. If one regards intelligibility in theology as secured by the demonstration that certain theological claims do not logically contradict widely-held convictions about the way the world works, then Tracy's proposal may be regarded as having achieved it. Kaufman's theological program, however, invokes a stricter criterion of intelligibility. For Kaufman, as shall recall, intelligibility is achieved only insofar as our constructive proposals can find some positive warrant in human experience.

---

33. Ibid., 126–31. For example, God as perfect agent can be described as *a se* insofar as God's "existence has no sustaining ground beyond his own continuous enactment of the pattern of his life" (128). Interestingly, however, Tracy suggests that the notion of God as agent rules out depicting God as timeless. It "commits us to thinking of God's life as having a temporal order." "Eternity," therefore, can mean only "existing at all times and in all places," and *not* existing above the fray of temporal succession (130).

34. Ibid. These affirmations, respectively, reinstate classical emphases upon God's "unity" and "omnipotence."

It may appear that Tracy's analysis of the complexities of the human experience of agency to just this. His representation of the "orienting" effect of embodiment upon every instance of human agency certainly resonates not only with human experience, but also with modern knowledge about human decision-making. Careful analysis of the role of this effect in Tracy's proposal, however, indicates that he understands it primarily as a constraint upon the capacity to act, which is thereby understood independently of embodiment. Showing that intentional agency can be understood independently, that the concept of nonembodied agency is formally coherent, does not suffice to demonstrate that we know what we are saying when we employ such language. Kaufman's thinking is less friendly to this sort of abstraction. For him, "agency" refers not to a logically independent feature of human life, but to a concrete phenomenon which has emerged in the course of a long evolutionary process. The modern matrix of ideas about the human capacity to act, he suggests, determines what we are able to make clear to ourselves about the concept of agency. And it leaves no room for understanding agency apart from the actual history of embodied life which has made it possible and which has nurtured it.[35]

The attempt to formulate a concept of agency by abstracting the capacity to act from its biological and social contexts, to put the point more strongly, takes agency-talk out of gear. By disengaging it from the matrix of associations in which it is embedded in our ordinary way if speaking, Tracy's proposal ruptures the actual grammatical context of the concept of agency which gives it meaning. Formal coherence may easily suggest clarity of thought, but this only indicates how easy it is to be "bewitched" by this sort of strategy.[36] In actual fact, we can have no idea of what nonembodied agency could be like. Our ordinary idea of agency cannot be analogically stretched in that manner, because such stretching would necessarily involve removing agency-talk from its ordinary linguistic habitat, from which it derives meaning. The idea of perfect agency, therefore, can have no possible warrant in human experience—it

---

35. Kaufman, *In Face of Mystery*, 331.

36. For a sustained analysis of the ways in which we may be "bewitched" by linguistic habits, see any of the later works of Ludwig Wittgenstein, most famously *Philosophical Investigations*. Kaufman has endorsed the use of later Wittgensteinian analyses of religious language for *critical* purposes in "Reading Wittgenstein," 404–21. Clearly this represents a radically different appropriation of "ordinary language" philosophy than that of Lindbeck and the Yale School, in which Tracy himself began his academic career.

fails to meet Kaufman's standard of intelligibility. Proposals, like Tracy's, which attempt to resolve the difficulty about attributing agency to God by removing limitations do not, therefore, provide a viable way forward for the theology of *God the Problem*.

Interestingly, however, the way in which Tracy identifies divine activity amid the welter of lesser agencies in the world bears some resemblance to Kaufman's. Tracy defines agency as a "complex of activity integrated into an operative unity."[37] One identifies this "operative unity" not only by the set of formal characteristics derivable from the notion of perfect agency, but by the more substantive and concrete set of action-predicates (or "dispositional qualities") discernible in narrative accounts of God's mighty acts.[38] Kaufman, we may recall, also sees action-predicates as the primary means for talking concretely about God. Concrete ideas about God are the products of imaginative construction, not deductive logic or direct religious experience of a transcendent subject. The difference is that, for Kaufman, attributing ontological status to predicates is reifying. The problem of representing divine activity, for a constructivist theology like Kaufman's, is to find some way of specifying the ontological independence (transcendence) of God without simply reifying the action-predicates contained in biblical narrative.

---

37. Tracy, *God, Action, and Embodiment*, 106.

38. Ibid., 152. Our knowledge of the particular features of God's character, for Tracy, is completely "story-dependent." In this way, Tracy clearly ranges himself with the Yale School.

6

God's Being Is in Becoming

THE TITLE OF THIS chapter is borrowed from Eberhard Jüngel's book on Karl Barth's doctrine of the Trinity.[1] This may well seem like a dubious decision on my part, because I have shown from the outset that in many respects the positions of Barth and Kaufman on God's nature and action could not be more different. For one thing, we have seen how Barth employs a strategy of rejecting modern knowledge in order to protect certain theological convictions from dilution, while this whole book has argued that Kaufman deliberately appropriates modern knowledge in ways that substantively contribute to his theology. In addition, Barth's theology thunderously purports to be ontologically realistic (even if we must judge that his realism is finally somewhat attenuated), while Kaufman's theology is forthrightly constructivist, eschewing the tradition's longstanding ambition to describe both God and mundane reality in an objective manner. Indeed, so far does Kaufman veer from this classical descriptive intent that it hardly seems appropriate even to talk about God's "being" in the context of Kaufman's theology. As we saw in chapter 2, his analysis of the very logic of God-talk would seem to forbid it. "God" means "mystery" which cannot be objectified.

These are important reservations. By way of self defense, I want to begin by suggesting that the notion of God's being points to a major question about Kaufman's theology that we have not yet resolved. Given that theological language is always constructed rather than derived from experience or from authoritative sources, how can we be sure that we are referring to someone or something real? In philosophical terms, what is the ontological status of the concept of God? Is God in some way distinct from the plethora of creative and humanizing trends operative within the world? Is there a way to specify this distinction, so that God

1. Jüngel, *God's Being Is in Becoming.*

may be ontologically located, even if not objectively described? In other words, is there a way in terms of Kaufman's constructivism to secure the reference of the concept of God?

Here I believe a comparison with Barth's theology will be instructive, because Barth's and Kaufman's programs both feature strong critiques of the reifying ontology of the Western metaphysical tradition, and each attempts to specify God's activity within the world and God's transcendence in a way which privileges events of historical becoming rather than a static, uneventful being. In fact, both projects culminate in a form of what might be called "radical theological historicism."

As Jüngel points out, Barth's objective theology can speak God's being only by means of a radical, historicizing reinterpretation of the concept of being.[2] As we observed in the first chapter, a reinterpretation of divine agency follows. God's purposes are not held in reserve behind the distinction between time and eternity, but are constituted in concrete acts.

"We are dealing with the being of God: but with regard to the being of God, the word "event" or 'act' is *final*, and cannot be surpassed or compromised. To its very deepest depths God's Godhead consists in the fact that it is an event—not any event, not events, in general, but the event of His action, in which we have a share in divine revelation."[3] Here, I will take this observation a step further, suggesting that Barth' theology radicalizes classical ways of identifying the uniqueness of God vis-à-vis other objects of experience or thought, which is the upshot of what theological tradition has called God's "transcendence."

For Kaufman, of course, both the concepts of agency and transcendence have become problematic. In attempting to resolve the problems associated with them, he constructs a "radical naturalism" which locates God within the world rather than beyond it, and he replaces the highly ambitious metaphor of agent with the somewhat looser, more modest concept of creativity. Upon close inspection, however, it will become evident that Kaufman's account of God also turns out to be less a repudiation of the concepts of agency and of transcendence than a radicalization of them. Though profound differences remain, this strategy of radicalization bears definite comparisons with Barth's. The comparison can be developed further than identifying a shared critique. In fact, I will

2. Ibid., 81.
3. Barth, *Church Dogmatics*, II.2, 263.

suggest that Kaufman's constructivist characterization of God, as much as Barth's revelation-centered one, utilizes the conceptual resources of classical Trinitarian thinking to critique the dominant substance tradition of Western theology and to offer a way to specify an ontological location of God within the nexus of worldly eventfulness. The radical theological historicisms they each develop are shaped in fundamental ways by the conceptual inheritance of Trinitarian tradition.

RADICALIZING AGENCY: CREATIVE BECOMING

As we have seen, the theological use of the concept of agency stretches it at least to the breaking point and perhaps beyond it. But for Kaufman, the language of divine agency has been vital to Western theistic traditions because it has served two important purposes. It has (1) provided warrants for construing the context of human life as meaningful or even purpose-laden; and it has (2) protected the transcendence or independence of God from being co-opted by hubristic agendas and idolatrous commitments (i.e., it has "humanized" and "relativized"). We saw in chapters 3 and 4 that Kaufman believes that the traditional picture of God operating as a discrete agency within the world is deeply problematic, and we tracked his diligent labors to construct a picture of the world as meaningful that does not appeal to such a notion. In this chapter, we will consider how Kaufman proposes to fulfill the second purpose of talk about God's action—securing God's transcendence.

Neither Kaufman's reservations nor his innovations on these points mean that the logic of divine agency has simply been subtracted from his recent theology. In order to see its lingering effects, let us begin by briefly recalling Kaufman's early account of God's agency sketched in the last chapter. Just as human agency may be understood as the orchestration of various intentions and purposes (e.g., passing a biology exam) into a series of "master" purposes (e.g., becoming a doctor), so God's agency maybe understood as the execution of a master plan by means of lesser purposes and intentions that are enacted by finite agencies. The master plan is hidden from view, and it is known only insofar as it is revealed in especially luminous concrete events.

Previously, we explored difficulties with this view. Here, we may note that this early account of agency yields an appeal to revelation that is at least superficially akin to Barth's. One may conclude from this that Kaufman's growing convictions about the constructive character of theology and his growing awareness of the problematic nature of talk about God have diminished the role of revelation for Kaufman and thus led him away from Barth. But it needs to be stressed that, from Barth's perspective, the interpretation of agency which generates Kaufman's appeal to revelation in his earlier work would be judged insufficiently radical. The language of "master plan" still invokes an essentialist account of agency. God first has a plan, and then subsequently enacts it in various ways. There is a transcendent identity, character, or purpose of God which is made clear by certain revelatory events but which exists apart from them. Barth, as we will recall from the analysis in chapter 1, offers a contrasting existentialist interpretation of divine agency. God's purposes are not in principle inscrutable, like the hidden subjectivity of an agent, but are publicly available insofar as they are constituted by God's concrete act of decision.

In this more radical interpretation of agency, the nature or being of the agent is located in the becoming of the act. In other words, God just *is* the concrete act of revelation in history. God's being is not an abstract, uncommitted being outside of history, but rather it is being that is essentially historical. In Jüngel's formulation, this means that God's being is ontologically and not just accidentally located in becoming.[4] Insofar as it is possible to speak of God *in se*, one has also to speak of God as already *pro nobis* in advance: one cannot go back behind the *pro nobis* because there is no neutral being behind it to go back to. Barth affirms the radicality of Thomas' conception of God as *actus purus*, but he further radicalizes it by adding *et singularis*.[5] It is not just that God's being is not to be separated from God's activity or power, but that it is not to be separated from *this particular* activity and power, the activity and power that is embodied in the Christ event. God's being is always also event. The point is that Barth's existentialist account of divine agency therefore makes it not only impermissible to speculate about God's being, character, or purposes apart from the history in which they become concrete, but also nonsensical.

Kaufman's alignment with Barth on this issue is obscured by the fact that his explicit account of agency remains somewhat essentialist throughout his writings. He agrees that God needs to be seen as event rather than eternal, static being. But, since he continues to regard agency

4. Jüngel, *God's Being Is in Becoming*, xxv.
5. Barth, *Church Dogmatics*, II.1, 263–64.

largely in terms of rational deliberation, he concludes that the notion of divine agency must be given up. The result is that it is only we humans who "act." For Barth, by contrast, God's lack of rational deliberation is precisely what makes God the supreme agent, since the gap between purposing and carrying out that makes agency difficult has been eliminated.

The difference, I suggest, has a lot to do with differing accounts of the proper conceptual home of the notion of "agent." For Kaufman, as we saw in the last chapter, the idea of agency is connected to our experiences of purposing amid a recalcitrant environment, experiences which have arisen over the course of a complicated evolutionary and cultural history, and to remove it from this context is to undermine its intelligibility. For Barth, on the other hand, "agency" talk is appropriate whenever power over events is leveraged. Our human experiences of agency do not exhaust or even define what agency has to mean. True to his revelational method, Barth insists that what we allow the particular, concrete exercise of divine agency attested in Scripture mark out the boundaries of the concept of action rather than imposing one from our own experience.

However, it is important to see that the overall effect of Kaufman's dismissal of classical, essentialist divine agency talk in relation to God and Barth's existentializing of divine agency is equally drastic, if not substantially the same. Whether we call it "action" or "activity" is less important than it may seem, because in neither form of radical theological historicism is there a supernatural, ahistorical sphere of purposeful deliberation that is subsequently imposed upon time and space. In both, both the source and goal of the creative and redemptive activity of God is inscribed in concrete events.

The larger point I am driving toward is that for Barth and Kaufman alike this existentializing of divine agency represents a radicalizing of divine transcendence. Neither accepts an anthropomorphic hiatus between deliberation and action. God is therefore ontologically located in history, and that means that God's transcendence cannot be understood spatially, in terms of a separate realm or a "beyond," where God exists somehow above or prior to God's action. The Platonic specification of transcendence as a realm of eternal essences by which Christian theology has always been tempted is eliminated once and for all, because there is no divine essence that is not already operative and therefore historical.

Clearly, for Barth this does not mean that transcendence itself has been eliminated. On the contrary, because Barth cuts the ground out from under attempts to specify God's transcendence by means of speculative theories of the beyond generated by human fantasy and projection, his theology deepens and radicalizes God's transcendence. Rather than a principle or theory, God confronts us as a unique and surprising fact, a fact which lies at the heart of space and time rather than somewhere indeterminately above it.

Again, one may balk at the dissonance between Barth's confident objectivism and the probing, almost torturously cautious tenor of Kaufman's theology that we have previously observed. But the difference in tone, I suggest, arises from the differing methodological commitments we identified in chapter 2 more than to substantive divergence on this point. For Kaufman, too, there is a facticity to God, and it is surprising—even "serendipitous." And, even though efforts to interpret or construct our ideas of God are always risky and deeply shaped by our own historical and personal perspectives, there is an obligation, rooted in the very logic of the concept of God, to respond to what is really going on in the world. Whatever we mean by "God," for Kaufman, we intend some connection to a reality which enfolds us and which sets the terms on which we must live.

But the similarities between Barth and Kaufman on this point run deeper than merely the intent to refer. They each specify God's uniqueness or transcendence by appeal to concrete activity in the world rather than to a speculative beyond. They both, albeit driven by somewhat different motivations, undermine Platonic associations of God with neutral being, and with ontological indifference to time and space. This is the lingering effect of Kaufman's earlier exploitation of the concept of agency. Even if the metaphor of "agent" is left behind, its central affirmation is retained: God is essentially historical. And in fact, Kaufman's movement on the question of divine agency draws him not further away from but actually much nearer to the radical theological historicism of Barth. Now, as we will see, there are no hidden purposes that are revealed in action. Rather, activity is all there is to God. God's being is eventful, becoming.

From the standpoint of the sort of radical theological historicism that Kaufman develops, the strategies of invoking either the perfection or the embodiment of agency that we considered in the last chapter repre-

sent ways to resolve the aporias of divine agency by means of speculative
theories of how a transcendent subject can interact with the flux of time
and space. Barth's existentialist account of agency represents an effort to
resist speculative solutions and instead to reach behind this aporia. It refuses to acquiesce in philosophy's imposition of ontological contest between transcendence and history. Kaufman's more recent interpretation
of God represents a similar refusal, if for somewhat different reasons. If
in Barth the transcendence of God is to be seen as already historical by
virtue of God's concrete decision, in Kaufman the divine transcendence
is to be located within worldly eventfulness because of the impossibility
of proceeding otherwise in an age in which we can no longer make sense
of a beyond. But the point is that in both cases, ahistorical speculations
about God's being beyond history are judged beyond the pale of acceptable theological inquiry.

As in Barth, then, Kaufman's theology specifies the transcendence
of God on the basis of a radicalized notion of divine agency in which the
traditional distinction between agent and action is erased. For Kaufman,
too, there is something like an existentializing of diving agency at work.
In the end, there is no "man behind the curtain," and that bracing fact is
part of the meaning of divine transcendence over human interests and
concerns. The anthropocentric charge of projection theories is avoided.
However, there is still an activity that precedes and envelops our action,
an activity that is real and which grounds human limits as well as possibilities. In these important senses, God is objective. God as agent just
is the eventful mechanics of divine activity: directionally oriented, serendipitous creativity.

RADICALIZING GOD: TRINITARIAN BEING

But on the basis of what conceptual moves does Kaufman make these
points? As in Barth, the equation of divine agency and divine action
does not entail a reduction of God to mundane events: God's being is
in becoming, not strictly to be identified with it. If there is no longer
a hiatus between deliberation and action, there remains a contrast between divine activity and temporal event. For Kaufman, however, the
safeguard against theological reductionism has an ontological as well as
epistemological support. The "proto-teleological" cosmology detailed in
chapter 4 is a sort of down payment on that, a way to begin to secure the
uniqueness of God and thus to fix the reference of theological language

and argument. Here, I will suggest that the philosophical fulcrum which provides much of the conceptual leverage for moving toward a full-orbed concept of God in Kaufman's theology is Henry Nelson Wieman's distinction between that which is "creative" and that which is "created."[6]

Kaufman's appropriation of Wieman is unique to his own perspective, and must be placed in context. True to his historicist convictions, Kaufman does not plunge headlong into metaphysics when he turns to the question of God's ontological location. More thoroughly than Wieman, Kaufman mines Western religious tradition for insight, and then proposes the employment of a normative criterion drawn from the tradition itself. In order properly and adequately to specify God's transcendence of the world in a way which does not run roughshod over modern naturalistic assumptions, Kaufman suggests abstracting a normative element of historic God-talk from its metaphysically dualistic, platonic associations. The normative feature that is identified is functional rather than descriptive, and therefore can be applied in the context of a number of different metaphysical assumptions and convictions.

This crucial feature of talk about God in the religions of the West, Kaufman argues, is its facility in sharply distinguishing what *is* going on in the world from what *ought* to be. The word "God" historically has operated, in other words, as a way of establishing a critical duality within human moral consciousness. Theistic language and belief points to a normative turmoil rather than to an ontological duality within our descriptions and interpretations of things going on in the world. The idea of God has had the remarkable ability to keep tension between "is" and "ought" in moral consciousness alive, thus preventing complacency, while allowing for the possibility (depending upon which concrete specification of God's nature and character is adopted) of relating them positively, thus preventing despair.[7] The upshot of theistic language, then, no matter how metaphysically imposing it may be, is that it enables (and perhaps requires) a practical posture of critical engagement with the realities of the world.

This interpretation of the normative function of God-talk highlights a slightly different sort of problem with philosophical attitudes associated with the term "naturalism" than does the charge of ontological reductionism. The abortive feature of most naturalisms, for Kaufman,

6. Wieman, *The Source of the Human Good*, 54–69.

7. Kaufman, *In Face of Mystery*, 328.

is not that they elide certain forms of existence that ought to be included in a complete inventory of beings, but that they collapse ideals and actualities, thus allowing and perhaps even encouraging postures of either complacency or despair.[8] Kaufman's "radical naturalism," outlined briefly in chapter 4, is in fact designed with the intent to formulate a perspective that avoids both this practical peril as well as the more overtly intellectual mistake of reifying poetic language about the beyond. The symbol "God," with its built in functional duality, plays a pivotal role in this perspective.

But there is a difficult conceptual issue lurking here. Since, for Kaufman, God is not an object which is directly available to human experience, the duality of God and the world, however practically important, cannot be directly experienced. As a result, the functional distinction between God and world which he abstracts from tradition, even if fundamental to theistic faith, is by itself void of specifiable content. Without some intersection with human experience, it remains merely a formal or linguistic rule for God-talk, and formal concepts without experiential content (to follow the Kantian formula)[9] are vacuous. The duality between God and world, therefore, cannot remain a merely formal or linguistic instrument in the sort of intelligibility-seeking theology Kaufman is after. Orientation in the actual world requires reference to its experienced realities, not to abstractions. God's relation to the world, therefore, must be specified in terms of some tangible model drawn from human experience.

In the biblical traditions, we may observe, frankly anthropomorphic models are suggested to specify and give content to this more basic functional duality. God's relation to the world is understood, for example, as akin to a "potter" and "clay." The world is the recipient of God's intentional actions, which are differentiated and specific, like those of any recognizably human agent.

Straightforwardly literal appropriations of this biblical imagery of course abound in difficulties, and the philosophical machinations of classical Christian theology may be understood as attempts to qualify the perceived excesses of literal interpretations of biblical anthropo-

---

8. Ibid., 458.

9. Immanuel Kant's famous formula portraying the reciprocity between conceptual powers and experience is, "Thoughts without contents are empty, intuitions without concepts are blind." See Kant, *Critique of Pure Reason*, 45.

morphism by offering other ways to specify God's transcendence over the world. Twentieth-century theologians have often reacted against the perceived reification involved in the kind of being-talk normally associated with these attempts. As we saw in the last chapter, however, the contrasting strategy of invoking a "scale of agency" does not easily escape the peril of reification. In fact, it plunges theology back into the murky waters of anthropomorphism from which classical theologians sought, understandably, to escape. For theologians sensitive to the dangers of reification, therefore, neither scales of being nor scales of agency can appropriately specify the duality of God and world. Renewed efforts to supply the needed model cannot make use of these kinds of conceptual tools.

In a section of *In Face of Mystery* in which this issue is addressed head-on, Kaufman is not very forthcoming about what this model should be. Ostensibly, he suggests the duality of "ideal" and "actual" itself as a replacement for discredited duality of a transcendent self and the empirical world.[10] This suggestion reflects a belief that the practical substance or function of God-talk just is this distinction, and that it can be understood independently of the reifying specifications which have been used to mediate between theistic faith and empirical knowledge in the past. Be that as it may, pointing out the normative importance of the distinction does not seem to offer any way of filling out the content of the duality in the way required. Where, we may be led to ask, does this distinction find traction in our actual experience?

Fortunately, however, Kaufman's proposal is more robust than the language of "ideal" and "actual" suggests. Like traditional theistic language, his own proposal actually invokes a specific mediating model for understanding God's relation to the experienced world that selects certain features of human experience as hermeneutically decisive. Kaufman's cosmological reflections of course pave the way, but the mediating model which allows God to be distinguished from his cosmology is founded on Wieman's distinction mentioned above. Rather than trading upon the felt distinction between self as actor and world as arena of (and perhaps obstacle to) action, as he did earlier in his career, Kaufman relies upon the notion of "creativity" not just as an account of what is going on in the world, but also as a logical contrast to particular instances or outcomes which may regarded as beneficiaries of creativity—i.e., as "created."

10. Kaufman, *In Face of Mystery*, 328.

The creativity that is identified as a pervasive feature of the universe, not reducible to any of its singular instances, is called in to define the "godness" of God as over against the plethora of finite occasions of creative advance in the world.

It may be noted in passing that the fundamental conceptual role of "creativity" in Kaufman is perhaps not as clear in *In Face of Mystery* as it is in two subsequent books, *In the Beginning—Creativity* and *Jesus and Creativity*. Previous analysis has shown that in the earlier book, it appears that creativity is placed alongside directionality as twin categories for construing God's relation to the world. While it is true that both are needed—creativity alone is too vague to orient human thought and action—their simple juxtaposition may obscure Kaufman's point that creativity is the more fundamental of the two. One may perhaps state the point accurately by saying that "creativity" is the proper noun while "directional" or "directionally-oriented" is the modifier. Accordingly, in his two most recent books the focus is on creativity.

In any case, Kaufman's model for specifying divine uniqueness relies heavily upon empirical insight, trading upon the observed distinction between the features of the world that support and enhance various creative trajectories and those which seem indifferent to or even opposed to them. The felt and observed tension between the creative and the chaotic provides definite content, then, to traditional language about God as a dynamic, acting reality in the world, giving particular shape to the normative turmoil implicit in the idea of God. As a result, though "God" does not reify human subjective awareness of intentional action, the idea of God does imaginatively hold together or "idealize" various trends in the actual universe which are experienced and known not only "intuitively" but also by the instruments of modern research and experiment.

Despite the facticity of events to which these idealizations refer, it needs to be observed that Kaufman has not become at this apex of his recent proposal a theological empiricist or realist. "God" remains an imaginative construct rather than an object of direct perception, important not for its capacity to aid explanation of events and processes in the world but for its capacity to orient human thought and action. For Kaufman, talk about divine activity, or of the overall movement of creative trajectories amid the chaotic welter of natural and historical trends, is important because human beings require some "center of value" to or-

der the exercise of their agential capacities so that the self does not frag-
ment into a confused array of motivations and idealizations.[11] Recourse
to talk about a single, overarching creative momentum, epitomized in
Western monotheistic language and reflection, is warranted by this practical necessity.

THE TRINITARIAN IMAGINATION

I have claimed that Kaufman utilizes historic Trinitarian motifs and not
just philosophical insights to critique classical theologies of being and to
advance his own version of radical theological historicism. It is time to
examine this claim further. As we have seen, Trinitarian language has an
important, though ambiguous, place in Kaufman's theology. On the one
hand, Kaufman eschews any alleged necessity to attend to this or any
other element of classical theological language just because it is featured
in a religious tradition. When he somewhat abruptly introduces of the
Trinity toward the end of *In Face of Mystery*, therefore, some justification
is required. Kaufman justifies its appearance by suggesting that it is, as
he puts it, "admirably suited" to summarize his hard-won conclusions
about God up to that point.[12] It is a convenient pedagogical device for
conveying the insights about the logic of "God" gained independently
of explicit Trinitarian considerations. We have also seen, however, that
the practical logic of the historically particular and thus already heavily
freighted concept of "God" as understood by Kaufman seems already to
feature a triad of familiar claims—claims about the mystery of God, the
importance of humaneness in the divine ordering of the world, and the
continual presence of God within the created order. A Trinitarian faith
already lodged in the Western concept of God, one might say, appears to
play a large hermeneutical role in Kaufman's interpretation of the world,

11. The phrase "center of value" is H. Richard Niebuhr's and expresses well, I believe,
Kaufman's own emphasis upon the morally orienting function of religious devotion.
For Niebuhr's most complete account of the phrase, see his essay, "The Center of Value,"
in *Radical Monotheism and Western Culture*, 100–113.

12. Kaufman, *In Face of Mystery*, 412. In this respect, Kaufman's assessment of
the appropriate role of Trinitarian reflection in theology is reminiscent of Friedrich
Schleiermacher's. The latter's almost reluctant treatment of traditional Trinitarian
doctrine in the conclusion of *The Christian Faith* is warranted only by the fact that
it "combines" several elements of Christian piety that are, however, best understood
independently of the doctrine of the Trinity. See Schleiermacher, *The Christian Faith*,
738–39.

and humanity's place in it, from which he attempts to construct a viable concept of God for today.

What we have in Kaufman's concept of the divine Trinity, in other words, is the culminating moment of a theological system which moves self-consciously and deliberately within a circle. Here as elsewhere in Kaufman, however, the circularity is not vicious. The attempt to find warrants for claims about creativity and ordering in the "macro-conclusions"[13] of modern science and collective human experience indicates that Kaufman's attempt to fashion a conception of God as Trinity is open to being shaped in substantive ways by non-theological sources of knowledge and insight. Moreover, the resultant shape of the concept of God reflects the significant contribution modern knowledge makes to Kaufman's account of God's relation to the world. God is less personal, certainly less anthropomorphic, and also less ontologically distinct from the world than either the tradition or the early Kaufman suggested. As we shall see, in fact, Kaufman believes that his reconceptualization of God as Trinity is uniquely compatible with the monistic metaphysical assumptions widely characteristic of a naturalistic age in a way which more anthropomorphic conceptions of God as agent cannot be.

On the surface, Kaufman's claim might well appear a bit too convenient. Some critics may regard it as all-too-predictable that a theologian would claim that the picture of God and world he has sketched apart from overweening reliance upon church dogma would, in the end, be found to be perfectly aligned with traditional convictions and claims. It is important, therefore, that we pay careful attention to statements made by Kaufman which indicate the respects in which he finds traditional Trinitarian thought illuminating. When we do so, we find that the Trinity is not only by happenstance a convenient summary of what he believes to be a viable conception of God for today, but that the contemporary value of this classical doctrine, for Kaufman, is rooted in a particular conceptual innovation which enables the revisionary theologian to avoid many of the most perplexing difficulties of theism as it has developed under the baneful influence of the Greek metaphysics of substance. This metaphysical tradition, it may be argued, is not only alien to the biblical picture of God and the world, but it is productive of a great number of intractable problems for theology. Most importantly for our purposes, by picturing God as a self-contained, self-sufficient being, the substance

13. Kaufman, *In Face of Mystery*, 429.

tradition raises difficulties about how God is related to other substances. Even if the notion of substance can be thought through clearly, the notion of an all-pervasive, active, yet metaphysically distinct divine substance is troublesome, particularly in a naturalistic age.

At this point the classical Trinitarian tradition provides an important conceptual resource, though Kaufman is characteristically ambivalent about its value. The concept of *perichoresis*, the mutual interpenetration of the persons of the Godhead, is a classical tool of Trinitarian thinking that was elaborated most fully by John of Damascus in the ninth century. Kaufman enthusiastically endorses *perichoresis* as a potential antidote to the abortive, though historically dominant, theological tradition of substance thinking. *Perichoresis*, he suggests, represents a decisive break with the substance tradition, suggesting that the persons of the Trinity are not separate, self-contained beings who interact by mutual consent or by necessity, but discrete but interpenetrating aspects of a single divine life. For Kaufman, the importance of the concept of *perichoresis* is that, by portraying the ultimate source of cosmic and human existence as a dynamic, social reality, it deflects historic Western (or Greek) fascination with stability, order, and being and it enables an appreciation of dynamism and interrelation as of ultimate metaphysical significance. It enables the theologian, in other words, to see the relation between God and world in historical rather than static terms.

On the other hand, Kaufman does not appropriate the perichoretic tradition without serious qualifications. He does not, for example, adopt the notion of interpenetrating personhood as a description of God's inner life, as Jürgen Moltmann does.[14] For Kaufman, as we have seen, attribution of personhood to the creativity at work in the universe takes ordinary person-language out of its appropriate context and thus suffers from intractable problems of intelligibility. Rather, the *perichoresis* to which Kaufman wishes to point is not the mutual interpenetration of aspects or dimensions of the divine life considered apart from events and processes in the world, but the absence of any clear ontological boundary between God and world. God is not an independent being somehow outside of the world, acting self-consciously to create, order, and redeem—rather, God just *is* creative, ordering, redemptive activity pervading the plethora of happenings which make up our universe. This classically Trinitarian conceptuality is appropri-

14. See Moltmann, *The Trinity and the Kingdom*, 10–21.

ated, therefore, to portray the fundamental intermingling between the being of God and activities in the world (roughly corresponding in theological tradition to the idea of the "economic" Trinity) rather than to describe the inner life of God (traditionally, the "immanent" Trinity).[15] Trinitarian language, like God-talk in general, only makes sense insofar as it is roughly translatable into a series of intelligible claims about the nature and purpose of our world. It locates the being of God thoroughly amid the becoming of worldly events.

The fruitfulness of the idea of the Trinity is tied in part, for Kaufman, to the fact that it is itself a perichoretic idea. The irreducibility and yet deep relationality between the conceptions of Father, Son and Holy Spirit included within it fosters the development of fluid and broadly flexible conceptualities which can account both for the complexities of our context and for the practical needs of persons and communities for orientation in the world. It both encourages and deepens, for example, Kaufman's own conceptuality of serendipitous creativity and directionality. By itself, the concept of serendipitous creativity may suggest an abstract and unprincipled fountain of novelty, just as the notion of God as "maker of heaven and earth" by itself might suggest raw, unprincipled power. For classical Trinitarian thought, christological motifs add concreteness of purpose to faith in God the Creator, preventing theism from collapsing into a functional pantheism which cannot make distinctions between activities in the world which serve God's purposes and those which do not. The interpenetration with properly theological and christological ideas, however, prevent the confusion in basic orientation that would result from construing Christ as some sort of Promethean opponent to the Creator. Kaufman's conceptuality for construing the world already approximates this perichoretic logic insofar as a specific directionality gives the type of specific content or direction to serendipitous creativity that is required for human agents who need to make discriminating judgments about what in their realm of experience is worthy of devotion, without portraying the former as anything other than the most authentic expression of the creativity which enables and upholds all events in the universe. As the Son does the will of the Father,

---

15. Indeed, Kaufman rejects the classical distinction between the economic and the immanent Trinity, not because he believes he can combine them, but because he believes that talk about an "immanent" Trinity of divine persons stretches our language beyond intelligibility. See Kaufman, *In Face of Mystery*, 494.

so directionality fulfills rather than opposes the fecundity of serendipitous creativity.

In Kaufman's interpretation of the Trinity, the first intention or motif of Trinitarian reflection, the ultimate mystery behind the becoming of events and processes in the world, is given specific content by the other two motifs: the trajectory toward humaneness brought to vivid expression in the death of Christ, and the ubiquitous presence of God in all events and processes in the world, symbolized in language about the Holy Spirit. These second and third motifs are seen, in turn, as paradigmatic rather than aberrant expressions of the creative fecundity of God expressed in the motif of God the Father. According to the perichoretic logic of the doctrine of the Trinity as understood by Kaufman, in fact, God the Father (creativity) is not fully the Father apart from divine activity as both Son (directionality) and Holy Spirit (presence).

Though Kaufman's characterization of serendipitous creativity as all-pervasive precedes his explicit discussion of the Trinity, his treatment of the third motif of Trinitarian language and reflection adds a distinctive note to his interpretation of God's relation to the world. The idea of God the Spirit, he suggests, points to a divine presence within every part of the created world. The ambition of this claim may easily be underestimated due to its familiarity, but Kaufman argues that it is sheer nonsense in substantialist thinking. According to the latter, distinct substances fill distinct regions of space and time, so that the presence of additional beings or realities is strictly inconceivable. According to the motif of presence, however, God and world are not absolutely separate or distinct substances, but interpenetrating and interconnected realities. Kaufman suggests that this model enables a more profound appreciation for and a greater degree of clarity about the classical theistic doctrine of omnipresence. On this (Trinitarian) model of conceiving God's relation to the world, God is not a being apart from or in addition to the set of (in principle) empirically observable realities of our world, but is instead "the very existence of things," interpenetrating, upholding, and ordering each of the events that comprise it.

The recognition of ubiquitous fecundity, of course, does not help agents choose appropriate ways to exercise their powers. The second, christological motif, according to Kaufman, provides the concreteness and specificity necessary for centered beings like ourselves to be appropriately guided amid the welter of cosmic and historical events and processes. Once again, Trinitarian language both anticipates and deepens the conceptual innovations of Kaufman on this point. A christologically shaped consciousness is directed to discern trajectories that support and enhance humane values, but these trajectories are vividly, and perhaps uniquely, exemplified in the events that surround the death of Christ. In *In Face of Mystery,* Kaufman adopts what he calls a "wider Christology," which sees the significance of Jesus not only in his person and work, but in the matrix of events in history both that make it possible and that carry its redemptive force through the responsive activities of his community of disciples. Focus upon these cruciform activities of Christ and his disciples as indicative of the cosmic trajectory toward the humane, for the Christian, show that the highest fulfillment of humane values is not the pursuit of relatively narrow self-fulfillment but the sacrifice of self-interest in service to others. This wider christological orientation thereby enables a sharper focus of devotion for adherents of Christian faith than would the recognition of vaguely humanizing trajectories in the world. Once again, however, this christological focus, in the context of a perichoretic logic, functions not in the face of but precisely in partnership with a piety that regards the welter of creative activities that pervade the universe as good.

Trinitarian language and reflection, once again, does not simply endorse or repeat Kaufman's cosmological concepts of serendipitous creativity and directionality. Rather, it both anticipates and deepens them. It anticipates them by orienting the theologian's attention in a particular way, so that the complex interrelationship of creativity and order is lifted out of the "blooming, buzzing confusion" of the experienced world. It deepens them by providing imagery which is both sharper and more evocative, and which is made intelligible by having been prefigured in Kaufman's presentation by a series of concepts which draw together widely acknowledged features of human experience. The unique, perichoretic logic of Trinitarian language and reflection, for Kaufman, enables a distinctively and fruitfully orienting perspective upon the world, and this fact serves to warrant the conviction that classical Trinitarian logic is pregnant with illuminating power that even the ideas of serendipitous creativity and directionality cannot exhaust. One might say that these concepts, cobbled together from human experience, represent Kaufman's skillful effort to prepare the way for a fuller doctrine of God which is at once faithful to the intentions of religious tradition and capable of genuinely orienting us in the world we know and experience.

Kaufman believes that his hard-won depiction of God as creative, ordering, redemptive activity is capable, in fact, of carrying out the most important function of more literally (or analogically) understood language about God as agent. It is capable of fostering, he believes, the same distinctive posture of critical engagement with the realities of the world which has been inculcated throughout the millennia of Western theistic teaching and practice. By portraying God as this sort of activity in the world, the Trinitarian model he proposes, like classical ones, avoids promoting a stance of either complacent acquiescence to the realities of nature and history or otherworldly indifference to them. Kaufman's Trinitarian God is neither for humanity by virtue of some merely transcendent decision unrelated to the time and space in which we human agents struggle, nor sublimely indifferent to human beings except insofar as they "succeed" in their environment. Rather, God is decisively for the particular natural-historical ferment which promotes human flourishing and which we can identify as operative within the experienced world. His theistic account of human life in the world therefore supports a posture of sober commitment, unsettling the status quo without resorting to utopias or to some other kind of purely negative, unapproachable ideal. The vision of humanization it promotes is both critical toward reality as we now experience it and deliberately connected to the naturalistic picture of the world characteristic of our age.

It perhaps does not need to be stressed that we have wandered a great distance from Barth at this point. I have suggested that they each arrive at a form of radical theological historicism in which the being of God is located in eventful becoming, and I have pressed the comparison because I do not believe that their differences should be allowed to eclipse their marked similarity in radically undermining taken-for-granted Western assumptions about ultimate reality. But the respective shapes of their constructive proposals are linked very much to their radically different methodological commitments, and we can easily observe how Kaufman's pursuit of an experientially-shaped conception of God eventuates in a drastically different theology from Barth's revelational and christocentric program. I conclude the comparison by observing that the differences between them amount to diverging specifications of the content of radical theological historicism. God is ontologically and not accidentally located in history: for Barth, in the history that culminates in Jesus Christ as the Word of God; for Kaufman, in the evolutionary and historical momentums that yield novel and to some degree human-izing configurations of value and meaning. And I repeat the assessment I urged earlier: an advantage of Kaufman's program is that he is able to draw actual human experience and empirical knowledge into his theol-ogy in a way which enhances its intelligibility.

REIFYING AND REFERRING

But where does all this leave us on the matter of reference? Kaufman's affirmation of the ineradicable fallibility ("mystery") of theological lan-guage certainly does not put him in a category by himself in modern the-ology, nor does his critique of reification in theological language. It does, however, pose difficult problems about the matter of reference which all thinkers in this category (Barth included!) must face. In Kaufman's case, if God is to be identified with the much looser concept of "creativity" rather than "creator," we have yet to answer the fundamental question: In what sense does language about God-as-creativity refer? We have so far considered the philosophical bases both for Kaufman's critique of reification and for his non-reifying specification of divine uniqueness or transcendence. In order to make clear his own account of reference, we will now situate him amid several options in contemporary theology which, unlike Barth, attempt to align theological commitments with hu-man experience.

Kaufman provides the lead here by urging that his particular form of empirically-engaged theological constructivism, while not laying claim to secure epistemic foundations either in revelation or experience, can "indirectly" open us to the reality of God.[16] We need to ask: what might this mean?

Theological Realism

First of all, one might take it to indicate that theological language inad-equately but genuinely distills a prereflective, experiential apprehension of the reality of God. In some revisionary forms of theological realism, religious experience is understood as grounded in the universal efficacy of the divine self-communication, and adequate theological conceptu-alities abstract from an inevitable unthematic awareness of God.[17] The

16. Kaufman, *In Face of Mystery*, 351.

17. See, for example, Ogden, *The Reality of God*, 1–70; and Meland, *Fallible Forms and Symbols*, 3–68.

"indirectness" here depends upon the gap between the richness of prereflective experience and the comparative poverty of conceptual language, rather than an essential incompatibility between human experience and language, on the one hand, and the divine mystery, on the other.

If Kaufman's theology may be construed as a form of theological realism insofar as it risks interaction with secular experience, however, it is not the sort of realism which regards God or God's activity itself as a discernible object of experience, and we may therefore immediately rule out this way of taking the claim in question. In an essay on the theology of Bernard Meland, Kaufman severely criticizes the notion that there can be a "direct empirical grounding" of theological reflection. This notion depends, he argues, upon a reification of the regulative ideas with which theology deals.[18] In Meland's program, Kaufman suggests, this fallacy shows up in his varying ways of writing about "mystery." While often using the concept to highlight human ignorance, in some instances Meland writes as if mystery were a "vivid empirical datum," directly accessible to human experience and thus adequate as an empirical foundation for theological reflection.[19] This "epistemologically positive" meaning of mystery represents precisely the use which Kaufman studiously avoids, and which according to Kaufman causes realists such as Meland to obscure the ways in which our experiences of ultimacy are decisively shaped, even constituted, by the conceptualities which are borne by our particular languages.[20] For Kaufman, as we have seen, experience of reality is always already conceptual, never purely and simply given and thus innocent of culturally conditioned meaning. The "rhetoric of 'realism,'" according to Kaufman, tends to blind us to the limitations of our thought and thus to diminish our powers of self-criticism.[21]

18. Here he calls it the "fallacy of misplaced concreteness." See Kaufman, "Empirical Realism," 136.

19. Ibid., 138.

20. Ibid., 140–42. Kaufman suggests that in Meland's case the supposed immediacy of his apprehension of realities in his experience is actually mediated by Whiteheadian categories, particularly by Whitehead's doctrine of "actual occasions." The experiential sources of Meland's theology are therefore alleged to be already shaped in crucial ways by a particular set of concepts.

21. Ibid., 143–44.

Theological Antirealism

Being confronted with the difficulties with theological realism may lead one read Kaufman as endorsing the view that justifiable talk about being "indirectly" opened to God implies no reference at all. It may be taken to indicate merely a normative perspective on human life. In Charley Hardwick's "valuational theism," for example, claims about God are construed as meta-assertions about objective value.[22] In the austere version of metaphysical naturalism Hardwick accepts, God cannot have "ontological inventory status."[23] Thus, similarly to philosopher of religion R. B. Braithwaite, Hardwick argues that the meaning of the claim that God exists has more to do with a way of life than with a reality in addition to those physical items which inhabit nature and history. Unlike Braithwaite, however, Hardwick believes that talk about God is cognitive, since it makes genuine truth claims.[24] But the truth of "God" is not the correctness of a particular metaphysical scheme, but that of a particular conception of objective value.[25] To deny God's reality, conversely, would be to deny that the values embodied in theistic faith are true or real.[26]

This way of taking Kaufman's claim has the advantage of being far removed from reifying forms of theological reflection that he criticizes, and also of cohering with Kaufman's interpretation of the idea of God as the site of moral turmoil. The problem, from the standpoint of Kaufman's

22. Hardwick, *Events of Grace*, 21–22, 64. See also Hardwick's "The Normative Argument for a Valuational Theism," in Peden and Axel, *New Essays in Religious Naturalism*, 99–110.

23. Hardwick, *Events of Grace*, 52–62. It is perhaps worth pointing out, however, that to ascribe to God the status of belonging to some "inventory," even an "ontological" one, seems wrong even to a large number of classical theists. For an account of this anti-reifying feature of the classical tradition, see Farley, *Divine Empathy*, 23–39.

24. Hardwick, *Events of Grace*, 54–71. Hardwick's view that theology construed as a "seeing-as" can be both cognitive and objectively true is therefore quite distinctive. For thinkers like Kaufman, the "seeing-as" character of theological vision casts doubt on the appropriateness of claiming objective truth. For others, it actually entails a non-cognitivist account of theological language. In Braithwaite's philosophical analysis of religious language to which I have alluded, theological claims are understood merely as meta-assertions about the subjective intent of religious persons and communities to live in a particular manner . See Braithwaite, "An Empiricist's View of the Nature of Religious Belief," 72–91.

25. Hardwick, *Events of Grace*, 158–206.

26. A problem with this view, we may note, is that it depends upon a moral realism that is only somewhat less controversial than the "ontological realism" about God that Hardwick dismisses because of its allegedly unacceptable degree of ambition.

position, is its severing of the concept of God from views of the world. Hardwick believes that an important advantage of his valuational theism is its freedom from inevitably controversial metaphysical ties. For Kaufman, however, the concept of God, though it does not necessarily imply the particular worldview in which it has arisen, nevertheless functions precisely as the "anchor symbol" of some overall worldview.[27] In Hardwick's vocabulary, "God" makes claims not only about the truth of objective values, but, even more controversially, about their cosmic support. As we have seen, God as creativity would make no sense in a world of eternal recurrence.[28]

The Indirect Referentiality of Theological Constructivism

The possibility of being "indirectly" opened to God may be taken to indicate, finally, that religious language and experience refer, but that reference to God is indirect even at the level of prereflective experience. In the theology of Edward Farley, for example, God is known insofar as God "comes forth as God" in human experiences of transformation from abortive postures of self-securing to those of gratitude and trust.[29] The experience of redemption is an actual effect of divine activity. Talk about God's redemptive activity is therefore talk about something real going on in the world. Through redemptive events, however, the believer knows God only as an "appresented"[30] reality—that is, as a bare, unapprehended implication of experience—and not as an object of perception. Like Kaufman, therefore, Farley holds to the final unavailability of God to human experience. Theology interprets experience, but it does not simply abstract from or thematize it in order to render an account of God. Like Kaufman, Farley acknowledges that claims about God are formulated with the aid of particular configurations of historical and linguistic tradition.

A problematic feature of Farley's position, from Kaufman's point of view, is connected with the word "appresented." Kaufman urges that

27. Kaufman, *In Face of Mystery*, 35–41, 70–82.

28. Early in Kaufman's career, this identification of God with temporal movement caused him to make a cosmological choice among two competing options: big bang over steady state. See Kaufman, *Systematic Theology*, 275–76.

29. Farley, *Divine Empathy*, 62–75. Farley's methodological point here is articulated in more detail elsewhere. See, for example, Farley, *Ecclesial Man*.

30. Farley, *Divine Empathy*, 99–101.

"appresentation" suggests a discrete object which can be known in quasi-perceptual fashion, thus effectively continuing the reifying theme of precritical theological reflection.[31] To be fair to Farley, he does in fact insist that God not be understood as an object, and that appropriate theological language is always bracketed by the qualifications supplied by the tradition of negative theology.[32] Still, Farley's theology is empirical in the sense that certain features of human experience are held to supply a firm basis, if not a comprehensive conceptual inventory, for making claims about divine activity.

Kaufman's program, by contrast, is more strictly constructivist. Talk about God is warranted not by "appresentation," but by the practical need to construe the ultimate context of human life as meaningful and supportive of human aspirations. "God," one might say, is a "postulate" of practical reason rather than an "appresentation" ineluctably given to certain varieties of religious experience.[33] As such, it embodies a mode of reflection which, like other kinds of thinking, involves acts of will on the part of the knower.

Despite these differences, I suggest that the use of the word "God" in Kaufman's program most nearly approximates this third position. By "God," Kaufman clearly intends to refer. As we have already noted, talk about divine activity does not refer to an agency which acts from beyond space and time, but to the mix of order and novelty that characterizes eventfulness in the universe, to the creativity which is realized in part by particular humanizing trends or movements in our world. Even though no supernatural agency is posited, this reference to a creativity that yields value-laden trends is nontrivial and controversial, since it entails that the world is characterized by something like "purposiveness" (i.e., a "proto-teleology").

31. Kaufman, Review of *Ecclesial Man: A Social Phenomenology of Faith and Reality*, by Edward Farley; and *Blessed Rage for Order: The New Pluralism in Theology*, by David Tracy, 10–12.

32. Farley, *Divine Empathy*, 111–22.

33. Kaufman uses the Kantian phrase, "postulate of the moral life," with reference to the status of God-talk in *An Essay on Theological Method*, 3rd ed., 29. As we have suggested, this language distances the reality of God from the grasp of religious and other forms of human experience. The crucial difference between Kant and Kaufman, as we have seen, is in Kaufman's "naturalistic" interpretation of "God," emerging with clarity only with the publication of *In Face of Mystery*. This move, as we have also seen, makes interaction between religious and empirical sources of insight both possible and theologically significant.

It needs to be stressed that the reference to the ontic reality of this creative and redemptive activity is indirect. The creating and sustaining forces of the cosmos do not impinge upon human consciousness in such a way that their reality qua creative and sustaining is incontrovertible. Creativity-as-such is not given as an "empirical datum." What are given, rather, are various kinds of trends and movements which are susceptible to being interpreted as instances of a more pervasive creativity. The theologian draws upon cultural and linguistic resources, primarily those embedded in the Western monotheistic religious traditions, in order to construe the realities of life in the world as creative and sustaining.

If differences in tone and vocabulary as well as a range of substantive differences can be overlooked, the methodologies of Kaufman and Farley may be understood as contributions to a common position on the matter of theological reference. Though the roles given to experience and to linguistic tradition in the two approaches differ, each program embodies both an insistence that talk about "God" entails references to actual transactions in the world and an acknowledgment that accounts of God's relation to the world require the use of conceptual resources which cannot be directly grounded in human experience. In terms of the polarity we explored in the first chapter, both are approaches with "discriminately interact" with human experience of the world.

Insofar as each rejects theological methodologies which seek to derive all of the content of disciplined God-talk from a single authoritative source, moreover, the position to which they contribute may be appropriately designated "constructivist." Risks have to be made; creativity is required. Theology of this kind, attending to possibilities within human experience and knowledge for "indirect" openings to the reality of God, does not rest finally in the rational adequacy of its account of the world (i.e., on its success as an ontology), but it its facility in poetically accounting for life in the world in a way which fits with our knowledge and experience.

Distinguishing "poetic" from "ontological" descriptive adequacy helps the theologian offer accounts of divine activity which capture the realistic intent of traditional claims about God in a way which is compatible with at least some forms of naturalistic metaphysics largely assumed in our culture. Accordingly, as in Hardwick, Kaufman's refusal to reify traditional theistic language helps him point to a kind of kernel of truth in biblical language which does not perforate modern naturalistic explanations of world processes. Unlike Hardwick, however, the descriptive component of biblical poetry for Kaufman is not entirely self-referential and therefore metaphysically indifferent. It is precisely this lack of metaphysical neutrality about imaginative religious language which grounds the distinction between "reifying" and "referring" in Kaufman's proposal.

For Kaufman, all talk about divine activity is poetic or imaginative, and should not be reified; but it is also realistic insofar as it refers, or intends to refer, to real activities whose existence and character may be qualified or even denied on the basis of empirical knowledge or metaphysical opinion. Heavy qualification or denial of these activities would break the back of theistic metaphors, so that the reference of God-talk is purchased in part by a certain degree of risk. More positively, the intelligibility of theistic imagery requires some at least suggestive articulation of a metaphysic which supports talk about God. Though the function of theistic action-predicates may be abstracted from biblical language for the purpose of reconstructing an account of divine activity, one may not simply cling to the functional meaning of theistic imagery. One is to some degree in the dark about the real significance of such talk until its reference is secured, and that requires either defending its original conceptual context (including claims about the world) or reconstructing it in a way that does not offend modern sensibilities. The meaningfulness of such realistic" metaphors, therefore, requires interaction with the relevant sources of knowledge and insight.

Though the vocabulary of "ideal" and "actual," and the practical intent it serves, are clearly reminiscent of the idealism of thinkers in the Kantian tradition, this dependence upon empirical knowledge for filling out or specifying the actual content of imaginative models for God's activity actually pushes in a very different direction. For Kaufman, in contrast to such diverse heirs to the Kantian legacy in theology as Barth and Hardwick, the model for conceptualizing God is not cut loose from knowledge about the causal realities of the world, but is in fact shaped in important ways by it. For Kant, as for Barth and Hardwick, a strategic retreat from the empirical is made in order to prevent modern knowledge from undermining what is perceived to be the essential content of religious imagery. What is distinctive about Kaufman's proposal is that he selectively conscripts empirical knowledge in order to re-specify the content needed to fill out the abstract functional imagery intrinsic to the logic of the imaginative, nonempirical concept of God. He thus combines a nonrealist, neo-Kantian epistemology with a strategy of engagement with empirical knowledge in order to support a decidedly realistic appropriation of religious symbols and imagery. As with more straightforwardly realistic strategies examined in chapters 1 and 3, of course, Kaufman's necessarily involves risks; but it also, I suggest, offers opportunities to revise and extend one's perspective in response to what is found to be really going on in the world in which we need orientation and support. In the next and final chapter we shall have occasion to assess these dangers and opportunities for Kaufman's project in more detail.

7

Creativity and Human Flourishing

M Y SYSTEMATIC CONCERN IN this book has been the relation between contemporary sources of insight about our world and
theological claims about divine activity within it. In the first chapter, we
briefly examined two relatively simple strategies for underwriting realistic interpretations of divine action in the face of the rapid advance of
knowledge and the growing breadth of human experience. To recall, we
may either (1) protect the tradition from the advance of modern learn-
ing by sharply partitioning religious insights from empirical knowledge,
or (2) openly embrace modern science, not only as a working body of
knowledge about the way things work, but as a new metaphysic, on the
same epistemic level and therefore in competition with traditional religious insights invoking God's activity. Each of these strategies, I have
argued, forfeits an important dimension of classical interpretations of
divine activity, which understood talk about divine action both as referring to real events and processes in nature and history and as disclos-
ing a distinctive, irreplaceable perspective upon the world. Our lengthy
analysis of Kaufman has sought to demonstrate that mediating alternatives which can recapture classical theological realism for a scientific age
are possible.

The time has come, however, to render an assessment. To what
degree has Kaufman succeeded in holding to a mediating position? Or
does his position ultimately fall back upon one of the admittedly simpler
strategies treated in chapter 1? To be more specific, we have now to ask
whether there is genuine, free-flowing commerce between theological
insights and empirical knowledge in Kaufman's substantive interpretation of divine activity, or whether a protective strategy is invoked at
decisive moments.

A pertinent way to test Kaufman's position on this question is to inquire about the place of human beings in the view of the world which has Kaufman constructed. The modern scientific picture of the world since Copernicus has of course profoundly diminished the cosmic significance of human life and history; but just to the extent that this trend has progressed, theology has distanced itself from cosmology. This reactionary trend toward non-interaction in modern theology appears to have been motivated in part by the need to protect an ages-long anthropocentrism in theology's account of God's relation to the world. We have seen this motivation in action in the theology of Karl Barth. We have seen, further, that there are genuine substantive similarities between Barth's and Kaufman's programs. We need now to ask whether Kaufman's own emphasis upon humanization drinks from the same anthropocentric well. In the end, does it stake too much on the prospects for human flourishing?

The answer to this question, as we will see, is complex. I will argue that there is in fact a tendency in Kaufman's theology to overstress the significance of humanity—though, as will become clear, this can be done in very different ways. Critics of constructivism may quickly rush in to point out that anthropocentrism is inevitable in such a theological method, because its criteria of adequacy are focused on the felicitous orientation of human action. One may think here of William James' interpretation of religion as the "will to believe," and the critics' charge that such an interpretations ends by "willing to make believe."[1] As in the case of James, the effect of Kaufman's tendency to overemphasize the humane is to diminish the "tough-mindedness" of his theology, and it also threatens its intelligibility.

I will point out, however, that Kaufman has been keenly aware of the difficulties with anthropocentrism, and his corpus bears the marks of a serious and ongoing struggle on this point. Indeed, any reader of *In Face of Mystery* and subsequent writings will know that Kaufman regards his critique of anthropomorphic accounts of God as also a critique of anthropocentrism in theology. Although it is not clear that the relation between the two is as tight as Kaufman often seems to believe, it is certain that his intent is to develop an austerely theocentric interpretation of God and the world that sharply diverges from the coziness of the worldview implicit in at least some versions of traditional theism.

---

1. James, *The Will to Believe*, 1–31.

It is for this reason that he has taken constructive steps taken since the publication of *In Face of Mystery* to clarify his position and to allay objections of this kind.

The most important of these, as we will see, is christological: what is the role of what Kaufman has lately called the "Jesus trajectory" within the broader sweep of cosmic history? His answer to this question, I will argue, yields a theology whose austerity goes a long way toward meeting the demands of realism embodied in the ideal of discriminate interaction with which we began. In other words, Kaufman seems now to have rendered full payment, in the precious coin of Christology, on his intent to construct an empirically-responsive theology. Its details will be disappointing to some, and it may be urged that Kaufman's emergent methodological purity has decisively positioned him exactly as his critics have long suspected. Indeed, as the cosmic significance of humanity diminishes, the existential commitment to the human project increases in proportion, rendering a kind of theological humanism that places him far beyond the classical Christian tradition in some respects. The chapter will be critical of some of Kaufman's moves here. However, I will argue that other clarifying moves in the area of Christology are possible, and exploring these may point toward developing Kaufman's theology in different directions. In any case, supporting this overall assessment will be the aim of this final chapter.

CREATIVITY AND HUMAN FLOURISHING: A DILEMMA

In 1981, James Gustafson wondered whether Kaufman's theology, despite its acceptance of modern assumptions about the seamless web of natural causes, really faces up to the possibility that what Kaufman had appealed to as a "rational assessment of the structure of the world" will turn out to be incompatible with the heavy emphasis upon God's benevolent and humane purposes in his portrayal of divine activity.[2] Gustafson was responding particularly to the account of God's relation to the world sketched out in God the Problem.[3] There, as we saw in chapter 5, a "rational assessment of the structure of the world" is rather sharply differentiated from a "first-person" account (or agent's perspective) of what God is doing in nature and history. The former is available through ordinary

---

2. James M. Gustafson, *Ethics*, 266.

3. Kaufman, *God the Problem*, 82–147.

empirical means, while the latter is made available to humans only in God's self-revelation. Empirical evidence, Gustafson seems to have been suggesting, could well turn this differentiation into a divide, yielding a theology which looks very much like Barth's not only in its critique of Western metaphysics but also in its isolationist response.

As we also saw, however, the gulf between these two points of view is not unbridgeable even in this early phase of Kaufman's work. Nor are bridges built only from the religious or theological side, as they are in Barth's theology. Rather, rational assessments of "the structure of the world" place limits upon what the theologian can legitimately say about divine governance. The naturalistic assumptions they embody and support, for example, rule out crude ascriptions of miraculous interventions in the course of nature. Instead, the whole course of nature and history is seen as a single, complex "master act" through which God accomplishes divine purposes through finite events and processes which can be fully explained in terms of ordinary causal analysis. Attributions of divine activity are thus not additional empirical insights, but the implementation of a uniquely religious perspective in order to see events in the world in a particular way. This dual perspective conceptual apparatus characteristic of Kaufman's argument in God the Problem therefore allows him to preserve the intelligibility of divine action talk while neither interfering with naturalistic assumptions nor evacuating theology of all empirical content.

The position articulated in *In Face of Mystery* and subsequent writings continues to invoke a duality of perspectives. Now, however, Kaufman appeals not to the hiddenness of a supreme agent's intentions in contrast to empirical knowledge about what is going on in the world, but to our capacity imaginatively to idealize certain features of the world in order to direct our affections and commitments appropriately. The perspectival duality invoked in this later work no longer divides God's hidden intentions from evident events and processes, but distinguishes the idealizing imagination of morally concerned human beings from the purely disinterested awareness of a plethora of actual trends in the universe which is cultivated by the scientific consciousness.

Whatever significance be attached to this change, Kaufman's critics may object that his newer program is even more protective than his earlier one. His theology, it may be alleged, continues to be characterized by a "hegemony of the moral,"[4] a dominance of moral categories over empirical knowledge which guarantees that his theology will not pay sufficient attention to natural and historical realities. I have engaged in the rather lengthy analysis of Kaufman's interpretation of God's relation to the world in the previous six chapters in the hope that a duality of perspectives does not in itself condemn a theology to this sort of defect. And indeed, for critics like Gustafson, the decisive issue is not whether theology offers a perspective that cannot be reduced to the level of empirical description (he, in fact, believes that it does[5]), but whether commerce between perspectives is allowed and encouraged by the position under scrutiny.

The analysis of this book has shown that there is considerable flow of traffic between modern knowledge and religious imagination in Kaufman's recent theology. The anthropomorphic way of construing God which seems to be native to the Western religious consciousness, for example, is replaced under the pressure of modern knowledge by what Kaufman calls a "process" God.[6] The concepts of serendipitous creativity and directionality of *In Face of Mystery* serve, in fact, to grant a strong shaping and constraining role for modern empirical knowledge in his renewed efforts to make sense of theistic claims about how God acts in the world.

But if this is so, do the conceptual innovations of *In Face of Mystery* effectively meet Gustafson's earlier challenge? The more naturalistic categories employed in his interpretation of the world which we have analyzed here certainly seem to provide resources for constructing a position that does. The point of Gustafson's criticism, however, is not that Kaufman's construal of the mode of God's activity in the world is insufficiently naturalistic,[7] but that his portrayal of the purposes it enacts is too

4. I am borrowing the phrase from Gustafson, "Theological Anthropology and the Human Sciences," 61–77.

5. In his *Ethics*, Gustafson consistently invokes a duality between well-established descriptions of the world rendered by modern science and the claims of religious piety. He rigorously denies that these different kinds of claims are incommensurable, but he is careful also not to collapse them. See, for example, his discussion of divine governance in *Ethics*, 238–42.

6. Kaufman, *In Face of Mystery*, 273.

7. Indeed, Gustafson's own rendering of the mode of divine activity is not radically different. Like Kaufman's, his account stresses what has traditionally been called "general providence," and does not include "particular" or "special" providence. Also, Gustafson

anthropocentric to fit the details about the world which we know. And so, while God is no longer pictured in Kaufman's more recent theology as performing distinct actions like those of a human agent (and thus cannot any longer be conceived as having purposes in a straightforward sense), one may well wonder whether concepts like "directional movement toward humaneness" continue to suggest an inflated cosmic role for human beings.

A further difficulty can only be mentioned here. It is that the use of the criterion of humaneness as the indicator of creativity's orientation (or, as in traditional conceptualities, "God's purposes") tends to underwrite a conception of value that is somewhat restrictive in scope. Other results of natural and historical processes (animal well-being and ecosystemic integrity, to take two contemporary examples) are kept from leveraging normative force. Further, even interpretations of the humane which do not privilege rational agency (non-Western ones, for example) seemed to be ruled out in principle. There are subtleties here, and the issues are complex. We will return to them in the next section.

The main problem is that the application of critical pressure on certain features of Kaufman's theology uncovers a dilemma. In simple terms, the reader of *In Face of Mystery* finds it at once very austere and at the same time persistently humanistic. God the "person," with whom we may be in intimate relationship, yields quite thoroughly to a nonpersonal "creativity." The anthropomorphic features of theistic tradition are forthrightly rejected. Yet, when the concept of directionality is employed in order to specify or give content to Kaufman's interpretation of divine activity, one finds that the directional orientation of creativity that is emphasized is toward an apparently restrictive if not parochial understanding of the human good.

Directionality is of course a highly formal concept, and in order to be useful it must be specified in terms of something more particular. One needs to know the actual direction of creativity, and not only that fact that it is "directional." And so, one cannot fault Kaufman for filling out the concept in some way. The question, rather, is: does his particular specification require that we regard humanity as the apex or on the leading edge of the unfolding drama of cosmic history? This would seem

---

is suspicious of the uncritically anthropomorphic imagery usually evoked in talk about divine action. His construal of God is agential only in a highly qualified manner: God is said to have "purposes," but not to have "intentions" (*Ethics*, 270–71).

to be quite at odds with evolutionary theory, which describes a sort of bush radiating in many directions rather than a straight-line upward march toward the free and responsible exercise of human agency. At first glance, one may wonder whether Kaufman's fully developed interpretation of the world is not as anthropocentric as his view of God is non-anthropomorphic.

Hence the dilemma: are we to take Kaufman as suggesting that human flourishing actually is the leading edge of cosmic evolution's creative advance, and thus acknowledge a host of empirical and theoretical difficulties for his position? Or should we rather take him as making the more modest claim that the directionality which expresses the religiously and humanly significant orientation of creativity is operative only within in the limited region of human history on planet earth?

The dilemma becomes more theologically acute when we notice that it impinges upon Kaufman's reconstruction of the idea of God as Trinity. What is the relation between the creative production of novelties in the universe and the redemptive trajectory of humanization which is witnessed and experienced in Scripture and tradition? How is the first "motif" or "intention" of theistic language, classically stated in the symbol of God the Father, related to the second (God the Son)? If humanization fully expresses the fundamental orientation of creativity, we are left with a host of difficulties and counterexamples: the bush-like character of evolution and entropic dissipation of energy, to name just two. If, on the other hand, the trajectory toward humaneness which culminates in the Redeemer is locally confined and unrelated to or even at odds with wider creative trends, the question arises whether a Marcionite contest between the two motifs is not at work. In other words, the subtle interweaving of the norms of intelligibility and theological integrity which we have been praising Kaufman for throughout this book is in danger of coming unraveled.

CHRISTOLOGY AT THE MARGINS

It is clear from his last two books that Kaufman's dilemma is at least partially resolved by grasping the horn of christological modesty, and that means that the rich Trinitarianism we examined in the last chapter is significantly modified if not vitiated entirely. In methodological terms, the norm of intelligibility is embraced, and attempts are made to mitigate the erosion of theological integrity. This should not come as a surprise. Kaufman's persistent question has been whether some features of theistic faith can be salvaged in an age in which explanations are scientific and in which the most pressing moral problems of the day raise large questions about human agency. In addressing this question, he has never promised to deliver a renewed Christian orthodoxy complete.

In any case, the task of securing the intelligibility of Kaufman's concept of God involves refining the ideas of creativity and directional trends and their relations to one another, particularly in relation to the stresses and strains placed on these and other theological concepts by contemporary knowledge and experience. I have noted already that Kaufman's more recent book *In the Beginning . . . Creativity* clearly subordinates the notion of directionality to a broad creativity that does not necessarily always support human well-being.[8] Indeed, in that book directionality seems to drop out altogether in favor of interpreting God simply as creativity.

This means that various facticities that from a human perspective are great evils are connected with divine activity. Cosmic and evolutionary trends may place constraints on human growth and well-being. History may undermine hopes for peace and for more humane and just political and economic orders. As with Calvin, "what experience plainly teaches" therefore needs to be entered into the account of God's activity, and the resulting picture places the well-being of human beings in the context of wider and much more complicated realm of ends.

The piety that is appropriate to these observations is, from the point of view of theistic tradition, somewhat chastened. Kaufman urges an austere reverence for the objectivity and complexity of the world which resists easy assimilation to a set of favored moral values and loyalties. By acknowledging that what we call "evils" are the offspring of divine creativity as well as what we call "goods," the good-and-evil axis is denied the right to specify the content of divine action, and the "hegemony of the moral" which concerned Gustafson is thereby rejected.

But that does not mean that Kaufman has stopped thinking about directional trends and given his theology over what H. Richard Niebuhr once called a "Unitarianism of the Creator."[9] In his latest effort, *Jesus and Creativity*, the trajectory of humaneness is brought to the fore once again, especially as it is sharply focused in what Kaufman calls "Jesus

8. Kaufman, *In the Beginning*, 60.
9. Niebuhr, *Theology, History, and Culture*, 52.

trajectory$_2$."[10] The events surrounding and following the life and ministry of Jesus of Nazareth are characterized in part by a growing momentum toward the responsible exercise of human agency on behalf of the other. Differentiating this trajectory from what he calls "Jesus trajectory$_1$," (the historical elevation of Jesus from a human being to a divine one about which the ecumenical creeds are written), Kaufman suggests that this particular historical trend like others arises out of the pervasive creativity of the universe. "Jesus trajectory$_2$," therefore points to a particular (and local) ordering of the creative energies of the world which provides real and tangible hope for human well-being. Redemptive possibilities are positively related to creative powers: goodness is connected to being.

But "Jesus trajectory$_2$," is not characterized in the most ambitious metaphysical terms: it is not seen as the only or even the most fundamental indication of where creativity is tending. In fact, the radically pluralistic implications of the concept of creativity are affirmed. The humane trajectory does not order the complexities of the world without remainder, subjecting everything to any kind of sweeping teleology. Rather, humaneness is identified as but one trend in a vast universe, operative only in this rather miniscule corner occupied by human beings who are being shaped by particular cultural traditions that enable and require the development of human capacities to act responsibly. Commenting on the identification of God with love in I John, Kaufman urges that "[T]his creative development—like many other distinctively human characteristics—came about only in the course of human evolution and history, as far as we know. It is quite unlike what has come into being in the interrelations of creativity (God) with many other spheres in the cosmic order; so the Johannine writer has really gone too far in suggesting that the God of the universe is simply love."[11] This more modest route allows him to affirm a genuine cosmic grounding of aspirations toward the human good while avoid excessive claims about the character of the world as we actually experience and know it. The result, we may say, is a christologically-informed theism that offers an interpretation of the world which is both distinctive and intelligible.

But it is important to acknowledge the cost that is incurred. A way to measure the price Kaufman has to pay for these refinements is to note just how restricted the trend toward humaneness now seems to be. If the

10. Kaufman, *Jesus and Creativity*, 16.

11. Ibid., 47.

trajectory toward the realization of our deepest aspirations for freedom is identified as one particular trend which is but one of many expressions of the cosmic creativity identified as "God," that which is redeeming, liberating, and agency-enhancing is pushed away from the center of God's purposes: it is "relativized."

In order to begin to discern the full arc of creativity, then, one has to take into account of violent and destructive features of the universe in general and of our own ecology—and also of various human cultures which rigorously and arbitrarily restrict human agency. These are all trends of cosmic creativity just as much as the trajectory toward humaneness. It is hard for us human beings to set aside our preferences for that which seems to offer support for human well-being. And, it is hard for us Westerners to imagine not explicitly preferring more agency-enhancing cultures over more repressive or collectivist ones. Kaufman offers theological support for both of these preferences. They are each identified with a certain directional trend which is connected with creativity, a trend which is sharply focused in "Jesus trajectory$_2$." But there are other trajectories that limit, conflict with, or are irrelevant to this one. And that means, as Abraham Lincoln once said, that "the Almighty has his own purposes,"[12] and these may not be visible as trends which we can affirm as moral.

We stressed earlier that Kaufman's view of God attempts to hold together what he calls the "relativizing" and "humanizing" functions of theological language. Clearly, his appeal to these two criteria is an assertion of the classical theistic union of power and moral goodness. But it must be stressed that goodness has been somewhat marginalized in his recent theology—or at least the goodness that is relevant to our own capacities and aspirations (i.e., "moral" goodness). There is perhaps an aesthetic order of goodness whose breadth is preserved, and a corresponding acknowledgment of it that is enjoined and supported in Kaufman's theology. But, in the end, the full coincidence of moral goodness (traditionally characterized as God's "benevolent purposes")

---

12. Drawn from Lincoln's second inaugural address, this phrase is the title of the last chapter of one of James Gustafson's recent books. For Gustafson, this is an important affirmation to make about God's relationship to human flourishing, and it appears that Kaufman's position has angled into the same affirmation. See Gustafson, *An Examined Faith*, 96–109.

and being (or reality) is set aside as unwarranted by our modern understanding of the universe.

We may note in passing that for Karl Barth, and also for process theology, God's power is rigorously reinterpreted in order to fit a moral interpretation of goodness.

> More clearly even than the definition of God by the abstract concepts of the infinite, the simple, the immoveable, etc., to define Him in terms of power in itself has as its consequence, not merely a neutralization of the concept of God, but its perversion into its opposite. Power in itself is not merely neutral. Power in itself is evil . . . If power by itself were the omnipotence of God it would mean that God was evil, that He was the spirit of revolution and tyranny *par excellence*.[13]

For Barth, the power of God must not be understood in abstraction from the selfless and other-empowering humanity of Jesus Christ. In Kaufman, there is a similar commitment to a highly moral account of goodness. But, for Kaufman, power is not reinterpreted to fit this moral commitment. Instead, a proposal is offered which admits that, more often than not, divine creative power and moral goodness are simply incongruent. Moral goodness is carried along by the power of creativity, but is regarded as only one expression among many. Relativizing power, not humanizing goodness, is preeminent.

It is easy to see that a Marcionite danger lurks here. More sharply than before, the redeeming efficacy of goodness seems to be at cross purposes with the amorality of creative power. And, indeed, Kaufman admits that his long-standing admiration for the doctrine of the Trinity has diminished in his recent work. "Hence, for those thinking in terms of something like a Jesus-trajectory christology . . . it is difficult to see how anything like the traditional doctrine of the trinity can still be advocated. Most of the vast universe, as we think of it today, is in no way affected by Jesus' life, death, and resurrection; it is only the human project and its evils, on planet Earth, to which the Jesus story—because of the healing and new life that it has brought—is pertinent."[14] The classically-minded theological critic will doubtless observe that he has at this point ventured a long way not only from Barth and from the classical Christian tradition on this point.

13. Barth, *Church Dogmatics*, II.1, 554.
14. Kaufman, *Jesus and Creativity*, 55.

Perhaps more importantly from the point of view of criteria internal to Kaufman's theology, it would seem that the capacity of his interpretation of God to orient persons and communities in the world has diminished. The movement toward a Marcionite disjunction if not separation of power and goodness means that Kaufman's notion of goodness—"humanization"—has in effect been secularized. While the humane trajectory embodied in Jesus is identified by certain values connected with the proper exercise of human agency and therefore crucial for proper orientation in the world, these values are not connected in any fundamental way with the reality of God. God may be said to support them in the sense that they are among the various features of the world to which creativity gives rise, but they enjoy no privileged status outside of their existential import for us. In other words, humaneness as a trajectory within the welter of cosmic happenings is no more central to divine creativity than are gravitation, entropy, etc. This means that a viable concept of God can actually tell us nothing about what the human good is. This difficulty is not Kaufman's alone, but appears in other austere forms of theocentric theology. If God is not, as James Gustafson admits, in some sense the "guarantee" of the human good,[15] we are dangerously close to saying that the good must be both defined and defended outside of the sphere of faith in God. In the end, the more God and the human good are separated, the more we are left on our own to decide what the human good is. For Kaufman, this dynamic has been pressed further than Gustafson, so that the norm we are obliged to follow in order to secure the prospects for human flourishing is finally self-referential, having to do with our survival in an ultimately precarious world.

Is there a way, within this perspective, to avoid this unattractive outcome? I am not prepared to rule out the possibility, and will return to it later. First, I will consider another angle on the problem that I have been analyzing here that develops this charge of secularization a bit further.

ECOLOGY, GLOBALIZATION, AND APOCALYPSE

Kaufman' theology since *Theology for a Nuclear Age* is developed against the backdrop of apocalyptic threats. The first to be addressed is the possibility of destroying human life by means of a nuclear exchange. This possibility, he urges, puts humanity in a fundamentally new situation:

15. Gustafson, *Ethics*, 271–72.

we now have the capacity to destroy ourselves. In the heightened responsibility for the human future that this elevated degree of power entails,
it is dangerous to think of God as a sovereign agent who guarantees
felicitous outcomes. More recently, Kaufman has stressed the possibility of environmental meltdown and thus the destruction of the ecology
necessary to sustain human life, again by means of our actions. Both
of these scenarios are apocalyptic in the sense that in them the human
future is abruptly cut off by the nemesis of human action gone awry.

If the history-ending possibilities which haunt Kaufman's theology
are apocalyptic, however, the redemptive possibilities he holds forth are
markedly anti-apocalyptic. The central point of *Theology for a Nuclear
Age* is that God is not coming to rescue us from our self-destruction. We
must rescue ourselves. This perspective continues through his mature
theology, and in fact is in many ways the substantive theme which unites
Kaufman's program from the late seventies through his most recent efforts. The irony is that a theology which ends by associating God with
power understood independently from goodness also and to that very
degree places human beings in control of their own destiny. It is ironic,
but of course far from illogical. For if divine creativity does not privilege
or guarantee human good, we are left on our own to secure it for ourselves. Christologically speaking, Jesus illumines the way that this can be
done, but does not reveal the heart of the divine ruler of the universe.

In apocalypse, human freedom is spinning out control and requires
divine intervention to institute a form of justice which originates with
and is defended by God Godself. In Kaufman's anti-apocalypse, justice
is secured by human beings shoring up the prospects for the ongoing
exercise of agency, or else justice is marginalized and suppressed, and
we allow the social and ecological fabric of human action to unravel.
In apocalypse, history is poisoned and needs rescue; in anti-apocalypse,
history is threatened anti-historical (anti-agential) powers, and needs to
rescue itself.

This dynamic of apocalyptic threat and anti-apocalyptic resolution
or rescue plays out vividly in Kaufman's interpretation of globalization. Eschewing the cultural relativism which characterized nineteenth
century forms of historicism and continues to influence contemporary
conversations about ethics, culture and politics both within and between
cultures, Kaufman argues that we need to find ways to forge broad agreement on issues of value and meaning because we are in the process of

becoming a single world through burgeoning communications technol-
ogies, economic interdependence, and the rapidity of cultural exchange.
We need agreement, however, not only to maximize possibilities resident
in globalization. On the contrary, cultural exchange opens the way for
more profound cultural contests. The specter of conflict looms amid the
heightening buzz of communication and exchange. Pressures driving us
toward a single interconnected world seem be placing us on a collision
course with each other. We may not, Kaufman reflects, survive much
longer in a situation of such unprecedented global volatility. Nuclear
holocaust and environmental devastation, possibly along with other,
untold horrors, lurk just below the horizon.[16]

But the resolution of this apocalyptic possibility, for Kaufman, is
not retreat to more isolated national or yet more local communities.
Rather, the solution is to embrace globalization and to seek to deepen
it further. Rather than retiring to private or sectarian enclaves, we are
to engage more rigorously in public discourse across traditions in order
to formulate a shared frame of reference in order to adjudicate disputes
and provide normative roadmaps toward a more humane world.[17]

Theology has no special competence to judge the merits of
Kaufman's hopes for a more robust and humanized process of globalization. Much would appear to depend upon global political, economic, and
perhaps religious developments which theology has no power to predict.
But how may we assess the anti-apocalypticism which undergirds it? As
I mentioned above, it clearly places human destiny in human hands to a
degree that would not been countenanced in the classical Christian tradition. As the nemesis which threatens history is a feature of history itself,
classical theology looks beyond history rather than within it for salvation. If history is broken, it requires healing rather than intensification.[18]

By raising questions about Kaufman's anti-apocalypticism, I am
not suggesting that old fashioned apocalypse is better, or is a more accurate or more pragmatic way of construing the human situation. Far
from it: I am simply querying whether the apocalyptic/anti-apocalyptic

16. Kaufman, *In the Beginning*, 45.

17. Kaufman, *Jesus and Creativity*, 105–9.

18. Of course, in the sort of classical theology which features a heavy dose of
Christology, one does not look toward the placid beyond of a second layer of reality on
top of this one or toward an eternal realm, but rather the beyond which is within history
(in fact at its heart) in the form of the cross of Christ. More about this will be said in the
final section of this chapter.

dynamic with which Kaufman joins issue throughout much of his theological work is ultimately a felicitous way of approaching God's relation
to the world. Why are threats the privileged locus for deciding the issue
of God's involvement in history? Is it true that apocalyptic threats fundamentally alter the theological situation? If, as Kaufman himself insists,
the internal logic of "God" includes relativization, how is that the threat
of human annihilation—even at our own hands—changes anything?
Why not just assume that the human project has a finite period of time
in which to carry itself forward, and that human failure to secure its
future is an ineluctable feature of our species mortality? It seems just as
plausible, in other words, to interpret threats under the aegis of more
fundamental relation of God signified by symbols of creation and ordering, for example, as it is to allow particular moments of existential threat
to reshape interpretations of God's relation to the world.

One way to get out from under the pressure of apocalyptic scenarios is to ask whether there is a way to connect the human good with
something larger—some larger, more inclusive order of value—than the
survival of the capacity for action (i.e., the "humanizing" trajectory). Does
human agency properly serve some end that has nothing in principle to
do with the continuation of the capacity to act? On Kantian grounds,
of course, it is somewhat hard to see how it could be so, and Kaufman's
theological anthropology follows the Kantian line. In order make this
clear, it will be necessary to digress for a moment to the topic of human
action in Kaufman's major work.

The central feature of human life, for Kaufman, is the power to act.
The account of agency he offers in *In Face of Mystery*, therefore, does
more than describe—it provides a central norm around which human
life ought to be organized. Like some action-theorists in recent moral
philosophy,[19] Kaufman develops a relatively comprehensive ethic out of
an interpretation of the capacity to act. The first responsibility of human
beings, he argues, is deliberately to take hold of our powers rather than
to shrink from them. Since this first norm (or, as he styles it, "categori-
cal imperative") is derived more or less deductively from his account
of personhood, it is not relative to circumstances.[20] Kaufman can wax
eloquent, however, about the ways in which our modern world both
demands and encourages with special urgency that this imperative be

19. See, for example, Gewirth, *Reason and Morality*.
20. Kaufman, *In Face of Mystery*, 201–2.

followed.[21] A corollary responsibility, he argues, as that we act "morally."[22] By this he means that it is incumbent upon us as moral agents to act in ways that support, rather than constrain or curtail, what Kaufman calls the "fabric of agency." In order for our capacities to act freely to be maintained and enhanced, in other words, the underlying conditions which make free action possible need to be protected—or, in cultures where they do not exist, developed. Finally, he argues, we are obliged to act "ethically," or to act in ways that can withstand rational scrutiny in light of the wider meaning one's actions have for local contexts and for the entire human community.[23]

Kaufman calls the ethic he develops on the basis of these three imperatives an "ecological ethic."[24] The terminology may appear strange, since the natural, largely nonhuman, natural environment which we now ordinarily connect with the word "ecology" does not play a significant role in his ethical reflections. For Kaufman, however, "ecological" signifies not so much the field of ethical inquiry, as what we might call the metaethical apparatus that underlies his explicit normative ethic.[25] It is "ecological" in large part because the moral imperatives it articulates are grounded in an "ecology," a context of human life that is ordered in a particular way. It appears that in *In Face of Mystery*, as we saw earlier, the world, or field of human action, is ordered toward human flourishing. And, since the most significant feature of human life is the capacity to act, acting in ways that enhance rather than constrict or diminish this capacity for oneself and for other is in sync with the way the actual world works. For this reason, Kaufman can talk about agency-supporting ac-

---

21. The increased agential powers of persons, and of the entire human community, in the modern world is in some respects, for Kaufman, a fuller realization of human being than was possible in the pre-modern world. Reading *Theology for a Nuclear Age*, for example, leaves one with the distinct impression that the peril of nuclear self-destruction represents for Kaufman the almost inevitable crisis of humanity coming of age.

22. Kaufman, *In Face of Mystery*, 203–5.

23. Ibid., 206–7.

24. The title of chapter 14 of *In Face of Mystery* (194–209).

25. I am relying upon a traditional distinction in philosophical ethics between *normative* ethics, or the attempt to elaborate a moral theory of the "good" or the "right," and *metaethics*, or the attempt to address the metaphysical or epistemological status of "good" or "right" language. I am characterizing "ecological" as a metaethical term in Kaufman because I believe that for him it makes a theologically important connection between moral norms and a metaphysic in the form of an account of divine ordering.

tivity as not merely supportive of a humanly-constructed contract, but as a "fitting" response to the way God has ordered the world.[26]

Now, to reiterate the critical question, this time in refracted form: Is there a larger order, one which cannot be invoked as a support for (or strand within) the fabric of human agency, to which human beings are properly responsible? Is there meaning to the notion of "fitting" human response to the realities that environ us which is not reducible to that which contributes either directly or indirectly to the capacity to act? And, if there is, may it be that the human good can in fact be understood in those terms? May the notion of human flourishing include the prospect of service to some larger reality that does not depend upon human survival? These are indeed hard questions. We should note, however, that, given a central place for humanization amid the richness of divine creativity, these questions do not arise with quite the same urgency, and one can talk comfortably about the "fit" between responsiveness to the world and support of human survival. But, when and as humanization as a trend within divine creativity is marginalized, they become unavoidable, and Kaufman's recent moves toward acknowledging the marginal status of the trajectory of humanization call for clarification on this point. To restate my worry: it is difficult to see how Kaufman can answer them within a framework which derives value from an interpretation of the capacity to act.

What would it take in order to provide an answer? It would seem, at minimum, to require a more straightforwardly ecological ethic—that is, one which features goods inhering in the wider fabric of nature whose integrity can be appreciated and supported without invoking human interests. Kaufman's ethic acknowledges the ecological nature of human agency: that its prospects are dependent upon a wider context which includes not only social conditions but conditions of nature as well. What it does not allow for, however, is the notion that human excellence or virtue involves commitment to the intrinsic rather than merely

---

26. Kaufman, *In Face of Mystery*, 208. Kaufman deliberately borrows from his teacher H. Richard Niebuhr on this point. For the latter's theocentric interpretation of morality, actions are "fitting" when they respond appropriately to the (divinely ordered) environment in which they originate. Interestingly, Kaufman's own more precise account of what God is doing (how God is ordering the world), presses the notion of "fitting" toward a more precise normative content. If God is humanizing activity, "fitting" actions are those which serve human flourishing. Niebuhr's moral theology had no mechanism for (nor, presumably, interest in) supporting such a definite specification of "fitting."

instrumental value of nonhuman goods—toward nature, for example, not just as the system of support for human capacities, but as an aspect of creation that commands our loyalty and respect for its own sake. It is interesting in this connection that Kaufman cites Jonathan Edwards' notion of "true virtue" as "benevolence to being in general."[27] While it is clear that Kaufman's theology provides warrants for piety or reverence toward "being in general" (the mystery of creativity), it is not clear, actually, that it supports moral commitment or loyalty ("benevolence") toward being in general.

To see the difference, we need to consider whether there are scenarios in which supporting particular features of the created order may suppress or limit the development of human capacities. Take the following, admittedly somewhat artificial, example: A local community is situated adjacent to a vital section of wetlands which several endangered species are known to inhabit. The local elementary school is crumbling, and lacks the technological infrastructure properly to equip its students with computer skills they need to succeed at the next level. Let us stipulate that there are no good locations for building a new school within the geographical area proximate to the community other than the wetlands. The community is forced to choose between building the new school and preserving the crucial wetlands. Without judging the outcome of this difficult decision (Of course it is to be admitted that in real situations there are likely to be ways out of the dilemma, even if they require greater expenditure of public funds.), we may ask whether there are theological reasons which may support a conservationist decision—not in the abstract (under a principle of "preserving God's creation"), but in the particular choice to suppress the enhancement of human agency for a group of people for the sake of preserving a portion of the natural environment which will do little or nothing to pay the human community back in terms of prospects for human flourishing.

Acknowledging a wider order of goods to which human beings are subject would perhaps be morally perilous for Kaufman, because it would tend to scatter motivation too broadly. It may induce us to take our eyes of the ball, as it were, desensitizing us to the hazards we face. Nevertheless, it is theologically important because it places the human prospect within a broader normative frame of reference, inclusive of creation as a whole. The human good presses beyond survival,

---

27. Kaufman, *In Face of Mystery*, 458.

toward self-expenditure in the service of wider purposes. In classical terms, human beings stand before God (*coram deo*). We are, as Jürgen Moltmann puts it, priests amid the created order, representing God before creation and the created order before God.[28] We have an important (perhaps irreplaceable) role to play, and yet our role is not self-referential, but oriented toward the well-being of the whole created order. Within this frame of reference, the force of apocalyptic scenarios is blunted, because less is at stake, theologically, in the continuation of the human project. Nuclear holocaust or environmental catastrophe would indeed be horrific, but perhaps neither would amount to a "disaster" or "enormous setback" for God.[29] More to the point, the prospective end of the trajectory of humanization within the broader array of trajectories, while catastrophic from a human point of view, is not incapable of being interpreted theologically. Nor does it render the human project meaningless: coming to an end, even badly, does not mean that the whole enterprise has not been worthwhile. And in any case, will it not be the case that God remains God?

Implicit here is a suggestion that we may fruitfully rethink the meaning of "humanization." The fulfillment of human being need not mean the maximization of human agency, but could mean responsiveness to the wider order of value inhering in or resulting from divine creativity. Humanity can fulfill itself—can be "humanized"—precisely in diminishing its capacities for the sake of a more inclusive end. In more traditional terms, the "purpose" of human beings is to "glorify God" and to "enjoy [God] forever."[30] The true fulfillment of human being, in other words, lies not in the maximization of human capacities, but in the service of a larger set of purposes which cannot be reduced to any sphere of value smaller than the "glory of God."

This is as much as to say that human beings may be understood christologically rather than understanding Jesus, as Kaufman seems to do despite his theocentrism, humanistically. That is, rather than construing Jesus as the brightest example of the trajectory toward humaneness which can be perceived on the basis of an anthropology constructed independently from christological insight, we may construe human being and its fulfillment in a cruciform manner, after the pattern of events

28. Moltmann, *God in Creation*, 220.
29. Kaufman, *Theology for a Nuclear Age*, 45.
30. Westminster Shorter Catechism, question 1.

narrated in the gospels but also broadly consistent with and even deeply informed by contemporary insight and experience, and in such a way that the human good is seen in its service (and perhaps suffering for) a wider array of values. In Christ, as H. Richard Niebuhr once noted, we find the highest ideals of power and love turned on their heads and are asked to acknowledge that true humanization may occur precisely as agential capacities are diminished or lost (i.e., in death).

To explore the point further, I want to return explicitly to the question of Christology and ask whether different moves here may provide the opportunity to avoid some of the less felicitous outcomes of Kaufman's theology within the strictures in which it operates. Actually, as may be evident, my suggestion is already prepared for by my previous comments about the meaning of "humanization." If humanization means service, perhaps even to the point of suppression of one's own capacities, then a Christology which features a heavy emphasis upon the ironic power of Christ's suffering seems to suggest itself.

Indeed, it seems that one may include a more robust doctrine of Atonement than Kaufman offers without violating his method. Of course, in order to do so one has to disengage the doctrine from the reifying conceptuality which depicts God as needing some sort of sacrifice in order to resume loving relations with humankind. But, once removed from that context, there is no apparent methodological reason why diminishment and death may not taken as instruments of larger creative trajectories. We need not venture far from Kaufman to find resources. His Yale mentor, H. Richard Niebuhr, for example, offered a vicarious interpretation of the Atonement which attempted to invoke the picture of Christ's innocent suffering in order to render an illuminating perspective upon the experienced realities of human history. The cross, according to Niebuhr, yields a perspective upon God's redemptive activity which enables the believer to regard those who innocently suffer at the hands of others in a distinctive way. They are neither tangible signs of a morally rational universe (people getting what they deserve) nor concrete proof that history is morally arbitrary; rather, they are to be seen as the bearers of the cost of sin which is enacted by the guilty. They are the means by which God calls the sins of creaturely life to account. This was an important affirmation for Niebuhr, since it meant that God the Redeemer could therefore be seen even in the brutalities of indiscriminate warfare during the bombing raids on European cities during the

Second World War.[31] The vicarious suffering of Christ thereby illumines God's redemptive relation to the world. Once again, humanly orienting answers to questions about what God is doing (where creativity is going) in the world can be sharpened by Christology without overtaxing the prospects for successful human agency. Indeed, in Niebuhr's interpretation of the Atonement, God's redemptive activity is most luminously active not in the willful obedience of the good, but in the uninvited suffering of those whose agency is deprived.

What does this accomplish, specifically within Kaufman's program? An obvious objection here is that the notion of a transcendent purpose being imposed upon human history from beyond raises all of the difficulties Kaufman has worked so hard to dismantle. But, although Niebuhr did not himself seem to envision such a move, is it possible to reconstruct what is most illuminating about Niebuhr's view of the Atonement without appealing to transcendent purposes imposed from beyond? I believe it is. What we need, first of all, is some way of accounting for the ways in which agencies may accomplish more or at least other from what they intend, generating a trajectory out of a disorganized, perhaps conflicting, set of interests and aims on the part of many (relatively) independent agents. The order or perhaps "purpose" would have to arise from the interaction between the agents rather than being imposed from the outside. This, we will recall, is just what Kaufman means by "serendipity."

Kaufman's resource for attributing serendipity to nature and history seems simply to be something akin to historical observation. It turns out that, upon inspection, things happen that amount to more than what might have been expected on the basis of studying the materials out of which the present and future are cobbled together by history. I believe this observation may be specified and perhaps deepened by contemporary complexity theory. According to the work of theoretical biologist Stuart Kauffman and his colleagues at the Santa Fe Institute, the emergence of complex forms of organization from simple, random or disorganized things may reflect as yet poorly understood laws of nature rather than mere random chance. The universe itself generates order out of any number of regimes of chaos which are characterized by randomly situated and often conflicted agencies. Kauffman calls this

31. Niebuhr, "War as Crucifixion," 63–70.

"order for free,"[32] and the important point for a theological perspective like Kaufman's is that there is no need to posit an external, transcendent agency in order to account for the fact that the world we experience seems to be capable of generating various forms of (serendipitous) order out of individuals bent on their own interests.

We need, secondly, a way of making use of the theory of complexity to interpret the specific operation of atonement as understood by Niebuhr. Such a device would give us the "how" of Atonement without appealing to an external agency. For example, we may reason in the following way: Undeserved human suffering at the hands of other human beings is a sort of moral chaos. There is something like a moral order governing historical events which generally rewards goodness and punishes evil. We may think of this in crudely prudential terms: some sorts of action are seen by one's peers as laudable and thus increase social prestige and therefore power; others are seen as deplorable and thus undermine social standing. But there are on the other hand numerous occasions in which human events exceed or otherwise fail to conform to this identifiable moral logic. Laudable action is disconnected from reward and deplorable action fails to yield the expected punishment. Undeserved suffering vividly portrays the breakdown, or perhaps just absence, of moral order. And yet, the regime of moral chaos or disorder which comes to light in cases of undeserved suffering is not necessarily self-perpetuating, in the way that entropic states are "frozen" and thus hinder transformation toward states of order. Rather, regimes of moral chaos in human history are inhabited by pockets of order in the form of consciences which are aroused by indignation or by guilt. That is to say, the being-felt of felt imbalances is already an ordering force which mitigates the rule of chaos. One might say the situation of moral chaos, when considered whole, is never in human history entirely chaotic, but is composed of a mixture or perhaps uneven assortment of chaotic and orderly elements. Occasionally, the two sorts of elements are poised in just such a way (in Kauffman's terms, at the "edge of chaos"[33]) that their interaction yields the emergence of new forms of order.

The civil rights struggle of the 1960s in the United States is a striking example. The protagonists of the struggle were motivated by a profound sense of unfairness rooted in the brutal contradictions be-

32. Kauffman, *At Home in the Universe*, 71.
33. Ibid., 86.

tween religious and political rhetoric about freedom and equality and the lived experience of African-Americans in the segregated South. The struggle itself constituted an "edge" between the organized system of law and precedent, together with a system of social relations and political arrangements that appeared to be intractable or even frozen, and the explosive frustration of oppressed persons. The borderland between order and chaos was powerfully and visually revealed in the marches and nonviolent protests, in which the volatility of the contradiction was not contained within the protest movement in the form of rage, but was channeled into the frozen system of law and order itself, resulting in untenable and unsustainable brutalities. Conscience was aroused, and out of this fertile mixture of order and chaos emerged a new order of law and precedent, and, slowly, a new set of social relationships and even a new image and identity for the South (the "new South").

When this kind of radical turnaround happens, we may say that what Kauffman calls a "phase transition" has occurred. The term "phase transition" is drawn from physics, where it indicates a change, for example, between solid to liquid or vice-versa. In Kauffman's usage, a phase transition is what happens when a fertile mixture of orderly and chaotic elements within an environment of human action spontaneously generates a new level of order, and the system of interactions is held together by an emergent logic which changes the basic character of the whole.[34] A theologian may see in the phase transition which characterized the civil rights struggle and other momentous historical changes an irreducibly theological component. What happens when conscience is raised through the vivid display of the racist system's brutality is *repentance*. One sees that the previous order of life was untenable both in moral and in pragmatic terms: it cannot stand. One is struck, additionally and more pointedly, by one's own participation and culpability in the maintenance and support of the old regime: I hold the firehose. One gains a sense, finally, of the twilight of the system of social and cultural meaning that held life together in the past: the old gods of clan and race cannot be trusted anymore. The cost for devotion to them is too great, and the dangers of anarchy as the flimsy order unravels are too real.

Note that in this use of complexity theory the scientific account of emergent orders does not absorb the doctrine of atonement whole. Interpretation runs the other way as well. Symbols of atonement un-

34. Ibid., 56.

earth a moment or a node within a natural matrix of order, disorder, and emergent ordering by which to interpret the process as a whole. The cross underscores the costs to be paid for change in social as well as natural orders. The generation of emergent forms of order is not simply an automatic or semi-automatic process, if by that we mean that they evolve easily and smoothly out of previous states. The clash of contending forces at the edge of chaos, rather, produces a rupture, a break, even a death. New orders emerge, graciously, ironically, often without the benefit of our foresight or planning,[35] but they do so at great cost to ourselves and to those who suffer at the hands of the orders that crumble away.

So again, what does this appeal to Niebuhr, now with an assist from contemporary complexity theory, actually accomplish in terms of the problematics I have identified in Kaufman's theology? For one thing, it incorporates the complexity of creativity within the sphere of the human, enabling us to view historical life as directional without being self-directing, and without being directed by a supernatural, anthropomorphically-conceived agent. It brings into sharper focus what we may call the tragic dimension of human agency, which is only a special form of the tragic aspect of life, which always brings about consequences it does not control nor can it intend. In theological terms, since the tragic results of this creativity within human affairs effectuate possibilities for repentance and renewal, we may say that human history is a bearer of costly grace. Exercising agency is salvific, or at least is a participant in a salvific drama, but not at all in the way expected.

Secondly, and closely related, it enables to view creativity as indeed operational within human agency, but not reduced to it. There is a definite *more* to divine creativity than self-directing agency, a "more" which surrounds, undergirds, shakes, contradicts, drives, even cajoles it, no matter what intentions may be visualized or expressed. This means that realizing our humanity means both more and less than maximizing agency. Humanization includes what Hegel once called the "labor of the negative"[36]: limitation, contradiction, and death. In the cruciform picture of humanization that emerges here, becoming human means service to a wider order of creativity that limits and redirects as well as supports

35. Indeed, as Reinhold Niebuhr argued, beneficial orders may arise in spite of our inability to seen them and our collective unwillingness to strive toward them. See Niebuhr, *The Irony of American History*, 151–74.

36. Hegel, *Phenomenology of Spirit*, 50–51.

it. Therefore, the movement of creativity in the historical realm is seen as embodied in wide array of human conditions and levels of conscious participation.

Thirdly, appropriating symbols of atonement clarifies and sharpens Kaufman's model of creativity in the natural order. It is not that vicarious suffering has to be seen quite literally under every bush, but that creativity has to be understood as of the sort of character which produces vicarious redemptive suffering in the historical realm. If humanization-as-agency is marginalized by the impinging realities both within and around human history, humanization-as-crucifixion is quite at home in the rather terrifying world of predation, the sudden and catastrophic collapse of populations, and the like. Creativity, in other words, has what may appear to us as a dark underside, both within human life and beyond it, but which is not devoid of theological value.

Obviously, the gains here come with their own costs. Not the least of which is the evocation of violent event which has never simply indicated the cost of progress but which has fundamentally disturbed the very idea of God. But it is offered here as an admittedly unlikely but, I believe, singularly effective way of refreshing and deepening Kaufman's project. With this resource, I suggest, the project of a naturalized Trinity, a Trinitarian way of construing ourselves and the world, need not pass away from the project Kaufman has been envisioning. Costly creativity and the work of the Redeemer, under the sign of the cross, can be seen as one great sweep of divine activity.

And, at the methodological level which has been the primary preoccupation of this book, neither need the project of an empirically responsive and theologically distinctive way of construing life in the world be given up. Again, and always with new resources and insights, the interminable conversation of theology continues.

Bibliography

Alston, William P. "Realism and the Christian Faith." *International Journal for Philosophy of Religion* 38 (1995) 37–60.

Augustine, Saint. *Concerning the City of God against the Pagans.* Translated by Henry Bettenson. Penguin Classics. New York: Penguin, 1972.

———. *The Trinity.* Edited by John E. Rotelle. Translated by Edmund Hill. The Works of Saint Augustine, part 1, vol. 5. New York: New City, 1991.

Balthasar, Hans Urs von. *The Theology of Karl Barth.* Translated by John Drury. New York: Holt, Rinehart and Winston, 1971.

Barrow, John D., and Frank J. Tipper. *The Anthropic Cosmological Principle.* Oxford Paperbacks. Oxford: Oxford University Press, 1988.

Barth, Karl. *Church Dogmatics.* Vol. 1.1, *The Doctrine of the Word of God, Part 1.* Translated G. W. Bromiley. Edinburgh: T. & T. Clark, 1975.

———. *Church Dogmatics.* Vol. 2.2, *The Doctrine of God, Part 2.* Translated by G. W. Bromiley. Edinburgh: T. & T. Clark, 1957.

———. *Church Dogmatics.* Vol. 3.3, *The Doctrine of Creation, Part 3.* Translated by G. W. Bromiley. Edinburgh: T. & T. Clark, 1960.

———. *The Epistle to the Romans.* Translated by Edwyn C. Hoskyns. 6th ed. London: Oxford University Press, 1950.

———. *The Word of God and the Word of Man.* Translated by Douglas Horton. New York: Harper & Row, 1957.

Beilby, James. "An Evaluation of Gordon Kaufman's Theological Proposal." *American Journal of Philosophy and Theology* 20 (1999) 123–46.

Braithewaite, R. B. "An Empiricist's View of the Nature of Religious Belief." In *The Philosophy of Religion*, edited by Basil Mitchell, 72–91. Oxford Readings in Philosophy. Oxford: Oxford University Press, 1971.

Brown, Delwin. "Mystery and History in Kaufman's Theology." *Journal of the American Academy of Religion* 62 (1994) 1209–18.

Burhoe, Ralph Wendell. "Prophesying Human Values." In *Science and Human Values in the Twenty-First Century*, 11–33. Philadelphia: Westminster, 1971.

———. "A Scientific View of the Role of Religion." In *Science and Human Values in the Twenty-First Century*, 135–60. Philadelphia: Westminster, 1971.

———. "Some Prophecies of Twenty-First-Century Technology and Religion." In *Science and Human Values in the Twenty-First Century*, 34–56. Philadelphia: Westminster, 1971.

———. *Toward a Scientific Theology.* Belfast: Christian Journals Limited, 1981.

Calvin, John. *Commentary on the Book of Psalms*, vol. 1. Translated by James Anderson. Grand Rapids: Baker, 2003.

———. *Institutes of the Christian Religion.* Translated by Ford Lewis Battles. Edited by John T. McNeill. 2 vols. Philadelphia: Westminster, 1960.

Cobb, John B., Jr. "Human Historicity, Cosmic Creativity and the Theological Imagination: Reflections on the Work of Gordon D. Kaufman." *Religious Studies Review* 20 (1994) 171–77.

———. "In Defense of Realism." In *Theology at the End of Modernity: Essays in Honor of Gordon D. Kaufman*, edited by Sheila Greeve Davaney, 179–200. Philadelphia: Trinity, 1991.

———. "Natural Causality and Divine Action." *Idealistic Studies* 3 (1973) 207–22.

Cobb, John B., Jr., and David Ray Griffin. *Process Theology: An Introductory Exposition.* Philadelphia: Westminster, 1976.

Collingwood, R. G. *An Essay on Metaphysics.* Edited with an introduction by Rex Martin. Revised ed. Oxford: Clarendon, 1998.

Cook, Martin L. *The Open Circle: Confessional Method in Theology.* Minneapolis: Fortress, 1991.

Davaney, Sheila Greeve. "Directions in Historicism: Language, Experience, and Pragmatic Adjudication." In *New Essays in Religious Naturalism*, edited by W. Creighton Peden and Larry E. Axel, 49–66. Highlands Institute Series 2. Macon, GA: Mercer University Press, 1993.

———. *Pragmatic Historicism: A Theology for the Twenty-First Century.* Albany: SUNY Press, 2000.

Dean, William. "Humanistic Historicism and Naturalistic Historicism." In *Theology at the End of Modernity: Essays in Honor of Gordon D. Kaufman*, edited by Sheila Greeve Davaney, 41–60. Philadelphia: Trinity, 1991.

———. "The Persistence of Experience: A Commentary on Kaufman's Theology." In *New Essays in Religious Naturalism*, edited by W. Creighton Peden and Larry E. Axel 67–82. Highlands Institute Series 2. Macon, GA: Mercer University Press, 1993.

Degler, Carl N. *In Search of Human Nature: The Decline and Revival of Darwinism in American Social Thought.* New York: Oxford University Press, 1991.

Dewey, John. *A Common Faith.* The Terry Lectures. New Haven: Yale University Press, 1934.

Drees, Willem B. *Religion, Science, and Naturalism.* Cambridge: Cambridge University Press, 1996.

Dyson, Freeman. *Infinite in All Directions: Gifford Lectures Given at Aberdeen, Scotland, April–November 1985.* New York: Harper & Row, 1988.

Edwards, Jonathan. *The Works of Jonathan Edwards.* Revised and Corrected by Edward Hickman. 2 vols. Edinburgh: Banner of Truth Trust, 1974.

Farley, Edward. *Divine Empathy: A Theology of God.* Minneapolis: Fortress, 1996.

———. *Ecclesial Man: A Social Phenomenology of Faith and Reality.* Philadelphia: Fortress, 1975.

Farrer, Austin. *Faith and Speculation: An Essay in Philosophical Theology.* London: Black, 1967.

Ferré, Frederick. "Unfazed by Mystery." *Zygon* 29 (1994) 363–70.

Finger, Thomas. "Relativity, Normativity, and Imagination." In *Mennonite Theology in Face of Modernity: Essays in Honor of Gordon D. Kaufman*, edited by Alain Epp Weaver, 204–23. Cornelius H. Wedel Historical Series 9. North Newton, KS: Bethel College, 1996.

Fiorenza, Francis Schüssler. "The Crisis of Hermeneutics and Christian Theology." In *Theology at the End of Modernity: Essays in Honor of Gordon D. Kaufman*, edited by Sheila Greeve Davaney, 117–40. Philadelphia: Trinity, 1991.

Friesen, Duane. "Toward a Theology of Culture: A Dialogue with Gordon Kaufman." In *Mennonite Theology in Face of Modernity*, edited by Alain Epp Weaver, 95–114. Cornelius H. Wedel Historical Series 9. North Newton, KS: Bethel College, 1996.

Geering, Lloyd. *Christianity without God*. Santa Rosa, CA: Polebridge, 2002.

Gewirth, Alan. *Reason and Morality*. Chicago: University of Chicago Press, 1978.

Gilkey, Langdon. "Cosmology, Ontology, and the Travail of Biblical Language." *Journal of Religion* 41 (1961) 194–205.

———. *Naming the Whirlwind: The Renewal of God-Language*. Indianapolis: Bobbs-Merrill, 1969.

———. *Nature, Reality, and the Sacred: The Nexus of Science and Religion*. Theology and the Sciences. Minneapolis: Fortress, 1993.

———. *Reaping the Whirlwind: A Christian Interpretation of History*. New York: Seabury, 1976.

Gordis, Robert. "Ecology and the Judaic Tradition." In *Moral Issues: Philosophical and Religious Perspective*, edited by Gabriel Palmer-Fernandez, 459–65. Upper Saddle River, NJ: Prentice Hall, 1996.

Gould, Stephen J. *The Panda's Thumb: More Reflections in Natural History*. New York: Norton, 1980.

Gustafson, James M. *Ethics from a Theocentric Perspective*, Vol. 1, *Theology and Ethics*. Chicago: University of Chicago Press, 1981.

———. *An Examined Faith: The Grace of Self-Doubt*. Warfield Lectures 2002. Minneapolis: Fortress, 2004.

———. *Intersections: Science, Theology, and Ethics*. Cleveland: Pilgrim, 1996.

———. "Theological Anthropology and the Human Sciences." In *Theology at the End of Modernity: Essays in Honor of Gordon D. Kaufman*, edited by Sheila Greeve Davaney, 61–77. Philadelphia: Trinity, 1991.

Hardwick, Charley. *Events of Grace: Naturalism, Existentialism, and Theology*. New York: Cambridge University Press, 1996.

———. "The Normative Argument for a Valuational Theism." In *New Essays in Religious Naturalism*, edited by W. Creighton Peden and Larry E. Axel, 99–110. Highlands Institute Series 2. Macon, GA: Mercer University Press, 1993.

Hartt, Julian N. "Encounter and Inference in Our Awareness of God." In *The God Experience: Essays in Hope*, edited by Joseph P. Whalen, SJ, 51–54. New York: Newman, 1971.

———. *Theological Method and the Imagination*. 1977. Reprinted, Eugene, OR: Wipf & Stock, 2006.

Harvey, Van Austin. "Feuerbach on Religion as Construction." In *Theology at the End of Modernity: Essays in Honor of Gordon D. Kaufman*, edited by Sheila Greeve Davaney, 249–68. Philadelphia: Trinity, 1991.

Hauerwas, Stanley. *Against the Nations: War and Survival in a Liberal Society*. Notre Dame: University of Notre Dame Press, 1992.

Hebblethwaite, Brian, and Edward Henderson, editors. *Divine Action: Studies Inspired by the Philosophical Theology of Austin Farrer*. Edinburgh: T. & T. Clark, 1990.

Hegel, G. W. F. *Phenomenology of Spirit*. Translated by A. V. Miller. Oxford: Oxford University Press, 1977.

Hick, John. *An Interpretation of Religion: Human Responses to the Transcendent*. New Haven: Yale University Press, 1989.

Holland, Scott. "*Einbildungskraft*: 1. Imagination, 2: The Power to Form into One." In *Mennonite Theology in Face of Modernity*, edited by Alain Epp Weaver, 244–54. North Newton, KS: Bethel College, 1996.

Huebner, Harry. "Imagination/Tradition: Disjunction or Conjunction?" In *Mennonite Theology in Face of Modernity*, edited by Alain Epp Weaver, 53–79. North Newton, KS: Bethel College, 1996.

Insole, Christopher. "Gordon Kaufman and the Kantian Mystery." *International Journal for Philosophy of Religion* 47 (2000) 101–19.

Irwin, Alec. "Face of Mystery, Mystery of a Face: An Anthropological Trajectory in Wittgenstein, Cavell, and Kaufman's Biohistorical Theology." *Harvard Theological Review* 88 (1995) 389–409.

James, William. *The Will to Believe and Other Essays on Popular Philosophy*. New York: Dover, 1956.

Jantzen, Grace. *God's World, God's Body*. Philadelphia: Westminster, 1984.

Jüngel, Eberhard. *God's Being Is in Becoming: The Trinitarian Being of God in the Theology of Karl Barth; A Paraphrase*. Translated by John Webster. Edinburgh: T. & T. Clark, 2001.

Kant, Immanual. *Critique of Pure Reason*. Translated by F. Max Müller. Anchor Books. Garden City, NY: Doubleday, 1966.

Kauffman, Stuart. *At Home in the Universe: The Search for the Laws of Self-Organization and Complexity*. New York: Oxford University Press, 1995.

Kaufman, Gordon D. "Apologia Pro Vita Sua." In *Why I Am a Mennonite: Essays on Mennonite Identity*, edited by Harry Loewen, 126–38. Kitchener, ON: Herald, 1988.

————. "The Christian and History: Structure or Process?" Review of *Reaping the Whirlwind: A Christian Interpretation of History*, by Langdon Gilkey. *Interpretation* 32 (1978) 194–96.

————. "Christian Education without Theological Foundations?" *Religious Education* 60 (1965) 15–18. Reprinted in *Radical Theology: Phase Two; Essays in a Continuing Discussion*, edited by C. W. Christian and Glen R. Wittig, 105–12. Philadelphia: Lippincott, 1967.

————. *The Context of Decision: A Theological Analysis*. New York: Abingdon, 1961.

————. "Conceptualizing Diversity Theologically." Review of *The Analogical Imagination: Christian Theology and the Culture of Pluralism*, by David Tracy. *Journal of Religion* 62 (1982) 392–401.

————. "Divine Power, Human Responsibility, and the Nuclear Threat." In *Readings in Christian Theology*, edited by Peter C. Hodgson and Robert H. King, 402–6. Philadelphia: Fortress, 1985.

————. "Doing Theology from a Liberal Christian Point of View." In *Doing Theology in Today's World: Essays in Honor of Kenneth S. Kantzer*, edited by John D. Woodbridge and Thomas Edward McComiskey, 397–415. Grand Rapids: Zondervan, 1991.

————. "Ecological Consciousness and the Symbol 'God.'" In *Christianity in the 21st Century*, edited by Deborah A. Brown, 72–95. New York: Crossroad, 2000.

————. "Empirical Realism in Theology: An Examination of the Some Themes in Meland and Loomer." In *New Essays in Religious Naturalism*, edited by W. Creighton Peden and Larry E. Axel, 135–60. Highlands Institute Series 2. Macon, GA: Mercer University Press, 1993.

————. "The Epic of Evolution as a Framework for Human Orientation in Life." *Zygon* 32 (1997) 175–88.

————. *An Essay on Theological Method.* AAR Studies in Religion 11. Missoula: Scholars, 1975.

————. *An Essay on Theological Method.* 3rd ed. Reflection and Theory in the Study of Religion 5. Atlanta: Scholars, 1995.

————. "'Evidentialism': A Theologian's Response." *Faith and Philosophy* 6 (1989) 35–46.

————. "Foreword." In *Theology at the End of Modernity: Essays in Honor of Gordon D. Kaufman,* edited by Sheila Greeve Davaney, ix–xii. Philadelphia: Trinity, 1991.

————. *God the Problem.* Cambridge: Harvard University Press, 1972.

————. *God, Mystery, Diversity: Christian Theology in a Pluralistic World.* Minneapolis: Fortress, 1996.

————. "God's Purposes in World History." *Pittsburgh Perspective* 9 (1968) 9–28.

————. "How Is *God* to Be Understood in a Theocentric Ethics?" In *James M. Gustafson's Theocentric Ethics: Interpretations and Assessments,* edited by Harlan R. Beckley and Charles M. Swezey, 13–37. Macon, GA: Mercer University Press, 1988.

————. *In Face of Mystery: A Constructive Theology.* Cambridge: Harvard University Press, 1993.

————. "The Influence of Feminist Theory on My Theological Work." *Journal of Feminist Studies in Religion* 7 (1991) 112–15.

————. "Is There Any Way from Athens to Jerusalem?" Review of *Foundations of Christian Faith,* by Karl Rahner. *Journal of Religion* 59 (1979) 340–46.

————. *In the Beginning—Creativity.* Minneapolis: Fortress, 2004.

————. *Jesus and Creativity.* Minneapolis: Fortress, 2006.

————. "The Mennonite Roots of My Theological Perspective." In *Mennonite Theology in Face of Modernity: Essays in Honor of Gordon D. Kaufman,* edited by Alain Epp Weaver, 1–19. North Newton, KS: Bethel College, 1996.

————. "Models of God: Is Metaphor Enough?" *Religion and Intellectual Life* 5 (1988) 11–18.

————. "My Life and My Theological Reflection: Two Central Themes." *American Journal of Theology and Philosophy* 22 (2001) 3–32.

————. "Mystery, Critical Consciousness, and Faith." In *The Rationality of Religious Belief: Essays in Honour of Basil Mitchell,* edited by William J. Abraham and Steven W. Holtzer, 53–70. Oxford: Clarendon, 1987.

————. "Nature, History, and God: Toward an Integrated Conceptualization." *Zygon* 27 (1992) 379–401.

————. *Nonresistance and Responsibility, and Other Mennonite Essays.* Newton, KS: Faith and Life, 1979.

————. "Nuclear Eschatology and the Study of Religion." *Journal of the American Academy of Religion* 51 (1983) 3–14.

————. "On Thinking of God as Serendipitous Creativity." *Journal of the American Academy of Religion* 69 (2001) 409–25.

————. "Philosophy of Religion and Christian Theology." *Journal of Religion* 37 (1957) 233–45.

————. "Philosophy of Religion: Subjective or Objective?" *Journal of Philosophy* 55 (1958) 57–70.

————. "A Problem for Theology: The Concept of Nature." *Harvard Theological Review* 65 (1972) 337–66.

————. "Reading Wittgenstein: Notes for Constructive Theologians." *Journal of Religion* 79 (1999) 404–21.

————. "Reconceiving God for a Nuclear Age." In *Knowing Religiously*, edited by Leroy S. Rouner, 133–52. Boston University Studies in Philosophy and Religion 7. Notre Dame: University of Notre Dame Press, 1985.

————. "Reconstructing the Concept of God: De-Reifying the Anthropomorphisms." In *The Making and Remaking of Christian Doctrine: Essays in Honour of Maurice Wiles*, 95–115. Oxford: Clarendon, 1993.

————. *Relativism, Knowledge, and Faith*. Chicago: University of Chicago Press, 1960.

————. Response to "The Christian Understanding of Human Suffering," by Langdon Gilkey. *Buddhist-Christian Studies* 5 (1985) 67–93.

————. Response to H. Victor Froese's "Gordon D. Kaufman's Theology 'Within the Limits of Reason Alone': A Review." *Conrad Grebel Review* 6 (1988) 26–28.

————. "Response to Hans Frei." In *The Legacy of H. Richard Niebuhr*, edited by Ronald F. Thiemann, 95–115. Harvard Theological Studies 36. Minneapolis: Fortress, 1991.

————. "Response to Ingersoll Lecture, 'The Psychedelic Mystical Experience in the Human Encounter with Death,' by Walter Pahnke." *Harvard Theological Review* 62 (1969) 26–32.

————. "Response to William Dean." *American Journal of Theology and Philosophy* 21 (2000) 73–77.

————. "A Response to William Klassen." *Mennonite Life* 52 (1997) 21–23.

————. Review of *The Being of God: Theology and the Experience of Truth*, by Robert P. Scharlemann. *Religious Studies Review* 9 (1983) 342–48.

————. Review of *Charles Peirce's Guess at the Riddle: Grounds for Human Significance*, by John K. Sheriff. *Mennonite Life* 50 (1995) 25–27.

————. Review of *Earth Might Be Fair*, by Ian G. Barbour. *Religious Education* 68 (1973) 525–27.

————. Review of *Ecclesial Man: A Social Phenomenology of Faith and Reality*, by Edward Farley; and *Blessed Rage for Order: The New Pluralism in Theology*, by David Tracy. *Religious Studies Review* 2 (1976) 7–13.

————. Review of *The Formation of Christian Understanding: An Essay in Theological Hermeneutics*, by Charles M. Wood. *New Review of Books in Religion* 11 (1982) 6.

————. Review of *God in History: Shapes of Freedom*, by Peter C. Hodgson. *Theology Today* 46 (1990) 442–44.

————. Review of *The Historian and the Believer: The Morality of Historical Knowledge and Christian Belief*, by Van A. Harvey. *Perkins School of Theology Journal* 20 (1966–1967) 45–47.

————. Review of *In Search of Deity: An Essay in Dialectical Theism*, by John Macquarrie. *Virginia Seminary Journal* (1986) 36.

————. Review of *Kant on History and Religion*, by Michel Despland. *Studies in Religion* 4 (1974–1975) 400–402.

————. Review of *The Nature of Doctrine: Religion and Theology in Postliberal Age*, by George Lindbeck. *Theology Today* 42 (1985) 240–41.

————. Review of *The Priestly Kingdom: Social Ethics as Gospel*, by John Howard Yoder. *Conrad Grebel Review* 4/1 (1986) 77–80.

————. Review of *Systematic Theology, vol. 3*, by Paul Tillich. *Harvard Divinity Bulletin* 28 (1964) 97.

————. Review of *Tradition and the Modern World: Reformed Theology in the Nineteenth Century*, by Brian A. Gerrish. *Theology Today* 36 (1979) 263–64.

————. Review of *The Uses of Scripture in Recent Theology*, by David H. Kelsey. *Interpretation* 30 (1976) 299–303.

————. "Some Reflections on a Theological Pilgrimage." *Religious Studies Review* 20 (1994) 177–81.

————. *Systematic Theology: A Historicist Perspective*. New York: Scribners, 1968.

————. "Theological Historicism as an Experiment in Thought." *The Christian Century*, March 2, 1966, 268–71.

————. *The Theological Imagination: Constructing the Concept of God*. Philadelphia: Westminster, 1981.

————. "Theology as a Public Vocation." In *The Vocation of the Theologian*, with an introduction and epilogue by Theodore W. Jennings Jr., 49–66. Philadelphia: Fortress, 1985.

————. *Theology for a Nuclear Age*. Philadelphia: Westminster, 1985.

————. "Theology, the Arts, and Theological Education." *Theological Education* 31 (1994) 13–21.

————. "What Shall We Do with the Bible?" *Interpretation* 25 (1971) 95–112.

Keener, Carl S. "Aspects of a Postmodern Paradigm for an Ecological Age." In *Mennonite Theology in Face of Modernity*, edited by Alain Epp Weaver, 115–33. North Newton, KS: Bethel College, 1996.

Klassen, William. "Mennonite Biblicism and Gordon Kaufman." *Mennonite Life* 52 (1997) 13–20.

Lindbeck, George A. *The Nature of Doctrine: Religion and Theology in a Postliberal Age*. Philadelphia: Westminster, 1984.

Mason, David R. "Can We Speculate on How God Acts?" *Journal of Religion* 57 (1977) 16–32.

————. "Selfhood, Transcendence, and the Experience of God." *Modern Theology* 3/4 (1987): 293–313.

McClendon, James W., Jr. "Four New Theologies: A Review Essay." *Perspectives in Religious Studies* 22 (1995) 183–91.

McCormack, Bruce L. "Divine Revelation and Human Imagination: Must We Choose between the Two?" *Scottish Journal of Theology* 37 (1984) 431–55.

McFague, Sallie. "Cosmology and Christianity: Implications of the Common Creation Story for Theology." In *Theology at the End of Modernity: Essays in Honor of Gordon D. Kaufman*, edited by Sheila Greeve Davaney, 19–40. Philadelphia: Trinity, 1991.

McLain, F. Michael. "On Theological Models." *Harvard Theological Review* 62 (1969) 155–87.

McLain, F. Michael, and W. Mark Richardson, editors. *Human and Divine Agency: Anglican, Catholic, and Lutheran Perspectives*. Lanham, MD: University Press of America, 1999.

Meland, Bernard E. *Fallible Forms and Symbols: Discourses on Method in a Theology of Culture*. Philadelphia: Fortress, 1976.

Midgley, Mary. *Beast and Man: The Roots of Human Nature*. Rev. ed. London: Routlege, 1995.

———. *Science as Salvation: A Modern Myth and Its Meaning*. London: Routledge, 1992.

Moltmann, Jürgen. *God in Creation: A New Theology of Nature and the Spirit of God*. Translated by Margaret Kohl. The Gifford Lectures 1984–1985. Minneapolis: Fortress, 1993.

———. *The Trinity and the Kingdom: The Doctrine of God*. Translated by Margaret Kohl. Minneapolis: Fortress, 1993.

Monod, Jacques. *Chance and Necessity: An Essay on the Natural Philosophy of Modern Biology*. Translated by Austryn Wainhouse. New York: Random House, 1972.

Morris, Thomas V. "Philosophers and Theologians at Odds." *Asbury Theological Journal* 44/2 (Fall 1989) 31–41.

Nagel, Thomas. *The View from Nowhere*. New York: Oxford University Press, 1986.

Niebuhr, H. Richard. *Radical Monotheism and Western Culture, with Supplementary Essays*. Library of Theological Ethics. Louisville: Westminster John Knox, 1993.

———. *Theology, History, and Culture: Major Unpublished Writings*. Edited by William Stacy Johnson. New Haven: Yale University Press, 1996.

———. "War as Crucifixion." In *War in the Twentieth Century: Sources in Theological Ethics*, edited by Richard B. Miller, 63–70. Library of Theological Ethics. Louisville: Westminster John Knox, 1992.

Niebuhr, Reinhold. *The Irony of American History*. New York: Scribners, 1952.

———. *Pious and Secular America*. New York: Scribners, 1958.

Ogden, Schubert M. *The Reality of God, and Other Essays*. Dallas: Southern Methodist University Press, 1992.

Ottati, Douglas F. *Meaning and Method in H. Richard Niebuhr's Theology*. Washington DC: University Press of America, 1982.

———. Review of *The Theological Imagination*. *Religious Studies Review* 9 (1983) 222–27.

Peacocke, Arthur R. "The Cost of New Life." In *The Work of Love: Creation as Kenosis*, edited by John Polkinghorne, 21–42. Grand Rapids: Eerdmans, 2001.

———. *Intimations of Reality: Critical Realism in Science and Religion*. Notre Dame: University of Notre Dame Press, 1984.

———. *Theology for a Scientific Age: Being and Becoming—Natural, Divine, and Human*. Enl. ed. Theology and the Sciences. Minneapolis: Fortress, 1993.

Peters, Karl E. "Pragmatically Defining the God Concepts of Henry Nelson Wieman and Gordon Kaufman." In *New Essays in Religious Naturalism*, edited by W. Creighton Peden and Larry E. Axel, 199–210. Highlands Institute Series 2. Macon, GA: Mercer University Press, 1993.

Placher, William C. "Thinking Our Way to the Ultimate Mystery." *The Christian Century* (May 19–26, 1993) 557–59, 561.

Polkinghorne, John. *Belief in God in an Age of Science*. The Terry Lectures. New Haven: Yale University Press, 1998.

———. "Kenotic Creation and Divine Action." In *The Work of Love: Creation as Kenosis*, 99–121. Grand Rapids: Eerdmans, 2001.

———. *Science and Providence: God's Interaction with the World*. New Science Library. Boston: Shambhala, 1989.

Proudfoot, Wayne. "*Regulae Fidei* and Regulative Idea: Two Contemporary Theological Strategies." In *Theology at the End of Modernity: Essays in Honor of Gordon D. Kaufman*, edited by Sheila Greeve Davaney, 99–113. Philadelphia: Trinity, 1991.

Pseudo-Dionysius. *On the Divine Names, and Mystical Theology.* Translated by C. E. Rolt. New York: Macmillan, 1951.

Rahner, Karl. *Foundations of the Christian Faith: An Introduction to the Idea of Christianity.* Translated by William V. Dych. New York: Seabury, 1978.

Rawls, John. *A Theory of Justice.* Rev. ed. Cambridge: Belknap, 1999.

Reimer, James. "Time, History, and Ethics." In *Mennonite Theology in Face of Modernity,* edited by Alain Epp Weaver, 227–43. North Newton, KS: Bethel College, 1996.

Russell, Robert John. "Special Providence and Genetic Mutation: A New Defence of Theistic Evolution." In *Evolutionary and Molecular Biology: Scientific Perspectives on Divine Action,* edited by Robert John Russell et al., 191–224. A Series on Scientific Perspectives on Divine Action 3. Vatican City State: Vatican Observatory, 1998.

Russell, Robert John et al., editors. *Chaos and Complexity: Scientific Perspectives on Divine Action.* 2nd ed. A Series on Scientific Perspectives on Divine Action 2. Vatican City State: Vatican Observatory, 1998.

———, editors. *Evolutionary and Molecular Biology: Scientific Perspectives on Divine Action.* A Series on Scientific Perspectives on Divine Action 3. Vatican City State: Vatican Observatory, 1998.

Sabatino, Charles. "Projection as Symbol: Rethinking Feuerbach's Criticism." *Encounter* 48 (1987) 179–93.

Schleiermacher, Friedrich. *The Christian Faith.* Edited by H. R. Macintosh and James S. Stewart. Edinburgh: T. & T. Clark, 1999.

Sonderegger, Katherine. "Gordon Kaufman: An Attempt to Understand Him." *Scottish Journal of Theology* 50 (1997) 321–44.

Stoesz, Donald. "Gordon Kaufman's Thought: A Monument to Modernity." In *Mennonite Theology in Face of Modernity,* edited by Alain Epp Weaver, 27–50. North Newton, KS: Bethel College, 1996.

Stump, Eleonore, and Norman Kretzmann. "Theologically Unfashionable Philosophy." *Faith and Philosophy* 7 (1990) 329–39.

Tarbox, Everett J. "A Dialogue between Gordon Kaufman and Ludwig Wittgenstein." In *New Essays in Religious Naturalism,* edited by W. Creighton Peden and Larry E. Axel, 235–46. Highlands Institute Series 2. Macon, GA: Mercer University Press, 1993.

Thiemann, Ronald F. "Revelation and Imaginative Construction." *Journal of Religion* 61 (1981) 242–63.

Thomas, Aquinas, Saint. *Selected Philosophical Writings.* Selected and translated by Timothy McDermott. World's Classics. Oxford: Oxford University Press, 1993.

Thomas, Owen C., editor. *God's Activity in the World: The Contemporary Problem.* AAR Studies in Religion 31. Chico, CA: Scholars, 1983.

Tillich, Paul. *Systematic Theology,* Vol. 1, *Reason and Revelation. Being and God.* Chicago: University of Chicago Press, 1951.

Tipler, Frank J. *The Physics of Immortality: Modern Cosmology, God, and the Resurrection of the Dead.* New York: Doubleday, 1994.

Tracy, David. *Blessed Rage for Order: The New Pluralism in Theology.* San Francisco: Harper & Row, 1988.

Tracy, Thomas F. "Enacting History: Ogden and Kaufman on God's Mighty Acts." *Journal of Religion* 64 (1984) 20–36.

———. *God, Action, and Embodiment.* Grand Rapids: Eerdmans, 1984.

———. "Particular Providence and the God of the Gaps." In *Chaos and Complexity: Scientific Perspectives on Divine Action*, edited by Robert John Russell et al., 289–324. A Series on Scientific Perspectives on Divine Action 2. Vatican City State: Vatican Observatory, 1998.

———, editor. *The God Who Acts: Philosophical and Theological Explorations.* University Park: Penn State University Press, 1994.

Troeltsch, Ernst. *The Absoluteness of Christianity and the History of Religions.* Translated by David Reid. London: SCM, 1972.

———. *The Christian Faith.* Translated by Garrett E. Paul. Fortress Texts in Modern Theology. Minneapolis: Fortress, 1991.

———. *Writings on Theology and Religion.* Edited and translated by Robert Morgan and Michael Pye. Atlanta: John Knox, 1977.

Ward, Keith. *Divine Action.* London: Collins, 1990.

Weaver, Alain Epp, editor. *Mennonite Theology in Face of Modernity.* North Newton, KS: Bethel College, 1996.

Weinberg, Steven. *The First Three Minutes: A Modern View of the Origin of the Universe.* New York: Bantam, 1977.

White, Vernon. *The Fall of a Sparrow: A Concept of Special Divine Action.* Exeter, UK: Paternoster, 1985.

Whitehead, Alfred North. *Process and Reality: An Essay in Cosmology.* Gifford Lectures, 1927–1928. A Free Press Paperback. New York: Free Press, 1969.

Wieman, Henry Nelson. *The Source of the Human Good.* AAR Texts and Translations Series 8. Atlanta: Scholars, 1995.

Wiles, Maurice. "Can Theology Still Be about God?" In *Theology at the End of Modernity: Essays in Honor of Gordon D. Kaufman*, edited by Sheila Greeve Davaney, 221–32. Philadelphia: Trinity, 1991.

———. "Conceptualizing Humanity, World, and God." *Zygon* 29 (1994) 357–62.

———. *God's Action in the World: The Bampton Lectures for 1986 .* London: SCM, 1986.

Wittgenstein, Ludwig. *Philosophical Investigations.* Translated by G. E. M. Anscombe. 3rd ed. New York: Macmillan, 1958.

Wright, G. Ernest. *God Who Acts: Biblical Theology as Recital.* Studies in Biblical Theology 1/8. Chicago: Regnery, 1952.

Printed in Great Britain
by Amazon